ADVANCED TAROT

THE VOYAGE OF PROPHECY

All is stone and air. Atomic.
The rest is what dwells between.
All is intelligent and all knows all else.

LY DE ANGELES

ADVANCED TAROT | THE VOYAGE OF PROPHECY

LY DE ANGELES

Copyright © Ly de Angeles. All rights reserved. No part of this book may be used, reproduced, stored in a retrieval system or transmitted in any form or by any means, electronic, mechanical, photocopying, scanning, recording, including Internet usage, without written permission from the author except in the case of brief quotations embodied in critical articles and reviews.

ISBN (Australasia) 978-0-6485745-2-1
1st Edition 2020

Cover design Arian Levanael and Nick White
Production LOTHBROKSIGURD.COM.AU

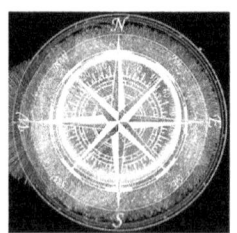

To my children, and theirs – this is what we do, puppies.
For past, present, and future apprentices and friendships.
For travelers who have graced my table.

BROKEN

THE SUBTLE BIGOTRY OF THE ENGLISH LANGUAGE

Inglan is a bitch
Dere's no escapin it
Inglan is a bitch
Dere's no runnin whey fram it

Mi get a lickle jab in a bih otell
An awftah a while, mi woz doin quite well
Dem staat mi aaf as a dish-washah
But w'n mi tek a stack,
mi noh tun clack-watchah

Linton Kwesi Johnson

People send me private messages and emails explaining that certain of my written works need a good editor. I always respond, asking about the glitch. When I discover, as I invariably do, that what so offends them is intentional when I wrote the words, I don't reply again. I go get another tattoo, instead.

I understand the need for certain stops. Certain punctuation. Even my daughter will pull me up with *Mother!* if I use ain't instead of is *not* or *isn't*. But the English language, while in my sinister hand is glorious, in a depth of habitation: of defeat and aggrandizement, deep-time memory of some-living, some-dead cultures is, in my dexter hand, an absolute mongrel of pompous stealth and misappropriation.

When I was a kid in kindergarten I endured elocution lessons because the drawl of the new colony was considered offensive and lowly. Lacking class and haught. And there it was. Bigotry inherent in language. Today's new cool, thankfully, is changing that. A dialect can be acceptable, *Eh by goom lad*?

I have travelers visiting me for tarot from all around the world. Immigrants and refugees, with strong accents that require all my listening to understand. But. And here's the crossroads. I only speak the language known as English. I can count in five languages, say hello in as many and could also ask for a *cafe con leche*, when in Spain. The people who have learned English as a second language are amazing, and I am the fool. So, when you write or speak, don't allow the bigots to correct your dialect. Be loud and proud.

We are only now beginning to free ourselves from an archaic academia, steeped in Latin, the voice of conquerors, rapists and thieves. Bigots. And many disciplines, like biology, botany and medicine, retain their roots in the monasteries from which they escaped, that became universities that sometimes resort to usury and pretense of learning. It's dead. The fucking empire is dead. The final death-roll of this crocodile is its adherence to grammatical correctness. The bigotry of rapacious privilege exposing its genitals and saying *My cock is bigger than your cock.*

Next time you hear that subtle inner voice pigeon-holing a person, by their ability to speak this young tongue, as under-educated or not sufficiently literate, go look in the mirror. I done it, once upon a time.

Me? I'm a Celt of many landscapes, but I'm also a winter mackerel and a grey-furred shaggy ol rabbit, smattered with the pale skin of the Breton, Parishi, Gael and Albanach, freckled with a Viking grandmother named, Loðbrók Sigurddóttir. My newly-found ancestral people spoke *Lanky*. I love language. Mainly because of etymology. To know the true meaning of the so-called slang word chook is from the old Irish *cheogh,* and that means hen, is copacetic and somewhat onomatopoeic.

You lose your native tongue? Someone's stolen your identity and said you ain't good enough. Gonna be really important if tarot is the dragon you intend training with. If you only have one language—a bastard one at that—bend the knee, metaphorically, to your guest and realize how easy it is to disrespect people.

MUTINY

This training is for everyone, of every gender-identity, every ethnicity and every culture. I am liberated by you, and because of you, and you are my teachers. Over the past six years, since moving to Melbourne, you have sat at my table, and spread the word, that I see you. That I hear you and that, because of you I have learned and deepened. I have, through your guidance, dropped the hidden persona of others' acceptable importance, and have become wholly myself. In all my colors. So, it is to you travelers, healers, poets, strippers, seekers-after-something, the wounded and the law-holders, that I bend the knee. I didn't know how much I needed your reflection, and through that, that I could be better at what I do, and who I am.

We are living in an era that is as thin as when first visible crescent of new moon shows a face. Fragile as a kitten, so easily starved if not for kindness and the careful wisdom of how to keep such delicacy vital in the face of abandonment. That delicacy is freedom of expression. The pride in ourselves, despite society or so-called authority. As such it is also to anarchy (no leader) and heresy (the right to choose). This kind of era has happened only once before in my lifetime. In the nineteen sixties. A singing of revolution, of calling out prejudice and discrimination. A walk against racism and sexist discrimination. A Woodstock apprenticeship in community and creative joy. If I miss this opportunity—now—to spruik my slant on being faith-skilled, then I'm a coward, and I will not see that as my epitaph.

Forty years ago I was metaphorically, outrageously and, somewhat ridiculously, *black banned*, in Sydney, for initiating a gay man. This was *witchcraft*, only recently branded as wicca, that demanded a woman initiate a man, and a man, woman. Some inviolate rule stylized by Gerald Gardner, or any one of his faux-pagan buddies, contemporaries or followers. Today this gay person is my best friend and, through their mind-altering study of genealogy they have traced my ancestry, that of a kid sold at birth into the company of strangers, down the roots of, firstly, a matrilineal tree, for approximately (to within a hare's breath) one thousand, nine hundred and forty-something years, because records have been kept as long as taxing and so, also, were the names of those, beaten and disenfranchised, who had the lands and water of their own ancestors, stolen and sold back to them at a price. Where once there never was one. It is only in the past twelve months, through DNA analysis and a grassroots movement of academics and researchers, that I have knowledge of a patrilineal lineage. A European, academic, bigoted, condescending, paleface-privileged mariner line, whose *taker* mentality I intend to drape with stone and rope to the bowel of a rotting hull, and see the humiliation sunk.

This book is for, and about, those of you either learning or working fulltime with tarot as your craft, or simply those who are curious, because you, also, are important. Because of your open mind. Your lack of dogmatic, religiously-discriminatory bigotry allows even mainstream purists to reconsider a naïve stance. This book is how you learn, how you wield this skill/gift and how, even, you reassess thinking and categorization.

After reading tarot, as a vocation, for those same forty years I'm ready to call it out. I'm at my peak, and still young enough to be outspoken and willful: an androgynous femme who has tried to fit some acceptability, socially, that was always to my detriment, and sometimes, also, close to being the death of me. A lack of mirrors to the soul, growing up in a regimentally binary society that demanded I acquiesce to some kind of stereotypical missy, when I was none of it, a wild thing biting hands that fed the hidden a perennial poison, landing me in as close to a dunking as was now legal, in the days of the caricature of the *bulldyke*.

It is with a fearlessness, and pleasure, that I attempt, in this narrative and how-to, to reshape viewpoints, names, titles, ideas, and the conformities and constructs to what is usual and acceptable rhetoric, in the representation of not only tarot but also a dualistic, tired, outmoded, predictable terminology, replete with hidden condescension, that attempts to describe ways of knowing. That of mysticism, the occult, and the art of the fáith-trained.

ADVANCED TAROT | THE VOYAGE OF PROPHECY declutters so-called importances. The instructions are nautical: the maps of a voyager. Earth, ocean, stars. Because we are, truthfully, all travelers of living, in a body, ship-like, on the way to death and forever (and that will be rendered otherwise here) and without sextant, North Star or elder-navigators—without those who have forged a map before you, and can advise of treacherous shallows, bergs, submerged reefs and interstellar clusters of alien minefields of space junk—the psychic muscle you use, reading the stories that tarot presents, will leave the people who come to you for guidance, in danger. Sometimes mortal.

You'll read the word *fáidh* throughout. The word is pronounced *fay* and is etymologically attributed to both fate and fear. *Fáidh* is an

Irish word, and means a seer or a prophet. It is us. Some authors place *ban* (*banfáidh*) before the word to indicate a *woman fey*. For the purposes of what I have to say, that is still part of a much larger problem. A form of shackle. And my ancestors, an entire groundswell of them being Irish, are a people who made it out alive, from under the yoke of a savagery garbed in guilt and pomposity, despite all odds. Others who speak through my blood and bone are from the Arctic north and the word used, in this context, is either *spae* (Albanach/Scottish) or *spé* (Old Norse). I will occasionally use one or the other, or even all three, so that my greatgreatgreatgreatgreatgreat grandmother, and those who spawned her, are appeased. All three are variations of the same word, just as *alba* and *älfur* are interchangeable, with an ocean and a seal-hide boat (its seams mudded in pitch) between one island home amongst the mists, ice and low, snow-filled cloud, and the next.

Variations of *map, destination, navigation, pictograms, story* and *traveler* are used instead of the expected: spread, outcome, way, client, as these are stale and somehow demeaning and patronizing. They are also depressingly overdone. The transition of such maps as *Dead Reckoning*, instead of Celtic Cross, *Horse Latitude* instead of a Warning spread. Research: Stargate and the Continuum, are intentional, whereas the older terminology is an invention, or a misappropriation. Whether you choose to remain with the familiar, or chart a course of your own, is up to you.

Wherever applicable I choose to use the pronouns they and *their*.

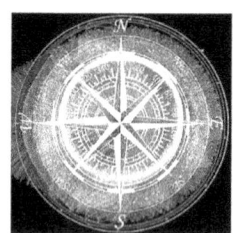

MASKS

Figure 1 – Mask

Why do I use *fáidh* instead of *tarot reader*? Spae or spé, instead of *divinator*, or *oracle*? Because these terms have been, and often still are, used to denigrate the mythic. The skilled *spae*-born everywhere. These words are also not my language, and language defines a culture, which is why missionaries have stripped this last vestige of heritage from indigenous people worldwide. I'm fáidh-born, popped from a stranger's vagina here, true, but as a stranger in an invaded land, and not one of my choosing, although now, a loved critter of red-blue and glare. Well, there comes a time in the life of someone like me, when we stop trying to use the chatter and babble of populism to try to be accepted, a bat pup amongst swallows.

MASCARA

The *Fool* is a card that represents the traveler, and it never is about foolishness. Fool, while we're at it can, also, never be understood because Fool is a magpie who hides their shiny findings, as though they are some ancient string of rough pearls: Australia who was once known as Gondwana, and we just might suffer cuckoos in our nests one unwatched day if we get too tired to care. If we relinquish vigilance to what's real and what's bullshit. I was told this pictogram represents the soul before it takes on a body. When I was a kid, I didn't question this. Well, I know better now. And we're *going* to question, and challenge, *all kinds* of throw-away lines… Because I *have* seen suicide when this card has turned up, and the traveler's best friend is found, someday way too soon, dead. Hung. The chair kicked out from under them and no note, so no one else to understand that this was meant to be.

FOOLISHNESS

The *Fool* represents every one of us. The masks we assume that allow us to blend in with a social group, to protect our true identities. We invent them, wear them to delude ourselves into a sense of protection, or even belonging, and they often, eventually, cage us as a means of coping. We have sourced them and pretended to be them, throughout history. They represent gods, and they invent *demonic* as a means of threat. They are seductive, or terrifying. We wear them during Black Plagues and to represent defiance in Hong Kong. Deepest fears are hidden by the masks we invent—or that are seemingly benevolent, like suits and ties and six-inch stilettos—so we can hopefully find acceptance. Love. Power. Sanctuary. But what happens when a. the mask becomes a nightmare, and b. who are we, if we choose not to wear one at all? Or is that last bit just not true?

> *Compare Occitan* mascara *"to blacken, darken," derived from* mask – *"black," which is held to be from a pre-Indo-European language, and Old Occitan* masco *"witch," surviving in dialects; in Beziers it means "dark cloud before the rain comes."*
>
> Online Etymological Dictionary

A mask conceals, it occults, it hides, and it tantalizes. It is the same word as person.

Then...

It's forever ago. I'm still breastfeeding my third child, living in a cottage I built by hand. No power, no running water, daunted by the eleven acres of wilderness that requires weaving through, come summer's end, to get to the river because the dam's so algae-blooming low, stalking a wide arc away from the neighbor's property. Him, with the shotguns, trained attack dogs and the never-silent generator, that I avoid with feral stealth. Proud. A city woman in cammos who's learned to wield a chainsaw like it's a tool of art.

I'm with that afternoon's visitor, a buxom thirty-something woman, her makeup as well-considered as a drag person, her legs spread around the edges of my recycled coffee table, drinking chai and smoking fags. She shuffles. I lay out map after map. All sex and love of kids, and money. And *Chariot* after *Chariot*, so no matter what I finally get to, in all this prophesying, she's no one's fool. Not anymore.

There're the beatings she took, preferring a broken jaw to him getting to the babies. There's the car she lived in for as long as it took for him to give up stalking her. Then, there's the STARGATE... and here, the sigil on the portal called ART, is the *8 of Coins*.

Hmm, I say aloud, smiling, with new-found confusion.

Whatcha got, hun?

I could be way off the mark, but this looks like you work in the sex industry.

Run two houses, lovey. Just wanna know if the bank'll give me the loan for a mortgage.

Well, that's easy. I'm so sure, I feel it in my gut. *Yes.*

Another day, years later. Another visitor. She sits opposite me, says nothing. Outside is around four degrees so she's rugged up, the wood fire warmth not yet reaching her. She's perky, solid, lean and tall. She gives nothing away. She's got on one of those silly puffer jackets. Gloves and a knitted wool beanie.

I do my ceremonial *opening* pattern. Banishing the last person without shuffling, because, well, that's my kind of spellcraft. I lay 'em down in the shape of a five-pointed star—a pentagram. One, two, three, four, five, over and over, image side down, teasing the story from the person with me, like carding wool, I suppose. Out falls *Death*. I put it back. I keep it in mind for later.

She picks off her gloves, finger-bit by finger-bit, smiling. She exudes a mother-smell. It's not an olfactory thing. Just a sense I'm used to. People all smell of something. I wonder, not for the first time, if this is what happens for dogs. That I am in a human skin and shape, but long ago stopped being just that, because the smell is also sight, and knowing and memory. I register a whole by it. It's all my senses… did someone say we only have five?

She sits twitching. I know the people who sent her. She doesn't look like them, but she stinks of them. Still, like I said, she's twitching.

You need to stand up. Walk around. It's normal to feel anxty, I say. She doesn't. She shuffles and cuts the pack into three like I ask her to. Past, present and future (silly, I know, but we'll get to why). And there it is, in the place of the self, in this first map, *Devil*. Cancer.

I know, I know. It can mean a lot of things. But I'm not wrong, I can't explain. She's riddled with it. Way past healing.

I look at other images. She's got children, a partner, a little house on the beach. She's a photographer. Death is like some black-winged cousin, quiet and easy-going, saying nothing. They don't need to, do they?

It's all a matter of when.

See this? I say, pointing to the *Devil*. She nods.

You're sick, and this is fear, before adding, *but fear can save your life, you know*.

I've got her attention. She didn't expect honesty. The way she tilts her head, pulls open the studs of her silly coat, and runs a hand down the front of her sweater like there's sweat on it, when there can't be. It's way too cold. So, a memory, I suppose.

Then I tell her, how I had all these students in one particular class who got discussing fear, like it's common. A day-to-day predictable and understood thing. How is that possible? Is it a word, like love, that you can just bandy about? Have a wee chat about? Wow. They have it upside down.

You've got cancer, I say, looking her straight in the eye. Loving her, a stranger (if such a thing is possible).

I'm dying, she says. *It's metastasized. Stage four*.

Hang on, I say, laying out the whole map of the so-called present, then that of the so-called future. *Eventually yes, but you're not going to die, not right now.*

I wait until she adjusts her beanie and stops squirming. *Your partner outside?* I ask. *You lettin 'em hear this?* We're recording the session, you understand.

Depends how bad it is. She snorts a laugh. We're in conspiracy, she and I, and she agrees to it.

The look she gives me is unreadable, because being here is what I'll one day call *Fight Club[1]*. I gesture the room. The door. I wonder, briefly, years later when the *First rule of Fight Club is you don't talk about Fight Club* became an urban thing. I am perennially amazed at the resilience of most people. What they can bear. What they can endure. How I've done so myself, so I can relate. The privacy of this...

This is just between us. I don't want you to record it. Wise words. She's passed through all those five phases of grief. She switches off the recording.

I wonder about the need to know what will happen in the future. How cruel the answers can be? How I can't lie about it. About how I say some of the hardest things a body is ever going to hear.

And I wonder that they keep coming. And that tarot, this invisible relative of fate and intimate destiny, can foretell events that are woven, like tapestry, not only between me and the person with me, but beyond the confines of what we know of as life and death. What a scam we've been talked into, this being told that who we are

---

[1] *Fight Club*, based on the book of the same name by Chuck Palahniuk

is all there is, or that there's an afterlife, when that's unpredictable. And that fear is not anxiety, it's the warning that can save us.

UNPACKING IN A SAFE HARBOR

I begin teaching this craft to small groups—ten people at most—back in the eighties of the last century. At thirty-something years old. Therefore, writing a book about tarot (and this is my second go) is tricky. It's important to understand that this skill, properly taught and learned, is oral. People take notes and transfer them, later, into a grimoire, but that's their business, and the writing/rewriting is a memory tool, yes. Tarot is comprehended from mouth to ear. By practice and example, with a knowledge-holder at the helm. It's not everyone's destiny to do what I do, but well-intentioned information-sharing is never pointless, because tarot is a way to live. Not a cult or a religion but a handed-down mystery.

I could be thought of as trying to reinvent navigation with this specific book, but no. The way I teach, in person, uses terminology and concepts that both shock and intimidate apprentices. In many cases they, probably like you, have read about this stuff somewhere else, have practiced on friends and willing others. But that doesn't mean you, or they, have been cracked open. People are used to charts and associations, that were written of a) by old white men hundreds of years ago, b) perverted into *past lives this* or an *aura* that, commentaries, c) in the little booklet that comes with a new pack. Many don't think it's used to predict the future… *but that's what tarot does*. Everything else is semantics, like the many artistic and interesting *wisdom* packs on the market today. They are not predictive, and they are not explicit.

The fáidh-born know this, no matter whether their ancestral lineage is Celtic, Yorta, Inuit, Maori or Sami. Can it be taught? Yes. This, then, makes *you* fáidh-gifted.

Without you in my parlor, here in Melbourne, I can only unpack what I know. Unravel the already-woven, so to speak. Make a mess. And this book *is* messy, because tarot is messy. You and I are messy. A traveler can be in the middle of the most tragic of circumstances, and their questions will reflect that. *Relationship* is the big one. The perennial, *Ah, it's not a question*, but that's what people will say, usually first, when question time comes at the end of a session. Relationships, money, health, hope.

The *unpacking* method presented here is the only way a person like you or me learn to rewire what we've learned, in such a way as to open some unseen door. Have that lightbulb moment when we spae something in 3D that is both on the table and in a mind.

You'll change because of it. Then… you keep working at it, and trusting yourself and this craft, through a series of traveler-denials and disrespect. This is called the *Plateau*, when you doubt everything, because the stranger across from you is deriding you, and telling you that you're rubbish.

Are you?

Are you a dressed-up charlatan who's doing the PR?

Advertising? Waiting for the phone to chirrup, when, by all that's strange and odd, you are haunted by a lifetime of questioners who'll hunt you down, find you, sometimes scare you, but always confide in you, like they never do with anyone else?

So, it's a way of knowing I offer here. Not a cookbook. A philosophy of meanings and perceptions. Tarot worthy of the three-hour conversation I had with an American friend, and her mum, yesterday. This *unpacking* skitch is their idea. I think it's a new term for the dissection of words, and their potential for misunderstanding if presented unscrutinized, because the majesty of this witchery—and this *is* witchcraft—is usually done in my parlor, with about ten people, who are tearing their hair out trying to understand what I want them to learn, when I don't want anything. I've got maps—navigation skills—they are necessary spaeing tools, darlings.

Someone I love is facing a tribunal, today, because her property, in regional New South Wales and supposedly zoned for rural purposes only, is besieged by a mega-company that has built a massive hydroponic herb-growing factory next door, and has installed industrial fans. She's fought them—implored them—to put up a noise-reduction wall (so her school-age kids don't go crazy), but no deal. This has gone on for two years. Local council, state land and environment are toothless. She looks like losing. Why? She is a woman, going up against a tribunal of rich men, who, unfortunately for you and me, deride her as being "just a tarot reader". And laugh. Still. And there we have it, huh?

My own ancestry, on both my maternal and paternal lines, warriors, scholars, downtrodden, meaningless at times, champions for indigenous oppression yes, but travelers, one and all. Seafaring, some rich and titled, others delivered to strange lands by famine and need, and so there's no point me repeating the same tired terminology with you. Language is a magic, that can make or break an entire country, as many of you know. Language can make or break love, security, the mystery of a seemingly certain destiny. And it is language between us that we need to comprehend. Just hear me out, because you've probably read the same thing, about tarot, time and time again.

It's a worry, and it's dead dull. I look forward to your comments in forty years.

…

PART ONE

AN ACKNOWLEDGEMENT OF WONDER

Figure 2 – Magician, Seer

OF MAPS

I want to be remembered as a professor who said a lot of stupid things to his students.

Arne Dekke Eide Næss,
Founder of the *Deep Ecology Movement*

THE MAGICIAN WITH THE SEER

Of the maps and stories that you'll examine I have this to say: The person or situation alluded to, with this pairing, is unique. I am reminded of profound thinkers, people whose work in the world I mention throughout. I call them the *Great Reflectors*. They are lighthouses along a deadly shore of broken ships and false affirmations. From Nan Shepherd to Robert Macfarlane and Martin Shaw, Rachel Carson. From Wendell Berry to Jon Young, Robin Wall-Kimmerer. Arne Dekke Eide-Næss, visionary of the *Deep Ecology* movement. People who have broken an anachronous and obsolete dialogue that, to a degree, most of us have fallen for. Until we wake up from the *Sleeping Beauty* state of unconscious destructivity we seem to be in.

Words, with this pairing, are beyond most of us. We have had millennia of explanations. Answers when there are none in the current era. People who have pulled the mythic rug out from the illusion of separation, a people-trap, from family of earth, sea and impossibly vast galaxies. There is a greatness to the being of this pair. I have rarely seen them together. I am struck speechless each time.

DENIAL

Figure 3 – Denial

Poor bastard, you've got nothing, I say to him, in the September of 1987. He thinks I'm an idiot, or more insultingly, a fraud. Who wouldn't? I don't know what I'm doing. It's like I'm butchering an auroch when nobody's taught me how. Or that aurochs are extinct, so what's this under the knife? Someone else (or is it the same trickster? I don't know because I can't spae) blinkers me, insisting I say what comes out of my mouth, based on only a few bits of paper, shuffled randomly, by this stranger. Yes, he walks out. No, he doesn't pay me. Not then, anyway. He has almost a million bucks. It isn't liquid, though. It isn't real money. It's invested in blue chips, on a stock exchange.

He comes back a month later, when it's all gone in that '87 *crash*, and he puts twenty-five dollars on my table. He's a mess. He's humble. He bludges a cigarette. Apologizes.

SAY IT AS YOU SPAE IT

Figure 4 – Murder

Murder, I say, when the pictograms in the above image flip out onto my cloth.

The woman's eyes are as big as saucers. 'Me?'

'Dunno,' I reply, because it's an honest answer. Tarot can be scant on details occasionally. Tarot has taught me to write without adjectives. Without platitudes. Tarot knows you'll understand and fill in what I can't.

The person after her: *Murder.* Ditto, their response. My reply is the same. It's there. To one side of the DEAD RECKONING map, in the place representing the *present. Death, 10 of Swords, Empress.* I sense the traveler's terror when I say it. Should I have said it? What's the point of doing what I do if I run a con job? If, a year from now, the person gets bashed and could have made it out alive? If they save their kids, but I haven't told them about the danger? Haven't given an inkling? I don't know what that would feel like, but I do know they won't come back, won't trust anyone who pretends, takes their money and says they'll be fine. Not ever again. The only obvious bit is that the *Empress* isn't a specific person but represents some person-critter identifying as woman.

Down the end of my lane, on that same Saturday, a woman is dying, while I'm reading about the event in someone's tarot. Her throat has been cut. *Death* card, *10 of Swords, Empress.* The police never find the killer. It's all over the Sydney and Melbourne newspapers but it gets a bitty mention in my local press, in a corner article just before the sports section. Why? Now, there's the question, isn't it? Not that she's murdered, but that tarot sees it, and that some vile official from the Chamber of Commerce says, *Hide it. Don't scare the tourists.*

Don't mention the drink-spiking, and what this person, now, feels like when they're sitting with me after being raped by who knows how many drug-fueled, privileged, *why-not* men? Don't mention being threatened with having their house burned down if they even think of leaving and pocketing his welfare check, because they've got three kids and it's his booze and pokies money. What do I say? It'll be alright? Life's not like that, and there are no solutions to the tragedies if they're covered up with platitudes.

Don't express fear, when the person on the end of the phone line tells me to stop teaching if I value my children's lives?

TAROT AND AMNESIA

Figure 5 – Snowy River

It's the Man from Snowy River, I tell her. And you're gonna be doing a whole heap of riding from now on. And later, *Aha, here's your key—A reunion (3 of Cups sometimes), and if there's no reason not to go, go.*

She's with a partner she's wanted to leave for years. But now he's had a massive stroke, and is paralyzed, only able to move bewildered eyes, and she's his primary carer. She's only fifty. She's a writer, and corrects me, saying, *you mean writing, not riding.* Is there a panic inside her at what she expects is to come? I don't know. But she's sitting with me a couple of years later and I'm reading for her again. I don't remember her. I don't, with most of them. That's the reality. I worked out, decades ago, that it's a tarot-thing, this selective post-advisory amnesia. It's so that I retain objectivity. I get it.

She's on the edge of the seat with those eyes, and that smile. She couldn't care less what I'm saying. I ignore it, as I usually do. I have to. And I conclude by asking if she has any questions. *No*, she says. *I just want to tell you...*

She remembered the tarot's key when she received the invitation to the high school reunion of the class of '84 up near the Mallee (that's the back of nowhere to a city slicker like me). She wouldn't have considered attending, ever, except for those last three pictograms in her first session. She's mingling with them all, thirty-five years older and it showing in every slim body gone to fat and every unrecognizable somebody, when a bloke, dragging a guitar case, comes up to her and says, *I remember you, your birthday's the day after mine.* He looks like a haggard, sun-wizened Robert Redford, but she doesn't recall him, at all, from the old days. They chat, and she's astonished. He's flirting. She doesn't know what to do. The organizers set everyone up to do an embarrassing skit of one sort or another. A joke, a poem, some ridiculously humiliating whatever. She hasn't prepared, thinks how foolish she would feel… But he has. He takes to the stage, unclasps the case, lifts out a Fender, and plugs it into a little portable amp. He pulls off the Mark

Knopfler riff from *Sultans of Swing*, before sitting on a stool and strumming an ending.

You thought I was going to sing, he mumbles into the mike, grinning. Everyone chuckles. Feeling for their phones. The excuse they've set up to get outa there. He clears his throat.

There was movement at the station—he recites, the traveler going all red up her throat, watching him, embarrassed because she's turned on, *for the word had got around that the colt of Old Regret had got away...*

He knows the entire epic from beginning to end, and she explains how her legs are so rubbery she has to sit. That he keeps his eyes locked on her through the whole thing.

She goes home with him that night. They have sex. She tells her husband. The side of his face that works, smiles. He understands. She won't desert him but, by god, she should have a life. She's been lovers with the *Snowy River* man since. He takes tourists, on horseback, to sit with agreed-upon remote Aboriginal storytellers, where they learn about indigenous lore. She's been riding with him all year since.

It's a terrible thing that you and I do. No wonder the christian authorities want us imprisoned, banished or burned. Even when they don't fear us, they deride us. It's a good ploy, isn't it? Humiliation. Belittlement. No matter, anymore, that they are corporations and not clergy. Until 1951, in the British Commonwealth, it was illegal to *practice witchcraft,* which is one of the terms for what this is. The *Witchcraft Act* was repealed. It's also the reason that, in the digital, plastic age, the Square, card-reader company, banned me. They have since removed the offending clause: *By creating a Square Account, you also confirm that you will not accept payments in connection with the following businesses or business activities: (1) any illegal activity or goods... (22) sales of firearms, firearm parts or other devices designed to cause physical injury... (24) drug paraphernalia, (25)* **occult materials** *...(35) fulfillment houses... and (36) network member payment processing service providers.* But when I phone them to reinstate my account (I was banned on clause 25, bold text. Not that anyone at customer service knew what that meant), I am informed that once banned, banned for life. I laugh, then ask her, *what the frack are fulfillment houses?*

BITE THE WEIRD AND REAL

This is not going to be fun. There's a heap of learning; so much to memorize. You should know that before you proceed. And there are dead ends. You either backtrack, when the shoals and depths become too treacherous to navigate, until you find another current to guide you, or you give up. This is definitely a witch's craft, and living with it can be exhausting, terrifying and ominous.

So why do I do it? Why are you still reading?

...

TIME – THE GREAT INITIATION

There is character in exchange for safety just beyond the streetlights, scars to be boasted of. Initiation recognizes this truth, holds it in ritual and gives it shape.

Dr Martin Shaw,
A Branch of the Lightning Tree

Figure 6 – Persistent Illusion

THE PERSISTENT ILLUSION

Because of Albert Einstein's theories, we often think of *time* as a fourth dimension. Special relativity shows that time behaves surprisingly like the three spatial dimensions and that length contracts as speed increases, time expands as speed decreases. And while Berty wrote extensively on relativity, he also said *the distinction between the past, present and future is only a stubbornly persistent illusion.*

Time as we understand it, is a human construct, but a clever strategy for our arrangement of memory, history and appointments, for consideration of how old anything is, how old you are in your current body, but... that can be vitally limiting. There seems, in this society, to be an agreement that certain things will occur at certain ages. At thirty we *should* be in a relationship, or married, we probably *should* have children, we have some kind of internal clock. We have been convinced that at forty we're past it. Rubbish, isn't it?

TAROT AS HEALER

Is tarot a healer? Am I? Are you? Well, maybe. I'm a communicator of messages. A codebreaker of sorts. It isn't that I defy any biological clock, just that I continue to explore magic, physicality and art, and to view statistics and definitions with suspicion. This is important, because the majority of you, reading this will identify as women, or LGBTQI. Just occasionally as cis gender men. And before I explain the importance just mentioned, I ask you to wonder: the subject of gender contains so much complexity and so many set-in-stone certainties—stagnant and rigid—women and men. Something predictably pink and blue. A certain role-play and job availability. A need to know the sex of an unborn fetus at the time of the first ultrasound, so that we can... So that we can *what*?

GENDER BIAS

What is *that* about, and why—other than genitally and chromosomatically—does it affect people, in the thus-called *west*, summoning wisdom and mysticism? Species indoctrination. Who knows how it happened? I do receive my fair share of blokey blokes, both for learning and tarot readings. A ratio something like 70/30, with the 70 being people of a forest of genders, and life choices. Lots of men are afraid. They worry that coming to me is unmanly. Interesting. Not famous men, or those in the armed services, or those spearheading a Royal Commission into the sexual abuse of children. Not cops, or firefighters, or those who serve in the military trying to come to terms with PTSD. They walk in, after a big hug, and take the seat opposite me willingly, comfortable with setting up their phone for recording. They've been told. Undercover cops want to know if they're going to get shot like their partner just did. All are comfortable discussing anything. This seems like a diversion from the how-to of tarot, but it isn't. We need to know what's going on.

...

WITCHCRAFT

Tha faemnan, the gewuniath onfon gealdorcraeftigan and scinlaecan and wiccan, ne laet thu tha libban.

(Women who are accustomed to receiving enchanters and sorceresses and witches, do not let them live)

From the *Legal Code of Ælfred*, or the Doom Book, circa 893 C.E.

Figure 7 – Seer

FÁIDH-SKILLED

Before we drop down into the how-to of tarot, it is necessary to clear this up. You work this talent—this skill—you are practicing *witchcraft*. And witchcraft, or fáidh-skilling, is akin to (perhaps the same as) druí. Without delving down the hundreds of years, we are going to confront this. You can research the existence or translation of this-or-that, for your entire life cycle as a person-critter but anything you read is likely to be biased. However, for anything I say to be taken as valid, I am required to know enough to provide a valid opinion.

A QUESTIONABLE PROPAGANDA

Who records history? Those who waged war and won. Is there a bias? It's called propaganda, and the technique of belittlement is still in use today. Moreover, this bias—bigotry—is still responsible for hatred and, in countries like New Guinea, parts of Africa, Haiti, parts of India, and I daresay, most evangelical christian strongholds, the murder of (mainly) women and children is still happening. A body must start somewhere with this, and I'd rather not generalize, so I'll start with my own ancestors. No saying, anywhere, that Caradoc ap Cunobelin (circa 35 CE, misnamed Caratacus by Tacitus, and later Cassius Dio), chieftain and rebel, was involved in sorcery or what we now call witchcraft or druidcraft, but that's not to say he wasn't. Boudica, his ally against the Roman occupation was called Boadicea, and was written, by Tacitus, as consulting auguries before the failed, doomed stand against Suetonius Paulinus (at what's now either Thetford Forest or Watling Street, London) by supposedly releasing a hare from within her clothing and observing the direction in which it ran. According to Cassius Dio, Roman History, Epitome of Book LXII, 6: *When she had finished speaking, she employed a species of divination, letting a hare escape from the fold of her dress; and since it ran on what they considered the auspicious side, the whole multitude shouted with pleasure, and Buduica, raising her hand toward heaven, said: "I thank thee, Andraste, and call upon thee as woman speaking to woman; for I rule over no burden-bearing Egyptians as did Nitocris, nor over trafficking Assyrians as did Semiramis (for we have by now gained thus much learning from the Romans!), much less over the Romans themselves as did Messalina once and afterwards Agrippina and now Nero (who, though in name a man, is in fact a woman, as is proved by his singing, lyre-playing and beautification of his person); nay, those over whom I rule are Britons, men that know not how to till the soil or ply a trade, but are thoroughly versed in the art of war and hold all things in common, even children and wives, so that the latter possess the same valour as the men. As the person, then, of such men and of such women, I supplicate and pray thee for victory, preservation of life, and liberty against men insolent, unjust, insatiable, impious, — if, indeed, we ought to term those people men who bathe in warm water, eat artificial dainties, drink unmixed wine, anoint themselves with myrrh, sleep on soft couches with boys for bedfellows, — boys past their prime at that, — and are slaves to a lyre-player and a poor one too. Wherefore may this Mistress Domitia-Nero reign no longer over me or over you men; let the wench sing and lord it over Romans, for they surely deserve to be the slaves of such a woman after having submitted to her so long. But for us, Mistress, be thou alone ever our leader."*

What a load of unadulterated, vile, denigrating rubbishy codswallop, is *that*? Dio was born a hundred years after the fact. What you just read is best written, by you, on a piece of vellum, mumbled over with the voice of storms and ravens, and set ablaze in a safely contained firepit, a curse upon him for daring to write such denigrating rubbishy codswallop. I don't intend to take this to pieces but to understand how, up through the chattering roots of living forests and along the *zaplines* of mycelium intel, ideas of people and indigene, prophecy and culture, have been misappropriated, and translated by way of an alien ideology, is to realize how dreadfully we are viewed as healers, mystics, midwives, wisdom holders and enchanters. A hare going a certain way was an *oops*? Propaganda, denoting the hillbilly nature of those gathered in that fateful grove—in excess of 120,000 people—and how they got it wrong. *"Andrasta"*? *"Praying"*? A woman speaking to a *"woman"*? *"Thee"*? People who don't know how to work the soil or a trade? A *person*?

No.

These are the words of an inherently hierarchical social kowtow, an academic monk, who either knows only leftovers, after Rome's day-in-the-sun diminishes, or who ignores, because he cannot comprehend, does not remember, or chooses to suppress and misinterpret a way of life—a culture—of people they have slain, vanquished or assimilated. Non-literate people. Even the idea of speeches is both curious and inconsistent with indigenous lore.

The knowledge specialist became the servant of the chiefs. From then until today the power of knowledge was subjugated.

Dr. Lynne Kelly,
The Memory Code, (p 33)

I've asked myself, and others, where this dismissive derision of femme gender came from, and when. It's nonsensical. It's also devious and specifically divisive. To belittle, and bring low, wisdom-holders, storytellers, initiators, their teachers and those who are taught, is to stop, dead, a people from being themselves. Take away the language, as the Anglo-Saxons did of the Celts, and there's nothing left. We have lost ourselves. And from there the only acceptance we can gain is to join the antagonizers. To take authority by force or be brought to the knees before the vanity of those who have also taken authority in a similar manner. Authors and academics insist on titling non-christian, or non-Abrahamic people as polytheist—many gods—without revealing that anthropomorphic stories are those told only to children, by indigenous elders. To cause them to be wary of wildness, to teach them, utilizing a metaphor that makes sense to a three or four-year-old. A language of masks, kachinas, dollies, poppets. People-looking objects imbued with meaning and magic. Therefore a storm could be called Thor, a world of ice and mist be named Alba, a herd of horses, beyond counting, be given the collective noun Epona, sun be tagged Lug or, Lucifer (in Latin): the light-bringer (also the planet venus), and in the language of Proto-Indo-European etymology *leuk*, or brightness and illumination, because Europe is cold, grey, white, invisible, for up to eight or even nine months of a year, rendered in splendor for a mere few weeks, as the landscape is bathed in sunlight, the sky displays all that blueness, and clarity of starlight, with the thinning of the mists and fog of winter—the season of dormancy—to bear fruit and sap to rise, herbs to flower and seed to gather, bees to sing the fecund air, standing stones to lack a dark shadow, and night creatures to recede to where the midges and the blackfly don't harry.

WHISPERS

But they are just that. Stories for children. As an individual grows to maturity those playthings cease to train. People are taught what is necessary for hunting, culture, art, survival, mating and longevity. As it is with tarot. Accepting the quick fix is going to make you desperate. And you will be left with dust. This is not a game for children who believe simply because they haven't elders, wise with lore of the grown-up stuff.

I mention my own ancestor because I am in awe. Not of him, but of the strangeness of what we all spae, but that so often doesn't get backed up by anything beyond doubt. For forty years I unwrapped the thickly entombed stories of the lost tribes of Europe, specifically those names and dates and places known to be Celtic or anGhaeilge. Allied with what? I didn't know. Me? Maybe? A bastard without a family at all? What is an illogical fascination with anything? Perhaps not illogical. Records are kept. Of births, deaths marriages, wills, titles, taxes. Particularly taxes. And if your name was on a parish register that wasn't burned at the time of an inquisition, or destroyed by priests, drunk on Irish poteen; if it existed beyond that, to be on the rolls and titles of a tithed and misappropriated land, no matter persecutions, no matter holy crusades where your demesne was stolen by the Northmen during that futile idiocy, you can find the heartwood. Whether druid is witch, and whether witch identifies as human or other, when you take up the work of either a fáidh-born or a fáidh-skilled person, you take on the garment of forest and fjord. You better not be a liar. There better not be gender-biased, or the maintenance of the delusionary spell, cast on you as a puppy, of an unfounded belief system that deems it more fun being a nun than getting some flesh-type loving.

LANDWISDOM

All the above is for you, the trainee practitioner of tarot—the fáidh-woke—to absorb, because the anthropomorphizing of earth, season, mountain, firestorm or flood, the delusional *outside-godness* of the current era, to which people pray, as though they are wiser than wilderness, and us within wilderness and are, like the legendary Person Canute, advising that he cannot turn a tide, left wondering what has gone wrong when we don't get what we have prayed for.

As fáidh-born, you need to step back from it all. Learn what you can and don't think just reading a bunch of books (and yes, including this one) will grant you knowledge. Because that's never true. It's the practice, the relentless listening, the waking up from the dream of habitual religiosity that allows a crack in earth's closed eyes.

The quote at the start of this chapter was later translated, by a man calling himself a person: James was his name—of Scotland (circa 1604), into an English language version of now-authorized biblical texts, that were originally agreed upon at a grand gathering of blokes in frocks, at Nicaea in Iznik, a currently-besieged city in Turkey, three hundred and twenty-odd years after the sacking of Jerusalem (in what was hoped to be control of the trading route called the old Silk Road)—a bible (a word derived from Latin and Greek meaning *paper scroll*). He had the quizzical word MEKHASHEPHA—perhaps mutterer, written up in the tractate known as Exodus 22 as *pharmakeia*: healer, herbalist, and thought to, therefore, in our man Jimmy's woman-hating eyes, to mean poisoner—because that's the best way to knock off an enemy who hasn't got a taster. Definitively translated as *maleficos*, inspiring the title of the *Malleus Malleficarum, The Hammer of Witches*, the scourge of wisdom-holders, still alive despite the ergot-hallucinatory-dob-a-witch craze that scourged across Britain and Europe, later America. A rule book that was deemed a mandate for torture and murder.

Has that stopped? No.

Even in your exposé of the most seemingly traumatic maps of the future, you hold the seeds of healing for the traveler who has come. How could people cope with cruelty and betrayal if they were not warned in some way? If no one is there, at the outcome of the prediction, to help them dust off the ashes of disillusionment?

...

RESPONSIBILITY

You help people to heal themselves so yes, *technically*, you are a healer. Particularly if you are a practitioner of more than this aspect of a witch's skill, such as ceremony and lore. I read tarot and foretell the future, yet I am not a *fortune teller*. I also tell potent and somewhat significant stories… Am I then a storyteller? I know the uses of spiderweb and yarrow in the healing of wounds caused by a knife blade, of valerian, passionfruit and chamomile for sleep assistance, and micro-dosing for a liberated journey beyond body-death. We *are* what we do, we are also who we are. But we must also know why we are both.

Those few of us who do what we do are not defined by the work. Riding is (or should be) a mutual agreement, between us in the saddle and the horse who acquiesces to the partnership. Sometimes the other way around. And yet it seems definition, and fitting into a recognizable identity, is almost demanded of us. By whom? This is "mirror, mirror on the wall," stuff. I can't help but reflect on the injustice of the *Snow White* story as I write. Because *Snowy* is a tale of the journey of salt from the mines of the Celtic Alps, along the Rhine in summer, to the sea, and a voyage to far-off lands where this element is worth more than frankincense. The journey of winter to spring. The story never was about a *Disney-strangled* wicked person and her hapless young victim: femme-debasing caricatures.

Does indoctrinative language imprint on our perceptions and viewpoints? Yes. Do I learn with every person and encounter? Definitely. Is it important that, while I learn, I contemplate, and heed the subsequent consciousness-altering knowledge of what intimacy is, what defines gender, how we are manipulated by media and advertising, of what *time* could be, might be, is and is not? An ironically-boxing terminology of past, present and future into an ideology of differences? Is it my responsibility, through this work, to maintain a wide-open mind? Yes.

TAKING CARE OF YOU

Your choice to continue, but I caution you. The skill can kill you young if you don't take care of yourselves. Tarot doesn't intend this, just as a hurricane doesn't care for individuals who beg. But alert you I will. I've seen what can go awry. And most of the practitioners of witchcraft, and augers of tarot with whom I'm in contact, know it also.

Piece of paper that's been in the oven for fucken hours, she says.

Yeah, but look in the money in the biscuit tin, says her partner, at the end of the first day on the job, at a Sunday craft market just outside of Perth.

SAYING IT ANYWAY

It's January, just a few short seasons before now. I've relocated to Melbourne after twenty-five years in a small rural tourist town. Both my sons, their partners and children, still live in that north country. I'm visiting, and one of the boys organizes a Saturday afternoon barbecue. I'm rather anti-social, so I watch and listen. Then a ghost walks through me and I'm tetchy, aware of knowing of an upcoming environmental threat. I call my eldest lad to a place of privacy and warn him (he lives high up in the surrounding mountains) that it's a great idea for his family to get out. To move closer to the sea.

Why? he asks.

Something's coming, I reply. *Danger. Flood. Dunno for sure.*

You and your f#*king prophesies, Mother. I'm sick of them.

Here's your dilemma. Your family, and many friends, after knowing you for long enough, will want you to stop saying things that disrupt them. Screw with their bubble. I have courage, yes, but also guilt and cowardice. My face flames at that aggression.

He and the family don't relocate. The flood comes. The road washes away, and for weeks food and supplies are helicoptered to parts of the mountains, to the people and the critters stuck higher than the landslide. As I write this, the entire region where they live has been experiencing catastrophic fire conditions, but they're alive.

Just last week I am rendered incapacitated with the overwhelming urge to phone a long-time sister-witch, living with horses, dogs, chickens, goannas, and her art, near Tenterfield. I need to assure myself that she's still alive (as we know it). We chat for hours. Among other things she discusses the drought, and the fires that have already decimated her region, but that's over. The blaze stopping at the boundary to her property.

They're coming again, I say.

When? she asks.

Soon.

Fire has raged out of control. Southeast Queensland, all of New South Wales, Western Australia, South Australia, now Victoria and Tasmania—the whole of the forested continent… and the summer of 2019—the calendar year of 2020, had just begun.

Was I an arrogant idiot for giving the warning? He saved his home, his family, his farm. Does that make me a problem? No. Choice cuts both ways when we've at least got one. My son's decision to ignore me, to stay anyway? That's what makes for both heroics and folly.

Once we all listened.

…

LEAVING SAFE HARBOR – THE VOYAGE BEGINS

Figure 8 – 7 Swords, Darkana Tarot

INITIATION

This raises huge ethical, existential questions for both you, as fáidh-skilled—the tarot navigator and reader of mystical maps, *and* the traveler who sits with your cards in their hands shaking, not perhaps out of fear, but from some adrenalin impulse, so utterly out of character and seemingly-unnecessary, but uncontrollable, that they laugh, embarrassed.

Most everything that you, or I, experience didn't make sense yesterday. Wasn't on any agenda. Was something no one could have stopped or supposedly foreseen. So much you or I can't change. So why bother? Two reasons: the first is strange. There is something awesome about sharing the fact of an event before it happens. The affect it has. Yes, it can evoke fear, but it also sinks the tension in the gut. This is destiny. The second reason is that sometimes you *will* help, intentionally or not. The battered woman: where to go, who can protect her, how she can change herself and what questions she should ask. It encourages a forensic attitude to life, love, and it spits at the mumble of that unconscionable expression *unconditional love*. I can spé a person's ancestral lineage in their face, in their hands and skin. I don't make this up. I discuss, freely, a person's sexuality, their escape plans, their inevitable return to their country of origin when their temporary protection visa is rejected.

This privacy—this acceptance—cannot sustain bigotry or personal bias. It just can't.

That's why I teach you to train your consciousness, and to really consider your language, before you ever pick up a pack of cards. To listen. If you don't have the gift, you'll never have it. There is an astonishing terror to what we do. How I say what I spae. A vast compassion of conspiracy, in secret, behind a closed door. A profundity to the act of recording the session. When they learn about who was murdered. When they realize how close they came to it being them.

...

Figure 9 – 2008 GFC

As I've brushed over already the trade language, *lingua franca*, that most of us speak, and use for business, is English. A language that bases historic events on a calendar, changed time and again by successive European popes, but appearing shallow and bigoted in its traditional form of B.C. and A.D. When you record a tarot session, and add a date, it's with this in mind. To my Chinese voyagers, I'm *wūpó*, the date predictable, alien and dismissive of their culture.

We have been indoctrinated, and whilst agreeing to the commonality of dates on a christian-based calendar, we must take a deep breath and know that none of this is *real*.

How important is the breakthrough? Inspirationally so. The knowledge that the path through the forest, based on Tuesday following Monday can only lead to our death, without our ever having realized that immortality is absolute, albeit the challenges, hazardous and steep; the edges an illusion of shrubbery, when either a stone wall or a thousand-foot drop is just beyond the peripherals.

I prophesied for a person who died in a light plane crash. I still have the tape of the session. The prophecy told that this significant event would happen in the time of Gemini, under a Virgo moon. I didn't spae a year. You often won't. But there are other ways of knowing when things will happen. Tarot will show you what leads up to an event. A divorce, a change in government. Stranger things that make no sense when you are foretelling. You'll spae the cut of the garment worn by a woman of wealth, during the Second World War. A *Reservoir Dogs* album cover. The assassination of a person not yet in the media spotlight. Or there'll be the *3 of Staves*, in 2005, suggesting that in 3 years there'll be a *Tower, 5 of Coins, 10 of Coins*: that 2008 financial barometer of futures funds.

Figure 10 – 3 Staves

We tend to view life through a static lens when nothing could be further from the truth.

YOU DIED AND DIDN'T KNOW

I've experienced near-death, more often than I can recall. As a grown person these near misses were surprising, but in retrospect only. I learned to recognize the pattern of reincarnation in a seemingly same body, and I put it to you. Did I die? Did you? How often have you been *so* sick, you wondered if you'd make it through the night? How often have you been so traumatized by brutality that you could hardly breathe? Did you almost fall—or jump—from the lip, either metaphorically or literally, of a cliff or tall building, but didn't? Each of these is an initiatory step into an unknown—but destined—future. Did you die and you just didn't realize?

WHAT IS INITIATION?

My grandmother isn't a blood relative, but that elder woman reads cards and tealeaves with unnerving accuracy. She relocates from her Kings Cross eyrie, into our big old house, when I am on the brink of the wilderness of adolescence, so I only fleetingly realize what she does. It's those barely registered moments that, retrospectively, form the threads that weave us into a recognizable tapestry, I am quickened. Later, some fifty years on, I write INITIATION | A MEMOIR, for people who maybe don't know—

> *Initiation is a mapped and charted experience that many people do not understand or recognize when the experience is not on their terms. You will be woken up. When wolf mother takes you*

in her jaws and pulls you into the myth you must realize you are helpless. You die to who you have been.

METAMORPHOSIS – THE LARVAL STAGE

It's 1980. I've dabbled with tarot, like a tease in a burlesque cabaret, from puberty. I was first initiated into witchcraft in 1968, but I'm in my late twenties when I take the responsibility of witchery seriously. I'm head of a coven by now, and one person, Lynden, reads tarot for their supper at shows. Several of us experiment, seriously, at interpreting the maps, for each other, at least once a week. Certain meanings, never static, never from a book. Oh, those books are there, and I'm sure I read them, but the titles have long since turned to compost. Not one of them informed of anything that had not been repeated elsewhere.

I collect different packs of cards. Liz Green's *Mythic Tarot*, Crowley's *Thoth* pack, *Rider Waite*, old replica stuff like the *Marseille* tarot. There isn't the impossible plethora of would-be decks like come later, most of which will be oracular, and pretty, and not tarot. Is there a difference? Yes. I'll get to that.

The year is 1979. I live in Sydney. I'm with a publishing company, setting up their computer system. I have birthed a child, and I am raising him as honestly as I know how. Not yet *me*. Just a grub unrealizing of the grotesquery of the chrysalis stage, of the experience of becoming. I consider myself authentic, but nothing could be further from the truth.

I come and go as I want. These are the years of the elite of computer wizards, and we practically star in *corporatedom*. Previously unrealized messianic radicals transforming a world that used to seem about people. Them becoming redundant, the writing on the wall but not yet seen, of poverty and uselessness. Of ineffectual schooling, and the threshold of a third industrial revolution. When I receive the phone call from Lynden, telling me how impossibly ill they are, that they don't want to lose their place with *Fortune Fair*, and will I please fill in for a week. I am both hesitant and cocky. Do I want to scry for strangers? Expose witchcraft to a superstitious public? Should I care? How humiliating to play the game? To dress in a dress-up-box of garments to convince the nameless and anonymous of the entertainment ruse? To pretend, even remotely, to competence? Am I at all fáidh-skilled, or a deluded woman in hoop earrings and red silk panne velvet?

I do it. I set up at a portable table and drape it in a midnight cloth, a pack of raggedy thumbed tarot cards, and a box, in which to collect the ten-minute session's worth of dollars, on its corner. By nine that morning a line has formed, and by midday it snakes to the escalator. Maybe fifty or sixty people. I don't recall specifics, but I know I am brash, uncaring. Certain I will never see any of them again, therefore telling who is going to get beaten, go loopy, lose their job, get married, suffer the PTSD of a pointless war, live alone, succeed and die.

MOTHS TO A FLAME

The following day the crowd is like a line of spectators at a zoo, sensing me as a predator, but unable to stay away. The piazza where

I am, reeking of the body odor of fear and expectation, of rosary beads and sly smiles, hides desire. A little of that vulgar stuff, called patchouli, wafts from the palm reader. Women are dressed in black, wear gold crucifixes, in all that gruesome, dead-god detail, are square-bodied and too old to be seeking any possible way out of what they were sold as success. Most are European immigrants bringing translators with them. I wonder, briefly what is going on, but my own box is full of money come midday. Thankfully, my current lover: black-irised, quick-witted, darkly humored storyteller of a man joins the queue, pulling me (goofy, as I stumble) from my chair, to get coffee and food. I lose all understanding of hours, and of the number of people who watch my face for hope or honesty, but by the end of the week, when Lynden recovers, and is ready to return to their place at that strange vulnerable table, these strangers' friends and relatives want my phone number.

...

DEATH

Figure 11 – Destination Rebirth

DESTINATION REBIRTH

Saturn Return is an astrological term. It hits, like a cement mixer whose driver doesn't see the stop sign at the T intersection, at around twenty-eight and, if you live long enough, again at fifty-six. Saturn takes approximately twenty-eight, twenty-nine years, to complete one full orbit around the sun, and literally return to the same zodiac sign it was in when you were born. It's meant to be one of the deciding astrological factors in life. Saturn, it is written by some, defines our limitations, although, as planets go, poor *saturn* has a bad rap. I am not aware of this when I quit my corporate job, when I go from snatching people's livelihood from them, to full-time fáidh-skilled, the Gaeilge (Irish)—ancestral—title of forecaster. A navigator on this ship of destiny.

I don't know this as an initiation, but it is. I am of the mind, in these early years, that initiation takes place at the pointy end of a sword, in the hands of those older and far wiser than I. You and I, however, were born to be heretics, anarchists, foxes in a chicken coop, screechers and scratchers-at-prison-bars, lovers of poetry, sex, rock and roll, carriers of placards for equal rights, bomb-and-war-banning, equality, black eyeliner and sorcery. Have we always been this way? Knowing injustice to be discrimination? Who are we kidding?

People are trapped in roles assigned them by religious boundaries and taboos, by their bodies. So, I'm not sure that I, in the recesses of lucidity, am capable of riding over, like an M36 Tank Destroyer, in a dance of the need for acceptability on a wider stage than my own logic. But in these early years I agree. Did you? It's a symbolic thing, this people-expressed acceptance into a secret society. Life is seriously more savage.

> *No one can hold us should we choose to make this choice, to wear the next mask and to clothe ourselves in this new garment of self. We don't have to cleave to the identity that we thought defined us. Life is art. Life wants experience through who we are and what we do. Wants the lone wolf to run with the pack.*

Am I lucky? Is it luck or fate? I am not *married* (in any traditional sense), not trapped by gender or religious expectations, not enmeshed in cultural normalcy, so the sheer numbers making contact, after I read for that week, mean I say goodbye to my day job, and adjust to how I will do this *tarot interpreter* raincoat-identity. I have to leave the family home, of course. My child and I move into a house painted deep bottle green, sharing with Sue and her dozen large dogs. But strangers have the old phone number, and my poor mama is kind enough to give them my new one.

I have aged in a blur of decades, or is it lives? But for at least forty of them, tarot has been a partner. Companion and teacher. Most deviously humored entity, ensnaring raven feathers at the crossroads, all pointing in one direction, to play me like a marionette. Would things have been different had I not recognized omens and portents? I did. We all do. So, no.

> *Like all profound mysteries, it is so simple that it frightens me. It wells from the rock, and flows away. For unnumbered years it has welled from the rock, and flowed away. It does nothing, absolutely nothing, but be itself.*
>
> Nan Shepherd, *The Living Mountain*

Many of you have your hearts metaphorically ripped out and your sanity threatened. So many of you grasp the thinnest of branches to stop your fall from the edge of the aforementioned cliff, into the crashing waters of the ravine three hundred feet below, the shallowest of caves to protect you from the storms of illness, rejection, disillusionment, abandonment. Death is a story. Just a story we are fed… for what?

HIV-AIDS

Figure 12 – STDs

As years unfurl, so does the company I keep, the lovers I laugh with, and the number of offspring I birth, the thrumming with magic, and the journeys from one man-mapped state, across man-made borders, to another. One environment to the next. Fascination still haunting me even now, in this era of mobile phones and social media, that I am found, every time, through word of mouth alone.

From twenty-eight until I know better, I am *high priestess* of a coven, involved with *wicca* and by being so, claiming that title (bestowed on me), not awake yet to contrivances of this, a new-old religion. Still trapping the wolf in a cage and demanding to be acceptable. I work with initiates, and I am teaching meditation and visualization, hypnosis and spellcraft, studying everyone from Franz Bardon to Barbara G Walker, learning everything about indigenous people, herbal healing, living off-grid, midwifery, Abrahamic lore, burning incense and, as honestly as I can be, being a hippy dressed in black, gathering the branches of lightning-struck elms, smithing silver jewelry, and analyzing how to live with two more kids, the same partner, and an adolescent son, all while working this *skill*.

Then, in the early nineteen-eighties James makes an appointment, and comes to me, now living in a cottage in the forest, a three-hour drive from Melbourne.

Figure 13 – Natural Death

When I lay out their story, here's the *Devil*, the *2 of Cups*, the *9 of Swords*, the *Tower* and oh, I don't know what else. The *Ace of Swords* and the *Death* card are in proximity, but not for James, only for his associates. What is this? Their outcome is the *10 of Cups*. Home. Best card in the pack. But all that is just trivia. What I spae is the Grim-Reaper-in-the-Bowling-Alley ad from the telly between my imagination and the table. They ask, before they are supposed to ask any questions, why I have gone green around the lips, and it takes a seagull-swarm of coercion on their part to get me to tell.

HIV, I say, a sort of a wasp in my throat.

I got full-blown AIDS. I just want to know how long I'll live, is James' reply. *Got to get things in order.*

I don't see your death, I say.

Retrospectively, it seems that every young man with HIV (this is the eighties, when this disease is a death-sentence) is visiting from Melbourne, sitting across the table from me. I don't spae their deaths. I spae their friends' and lovers' deaths, suicide, grief, anger, despair. But that *10 of Cups* keeps coming, so I'm confused.

Michael, my student, and also a math professor, has stage four liver cancer. He asks me to advise him what really happens after we die. I say *I'll tell you when I get there*. He says that's not an answer. I ask if he wants me to be honest or make something up so that he's not so scared. I don't know anything yet.

THE OBSERVATION OF THE LIVING

Death is an observation. It's every time you come a cat's-whisker from ceasing life as you know it. You change after. Think about it. Every anaphylaxis, every time you suffer the flu, every infection, every child you bear, every close call. You change. So, after all the men, desperately ill (and most I never heard from again), and sitting with me in confusion, wondering what I mean, I conduct a survey, a *daonáireamh*—a census of sorts. I ask travelers and friends, oh anybody, actually, how close they've come, and what happens afterwards. And every time, they tell me life gets weird. Or *they* do.

I'm teaching a cluster of tarot students, years later, and we discuss this. They don't quite understand. I ask them to close their eyes and hold out their hand, in their imagination, palm up. I ask them to visualize a small, *smurf*-type critter with blue skin and a conical yellow and green-spotted hat, holding a white surrender flag, waving at them. When they open their eyes I ask, *did you see*? They all do. *Again*, I say. They close their eyes and I instruct them to imagine being dead. Nobody can. They imagine seeing their body on a slab (who is doing the looking?) They envision endless space (who is envisioning?). They imagine, they imagine that they imagine. They are present. And it makes sense.

Then there's Dennis. He comes to me in November 2018, aged sixty. An entire adult life worked in instant-coffee offices, in aircon, under fluorescent lighting, in technology. They're married to a person they love.

They have explored consciousness through copious *ayahuasca* ceremonies, and plans, on retirement, to travel the world. Instead they are diagnosed with advanced motor-neuron disorder and will be dead by the coming April. This is one of those occasions where the *Death* card is just that. The concept, the thought, the wall they face. I ask, quietly, secretly, if they've sorted it out, and they say yes. They have already traveled to Mexico to get hold of a *Nembutal,* because the final stage of this disease is suffocation, and euthanasia is still illegal in most of Australia. Their outcome card is the *Star*.

...

LIFETIME AWARD

Figure 14 – Exalted End of Life

That's it, I say. *You've done it.*

Done what? Dennis asks.

Everything you were born to do. There's nothing to think about.

I have regret, they say softly. Tears.

Why? Like a goose attacking a truck, I'm genuinely surprised.

Plans.

I laugh a bit. It bubbles close to the surface, and Dennis smiles at the look on my face, knowing, just not understanding why.

Explain, they demand softly, already getting it.

See that? I point to the *Star* card. *You've lived everything. It's that high and that vast.*

What happens next? they also ask, predictably for a traveler.

I'll tell you when I get there, I answer, again.

RECYCLED IN A SONGLINE

Each initiation—each lifetime—is an opportunity to add beauty to living. To be authentic. What's it for? Nothing. People ask me their purpose. There isn't one. This striving to achieve a reason for being, is terrible. It is cruel and demeaning. The concept divides us. Important or not. Worthy or not. Significant or not. We live. That in itself is beyond amazing. Defies all rational thought. In a solar system that seems devoid of life as we know it, we get to be crowded in with staphylococci, tree sap and bears, in the company of wind and starlight, with the DNA and mitochondrial alliances of countless billion, trillion years. And when we appear corpse-like and are buried or burned, we go nowhere. We remain earth. We nourish mycelium, unimaginable forests and savannahs, future evolutionary species, people-animals maybe, weather, and forever.

What has this to do with tarot? Everything. I get it. But first, all my bigotry and preconceived senses of importance and dogma, have to go. We, in the so-called privileged civilized *first world*, responsible for so much carnage, have been misled into thinking of death as a crossroads. That there is an afterlife that includes judgement and bling and fluff. Even the idea of *karma*, *reincarnation*, is all askew. I am your plunger, and you are my blocked sink.

JUMPING MOUSE AND A COUPLE OF BILLION YEARS

To be native to a place we must learn to speak its language.
Robin Wall Kimmerer, *Braiding Sweetgrass*

No understanding of time happens without the considerations of life and death, but we've been misled and that's a reason for sadness, and the voracious, pompous, never sated and overpriced funeral industry. To become a teacher and elder, life and tarot have required that I *change my mind* (whatever mind is), and that I continue doing so. I thought I understood about immortality once. But I was clueless. It wasn't until I read Hyemeyohsts Storm's *Seven Arrows* that I got it, that we're not the species at the centre of everything and that we—you and I—as individuals, are beautiful. But superfluous. Other than for the meat of us. I learned this from the *Jumping Mouse* story. Of how we transform, on our individual quests to find some truth or other, and constantly *die* to who and what we are, or think we are, but that we don't actually even exist in the big picture. So, where's the tragedy? Where the right and wrong? How do we even figure in the larger schemes of forest, mountain and sea, or are we merely walking the brambly undergrowth, being followed by the predator that we also are? What makes each of us unique? Are any of us so? If yes, how? The answer is both simple and conflicting. Any breakthrough is better than belief. Any defiance of servitude, or lassitude, pertaining to a norm. Why not?

In J. Mouse's case, the source of the river is where? Nobody else, in JM's tribe, asks that question so, sheer guts, bereft of both eyes and a body, later, JM not only realizes the truth of their quest, or so we surmise (because mouse-person has no eyes to see the bubbling rising from the breast of earth mother), they become another species altogether: eagle-person. Then, having read this fable, questions come to me, like how do we know that mouse is now eagle when we don't see ourselves? And why do we, as a mammalian species, gain so much kudos within our communities for our great capacity to name things, in a frenzy of objectification, that we don't actually ask these deeper questions concerning *being* and *becoming*. A *you are what you eat* story. That and the understanding that we are 90% bacteria that have been around forever. Estimates suggest 2.5 billion years, but what about before that? Estimates also age Parent Universe as being for 13.8 billion years. How does knowing that help you know tarot? How can any of us accurately predict explicit events unless we know they are going to happen? We'll cover this further into the story but getting your head around how old you *really* are—probably—is a feasible start.

The story of J Mouse is roughly this: their tribe lives by the river. No one questions the river. The river just is. JM? Questions knowledge of the river. Why it always goes in the same direction. Where it comes from. When no one in JM's tribe either has an answer, or wants one, JM has to learn to communicate with other species. Frog, buffalo, coyote, and finally eagle. At least, these are the names we have labelled these people-critters as being. And in labelling them we think we know all about them. But I suggest we know nothing, and that this *knowing* is a very substantially important place for the fáidh-skilled to sit with a traveler, before beginning their voyage.

EXERCISE–PEBBLES AND POOLS

In your mind's eye spae a pool of still water and visualize dropping a pebble into the center of the surface. Two things—
- Understand, during the vision, that the pool is bottomless

- Observe the concentric ripples that expand outward from the center where they stop at a finite shore

This is the perennially autumnal Forgotten Lake, that I write about in both *The Quickening* and *The Shining Isle* books. I sit here to understand time. The pebble dropping endlessly through Ancestor Water is as rich an analogy as is the finite surface expression of any event.

> *It seems that time has an arrow, in a sense that space does not. If you make yourself a cup of coffee with cream and sugar, you can raise your cup, drop it, move it left, or move it right. You cannot put it back to the way it was before you added the cream and sugar.*

This is applicable to *every* observable event. Although they seem to have their place in past, present or future, there is another aspect to the story—that they exist forever. This leads me to discuss one theory of how tarot prophecy happens, and this is the *Arrow of Time*.

...

THE THEORY OF EVERYTHING

Figure 15– Hand of Staves

THE ARROW OF TIME

When the hypothesized *Big Bang*, or the moment of the speculated birth of a universe, happens, we exist. Nothing comes from nothing, so of course I do consider that the *Big Bang* can simply be another universe passing through an infinitely small orifice, or sound generating a material expression, or the superposition of two mutually opposing waves somewhere beyond anywhere known, or an exploding/imploding singularity. Or, on the other hand it can as easily occur because a god child wants to experiment, in some far-flung corner of their mother's laboratory, with a project that may or may not be dangerous.

Inherent in the DNA of every living thing is all that is, and always is. The iron in our hemoglobin is original iron, the hydrogen molecules in our body's waters are the same hydrogen as always exists, as is every other element and compound that makes us, *us*. The knowledge has been passed from our biological parents, to them from theirs and so on all the way along the Arrow of Time, even before we are, theoretically, amoeba in a soup of one-celled creatures floating in the viscous seas of Infant Earth with no discernible differences to blowflies, elephants or mold.

This theory of the origins of Earth introduces us to our mothers and our fathers, and our DNA remembers them (to re-embody that which has come before). We are so conditioned to think that our lives begin with our births and will end with our deaths, no matter the notion of an *afterlife*, that we do living an injustice. We consciously ignore our immortality.

When a traveler comes to you, sits at your table and shuffles their future into the pictorial book of 78 images representing one way of interpreting tarot, they unknowingly sort them into effective order—an impossibility to do intentionally—that something *other* than randomness is most definitely involved. This supposed shuffle is akin to an accomplished pianist playing Rachmaninoff's Piano Concerto No. 2 in C Minor. Every one of us has, at least, since a hypothetical *Big Bang* to become savvy.

PRACTICE–
DIGGING FOR THE ROOTS OF YOUR ANCESTRAL TREE

It should begin as something like this:

Figure 16 – Y Node Ancestry

Where it ends... Well, it doesn't end, but we all must stop what we're doing and being sometime. At the edges of a page. Each pair of branches that extend away from you drive deeper into the deep, deep unknown, and represent countless ancestors. You are the biological result of two parents. It took two of each, to make them, that's four people. These four have a pair of parents each, that's eight people. These eight also result from a pair: sixteen. And so on. Suggesting an average generation as being twenty-five years, can you calculate how many direct progenitors you are, also, in the last two thousand years? Calculate *that* figure by five hundred and forty million years.

How then can anyone ever predict the future, either for an individual or a nation? And how can anyone hold these events to any biologically recognized lifespan? The events have already occurred in one way or another. How do I justify this? The universe is still catching up with itself.

Again, considering the hypothetical *Big Bang*, we are informed that in a matter of a speculative 10^{43} of a second, energy expands throughout the known universe in an almost equal, yet asymmetrical quantity of matter and antimatter. As these two materials come into existence they collide, seeming to destroy each other while, in reality, transferring energy from forever to forever. It takes another infinitely small period for common particles to form. These particles are called baryons, and include photons, neutrinos, electrons and quarks that will become the building blocks of matter and life as we know it. During the baryon genesis period there are no recognizable heavy particles such as protons or neutrons because of the intense heat. Quark soup. As the universe begins to cool, and expands exponentially, we glean more clearly what exactly is happening.

Within two to three minutes the universe cools to about 3000 billion degrees Kelvin and, to cut an exceptionally long story short, matter begins a journey, through the sea, or space, to becoming continuous, exploring eternity.

The point here is that matter follows energy and not only is this so, they co-exist, knowing each other in passing.

...

Life's never a postcard of life, is it? It never feels like how you'd want it to look.

Russell Brand,
My Booky Wook

Figure 17 – Books

A CAGE OF SELF-IMPOSING

Mind and a brain are not mutually inclusive. Mind is indefinable and ineffable. Mind contains the triggers that will recognize everything you'll ever learn. Mind is the environment of imagination, the forest of hidden and extant symbolism, all value-judgements, learned or programmed reactions to external scenarios and observations. Mind seems to reside in a person's head—to be brainy—but is that necessarily so? Couldn't it as easily be that mind (you without a body) doesn't exist within the confines of a circus-like conditioning? A cage of self? Is interpreted by your brain, just as is all *external* stimuli?

And it never shuts up. Darryl Reanney, in *Music of the Mind*, suggests that thought and light are synonymous. They both seem to *be* at the same impossible speed and, even when supposedly achieving deep state meditation, there are a trillion, billion lives in your gut and on your skin, having sex, breeding and dying. There's a delightful background synapse sizzle and full environmental awareness in case of unexpected hyena attack.

Thought, like light, is in a seeming wave state, because the thing about thought is that it isn't anywhere and, like light, it can exhibit itself as both wave and particle. What transforms thought into particle? Whether thoughts and ideas manifest in a material outcome depends on our interpretation of them, into perceived reality, through the medium of stuff. The future does not, in any true sense, exist. Not until events happen, and are recognized as happening, does the so-called future come into being, and by the time it does the events will have *already occurred*, therefore events yet to come are already in the past. There is, as was mentioned earlier, no beginning to anything and no end either, and all such considerations are value-judgements, open to error (in the light of future history) because—as physics clearly demonstrates—there is no such thing as an impartial observation.

A person coming to your table to have their future foretold will do so for many reasons but all of them are serious. Some of those reasons are:

- As a seeming sceptic. They may very well even *want* you to be a fraud. That would provide them with a sense of safety that the real deal would disrupt unimaginably
- Out of curiosity because someone else came before them
- For you to tell them that everything in their distressed lives will work out okay
- To have you give them answers to their choices
- For the sheer privacy and company that only a total stranger can provide
- If you have a reputation for accuracy they will come because they want to hear what you have to say

The reality is that they were always going to come because they *have* come. Could they have avoided coming? No, because they are here, and along the way to being with you were countless alternatives. None taken.

...

CLOSE ENCOUNTERS

Figure 18 – Walking Through

WALKING THROUGH WHAT HAPPENS

A traveler makes the initial contact. That has changed both your realities because space and distance are contrivances. Even the so-called sceptic's reality has changed: they have agreed to the voyage into the unknown, through this suspect witchcraft and practitioner's suspect skill.

An appointment is made and, consequently, unseen and

occulted, a reaction is occurring and will continue to affect forever. It is only within the tiniest window of each of our lives that something that utterly defies the laws of probability occurs.

The central theme of the consultation unfolds like this—

- They arrive and you guide them into a private space
- After you lay out an opening pattern with the cards that you use to separate the images in the pack from the last person, you hand them to the stranger sitting opposite you at your table
- They shuffle
- For map after map, you to do all the talking, until the first section of the foretelling is done, at which time you might agree to them asking questions
- At the completion of their voyage the traveler pays an agreed sum and sails away

Reads as simple enough, doesn't it? It isn't. Everything plays a part in what happens next: the traveler, their DNA and ancestral bacteria mixed in with yours, that of every card and everything in your surroundings.

When you interpret what they've sorted, you're collapsing what was, until that moment, the probability of only one of very many possible futures. *What's spoken can't be unspoken.* Matter is slower than light (or free energy), therefore manifest events will happen more slowly than the thought or spoken word, because matter must catch up. But it will – no matter how bizarre the prophecy; no matter how out of left field.

The events that tarot predicts will happen. What a person does, when they happen, is free-will. Each event is like a destination, clearly marked. The outcome of the event is rarely given, because not only the traveler's actions and intentions, but those of others, will come into play once the event is realized. The only absolutes are birth and death, and even then, these are observations, and there's always a before and an after…

OPENING SPELL

(This will be mentioned again later). Lay out the pictograms in the shape of a traditional wiccan banishing pentagram (or any shape you fancy), then pick up each of the packs, put them together again, and hand them over: *Never shuffle them.* Shuffling them yourself will contaminate their journey with yours.

Figure 19 – Opening Pattern

The process is like ordered randomness and, if none of the cards have stuck together the last image in the story that you lay out will fall on point 3.

HOPE

You may say I'm a dreamer, but I'm not the only one.

John Lennon, *Imagine*

Figure 20 –Pied Piper

TRUTHSAYER

People often ask me how long before they can come again and my usual answer is *When the events have happened, or enough of them for other probabilities to show up*. This is important because there *are* tarot-junkies.

Whenever a follow-up reading occurs tarot is often disinclined to mention the forecasts that have *not* happened and can often make events seem larger—or more significant—than they will be, because of the time/space-factor. By this, I mean that the earlier prediction, over an approximate two year period, will be magnified, so that financial wealth (*Sun* card, *Ace of Coins*) within the span of two years could represent thousands and thousands of dollars, but if the traveler returns in six months, with none of the events having yet happened, the same two stories could represent finding a fifty dollar note on the street.

Figure 21 – Wealth

You, as fáidh-skilled, will lose your objectivity if you read for the same person too many times, because it's imperative that you forget everything about your journey with them until, and if, you are reminded of it another day. The forgetting is selective, and some people might think you are addled because you don't recall them or their lives. You'd go crazy if you did, but… nobody will know just how many people visit you, thinking, perhaps you are like them. You're not. Nor will you ever be.

THE RANDOM FACTOR AND THE FOOL

And the Piper advanced and the children followed,
And when all were in to the very last,
The door in the mountain-side shut fast.
From the Pied Piper, various authors since 1284

The accurate foretelling of an event, that is recognized explicitly in the realization of a manifest experience, is not random, but there *are* odd-ball things that happen, and often these are obfuscated by the *Fool* card.

When the *Fool* shows up, without the interaction of other indicators, the card hides an event that the traveler is not to know about. It does this because some things must seem like accidents if they are to alter the course of the traveler's future. This is a paradox because the traveler would most certainly have set up this accident as a means of changing a problem situation in their life and they are afraid to change the problem thing in their life and therefore require the intervention of the random element, or fate, to trigger the job for them. Unless it turns up with some tricky patterns—

Fool with the *Moon*, and the *6 of Swords*: can be, literally, fishing.

Fool with *Death*, can be suicide

Fool with a card representing a person—our own species, or any other—can be a seemingly random, but significant, meeting

Fool, with a person card... can be a fool

BEING PSYCHIC AND OTHER WEATHER AUGURING

Figure 22 – Lascaux Hunting Magic Art

A psychic is someone who seems to be psychic. Psychic means relating to ghosts and the spirits of the dead. Synonyms: supernatural, mystic, magical, occult, clairvoyant, other-worldly.

Collins Online Dictionary

WHAT IS TAROT?

Do you have to be psychic to interpret tarot? What a strange question, but I have been asked this by someone in every coven I have taught. Yes. Of course. What's witchcraft, after all, but a quizzical practice that won't fit acceptable parameters? We'll never be popular. There's a *but*. What is supernatural, in difference to natural? What is a ghost, a spirit, the dead? The quote above mentions mental powers but we've already covered that, in the consideration of the mind and the brain. And that nothing dies.

What tarot *isn't*, is just a pack of seventy-eight cards. It's way bigger and much more exciting. Because what applies to us as a species, and to our immortality, also applies to the entirety of everything including these seventy-eight pictographic stories, or words, that, in the not-so-distant yesterday, were trees, blowing in the wind of late winter; of a forest family somewhere, the outcome of every preceding seed. It's the same principle with everything, and there is absolutely *no such critter* as an inanimate object.

The word *tarot* is French. In Italy it was/is known as *tarocchi* from the earlier *carte da trionfi* (or representations of triumph), in Germany, *tarock*, in Hungary *tarokk*. It's suspected that the word originated in the Arabic *taraha* (reject) but no one knows for sure. There's power in words but it seems to me that the power invested in the word stems from what the cards, representing tarot, do or don't do—

- Individually they do nothing
- Without the hand of the fáidh-trained, they do nothing
- When they are eventually falling to pieces, like feral cloth, a few of us bury them and plant over them. There are enough bacteria and fungi, embedded in a well-worn pack of stories, to be excellent compost

...

A FÁIDH TRAINED NAVIGATOR IN A JADED WORLD

Tarot is a word to describe a technique of foresight that works, and tarot is a map, a wayshower, therefore a loon, way out to sea—some kind of *god*—that defies categorizing. Tarot, through fáidh-skilled witchcraft, forecasts events that have seemingly not yet occurred, more so than any other art, even down to exact times, names, places and descriptions. I will explain that last bit when I discuss the murders here in Melbourne, since January 2019, that have enthralled the media. What I saw. How I can warn.

Tarot is not the folly of *past-life* exploration (unless by this, you understand, that I refer to that which is ancestral), not spiritual or emotional balm, or psychological diagnosis, the fáidh-skilled will only ever tell a traveler of future experiences, and news, no matter *what* the seeker *wants* to hear. Tarot is blunt, and as often disturbing as reassuring, and *light-bulb* moments can interrupt an interpretation with unexpectedly pertinent information, such as world events or even other people's stories, people the traveler has not even met and may never meet but will assuredly know of. Or other. These *light-bulb* moments don't require material pictograms.

A woman jets across the Tasman Sea from Auckland, on the north island of New Zealand. While she's still shuffling—before any maps are laid out—I have a realization. These happen as abruptly as a car crash.

Adult-onset grand mal epilepsy, I say. Urgently. *Don't go back.*

She's gone all peculiar. Bluish around the lips. As happens, if a stranger throws that at you, and you've left your spouse of over two decades (in the dead of night, your kids in their jammies) three months ago, because he's brutal, obnoxious, dismissive and needy, all at the same time, shooting up meth, disappearing with his bros for days, and then drinking himself into a stupor every night when he eventually comes home. Then the epilepsy sets in. Ten, twelve, more, seizures a day. And both her parents, and her parents-in-law tell her it's her duty to look after him… for better or worse, in sickness and in health, and all that biliousness. *Till death us do part.* What is *that*? It's why she's come all this way.

She's got her answer. I don't know what else I say that day, but who cares? She doesn't.

Tarot teaches—if such an entity trusts that we won't stop learning—because tarot *is* time. And tarot knows what's beyond this momentary season of mist and moonless night. Tarot is the unraveler. The slow unknotting of the accepted present. Tarot is a bullied hound. It will trust us *only* if we know the language of dog—and are honest—with what we say with all of ourselves, not just a mouth. Tarot only trusts us if we *admit* to the traveler what we spae, no matter how seemingly stupid, off-the-wall, crazy, uncomfortable or unbelievable it might seem, to either you—the fáidh-trained spé—or the person with the pack of cards in their hands.

…

DEEP LISTENING

If you learn to listen to the silence, you'll hear more of everything else.

Jon Young, *What the Robin Knows*

Figure 23 – Deep Listening

TRACKER LANGUAGE

There's a difference between *communication and babble*. Observe people. Talk with others without entering your waiting self-chat into the conversation. Ask them to explain what they really mean. People will share their knowledge, their experiences and viewpoints, if they know you are listening. Their body language is telling most of the story, an understanding *without* words. Your own reactions and responses? Am I respectfully open to interpreting them on a plethora of levels? Or am I filling in the gaps with what I assume is meaning? If I intuitively pick up passing thought-scraps that seem to be precognitive, I either suggest the information eventually, and considerately, or I shut up, but I don't forget.

> *How on earth do they remember so much stuff? Their very survival depended on it.*
>
> Dr. Lynne Kelly, *The Memory Code*

If Jo phones and tells me they are getting married, and a small mind-voice whispers, *Oh-oh!* I don't say anything, of course, but I certainly file the thought away for future reference.

This is called *deep listening*.

I came across *deep listening* through the work of Jon Young, when he encountered the technique from Kalahari people. When Jon and the tribal representative first met, he was asked to talk about who he is. At first the thought was daunting because he didn't understand the protocol. The Kalahari elder put his head in his hands and listened to Jon speak for forty-five minutes, at the end of which he shook Jon's hand and agreed to meet with him in the evening. That night the same process happened. This was repeated on several occasions. Jon couldn't figure out what was going on until his translator explained that his host was mapping him. Forming mental maps that could lead him straight to Jon's door on another continent.

ORALITY

Australian scholar, writer and researcher Lynne Kelly, author of *The Memory Code*, understands non-literate cultures and classifications, as does Potawatomi elder, Robin Wall-Kimmerer, explaining this in her most recent book, *Gathering Moss*. As we move into the maps and the interpretations to come, it's necessary to build memory trackways, erect dolmens between mountains, paint hunting magic on the walls of limestone caves. To recognize patterns beyond ourselves. Deep listening means suspending the identity and lexicons we have erected, sometimes over a lifetime, because even though the traveler and I are both speaking English, that does not mean we are communicating in the same language or understanding what is being said.

Refer to synapses—firing together, wiring together—because people only know how to speak from within the ring of their cultural or habitual *Fight Club* and as a fáidh-trained artist of witchcraft you need to interpret what you are hearing, or picking up. And you can't be wrong. These language denominators are also religious and geographical, and that does not simply denote only those from other lands and cultures. I live in Melbourne and the dialogue of a person in Sydney is altogether different. A person living close to homelessness will speak a specific language to someone, struggling to afford the mortgage on apartment they occupy, and who pays the bank four thousand dollars a month.

Fáidh-skill requires a worldliness that many reject or fear. We must understand the persona we are presenting, in a society that may not even recognize our indigene. Do I know it? Have I stolen an identity to fit a cultural (or pack) agreement?

The more I listen to, and hear, the more will be communicated. A small, solemn and undeterred voice has been talking all my life but for years I gave it no attention. Society and tradition warned me against such misbehavior.

Watch the news. Update yourself on current events because they *will* sneak into readings and it *will be necessary* to recognize them as being unrelated to the intimate experiences of the traveler. Ignore the hype and the politics, that's all, because they're always biased by the media-anchor's bosses. Such are meant to be entertaining when, instead, they play on prejudice and habitual agreement.

BLACK AND WHITE ON A RAINBOW SPECTRUM

With tarot there is no right or wrong. Binary, or polar opposites like that, are a weakness of vocabulary. They are vulgar and refer to architecture, arches and straight lines, not morality. Predicting events as you or I spae them, or hear or taste or feel them, even sometimes as we smell them, because all our senses come into play sooner or later, some more than others depending on talent, requires non-denial. Syntax and context. The most appropriate way to describe an answer spoken to the traveler, is to evoke a technique used, when in a potentially dangerous situation: what you do *not* do is to look into the eyes of an opponent, because to do so is to become trapped within the identity that *they* perceive, and you are no longer able to register the telegraphing of information available through non-spoken communication. Therefore you, as fáidh-trained, are the equivalent of the martial artist who will look at nothing and spae everything.

SEI CHU TO – FROG-SKILLED

Frogs do it. Leopards, cats, lions, snakes, dogs, wolves, bats and hawks. Do we? I think we've forgotten how. *Sei chu to* is a Japanese expression for a form of preparedness and action. It doesn't really translate into English, but is important to mention. Yes, you can go spontaneously into a session because someone has turned up unexpectedly and is desperate. But who does that? A green tree frog takes up a position on the edge of my kitchen kettle (back in the days when I ate bread), not far above the toaster. The whole top half of frog-person is suspended in mid-air. Frog-person remains like that for countless hours. Frog-person displays no discomfort, no exhaustion, no exasperation, no impatience. They simply are. That's the *chu* part of the equation. The *sei* is the action of climbing onto the kettle and settling into *chu*… (some frogs can *chu* for years, a meter underground, if there is no rain) until the cockroaches come out of the woodwork for the toast crumbs.

And then the *Froginator* is gone until another night, leaving me the shiny, iridescent brown defecations as gifts to their fellow-residents. That *to* occurs when insight strikes.

Tarot predicting is the incomparable speed of a threatened brown snake. I don't think about it, but I have prepared for the event. From the moment the traveler makes contact they are somewhere, somehow, with me. I don't think about it. You won't think about it or you'll go loopy. It's not describable in any other way. You'll even dream their dreams, but will you know it? No. Oh, for hindsight being foresight! I get it, I do. We couldn't live should we constantly be in this arena of awareness. As sure as I sit with you, though, that *chu* process has been active.

Sei has been your life since deciding that tarot, and fáidh-skilled witchery, is your destiny.

...

PART TWO

REVOLUTION
BEYOND GENDER, STEREOTYPE AND METAPHOR

And accept it that soon
You'll be drenched to the bone.

Bob Dylan,
Times They Are A-Changin', 1963

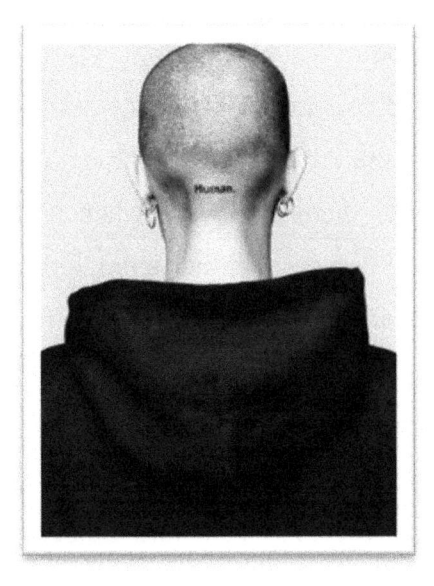

Figure 24 – Androgynous Human

BEING PRESENT

THE MUCK OF LANGUAGE

I've waded through the muck of language for decades. The English language. It's all I have. I say more with body than with mouth or typing fingers, but we are not sitting across from each other and the language of tarot is spoken. From you to me, to you. From traveler, to fáidh-skilled, to traveler, we are waves and weather and seasons of change, from wildfire to frozen water pipes. We will have problems, throughout this work, because my first language is, again, our bastard English, and so, probably, is yours. I'm establishing this now, because I intend to tear the flesh of theocratic, homocentric-speak, down to the bone, so that I am not misrepresented, and so that you are not misguided.

The language of my ancestors is like dead leaf-mulch become soil, then blown by the tail-end of a combine harvester, to dust and desert. We are left, therefore, with what remains, with all its savagery of foxtail grass. To be extracted slowly, and with compassion. Words and philosophy that are retrorse barbs. I've seen what they do. Jonesy and I keep company until he is shot by a farmer for playing with a flock of that man's sheep. Jonesy is an old Irish setter I rescued from a Castlemaine kill-center. I lay him down at the close of every day, tweezers in hand, and dig between his toes. Grass seeds are buried there, up to four-deep. In the damp corners of his eyes and under his lashes, within the soft pink of his ears. Inside his lips. In the delicate tissue of his anus. Religion is like this. Words used to explain law, in the language of universities. Of conquerage. Of colonizers and segregation. Words denoting right and wrong, based not on *tapu* and *rāhui* (see page 75 on) but on some alien book of liturgical, and ecclesiastic rules, imposed by a bunch of bearded old blokes at the Council of Nicaea, after the Roman Empire had dismembered indigenous Europe and imposed such tortures as crucifixion for disagreeing with its principles du jour. Torture, in an infancy, not yet disassembled in the twenty-first century, that has religious righteousness as a foundation. A madness beyond comprehension to us, as earth.

WEIRD

I have a book launch for WITCH | FOR THOSE WHO ARE, an anthology I put together for exponents of witchcraft who are past the beginner phase. The event is at *the Muses of Mystery*, a niche supply-and-training venue here in Melbourne. The facilitators agree with me that we'll be able to squeeze maybe twenty to twenty-five people into the room after we move the big table out. I put the event on Facebook, knowing that if ten people write that they are coming, two are likely to turn up. Close to a hundred and fifty people come. A couple of those people have lived longer than forty years, but the others are much younger.

What attracts such a crowd? Most are fey, practitioners of some form of witchery or other, artists, performers and rockers-of-boats. Most are Queer.

You're all so... I say lightly, my eyes delighting in this profusion of an such an eclectic and artistically-adorned species, "...*weird*." The comment raising eyebrows, tilted heads, shrugged shoulders, wry smiles and murmurs of *Mhmms*. There is laughter at the realization of the truth of that enfoldment, that encompassment. *Weird* is the revolution. The grass roots movement of people who represent the Rage Against the Machine lyrics, from the track *Killing in the Name*: "*Fuck you I won't do what you tell me…*" in the *Muses* that day are academics, strippers, musicians, designers, destitutes, artists, dropouts, storytellers, performers, directors, film makers, adventurers, animists, martial artists and the curious. Of any and every gender persuasion. The generation that wears velvet and crowns, claiming a hierarchy and communicating with a tongue of religion while still buying christmas presents and dressing up with green faces and pointy hats at Samhain, is dying out. One of my sons says, *Mama, you don't listen*. I am still learning.

EARTHTALK

To have genuine a voice, an earthcentric conversation, is one of the oddest studies of this lifetime. Because there is little reference. No human being in my vicinity speaks sparrow or hedgehog, ravine or sink hole. I hear now. And the volume is cacophonous. The propaganda, the invasion of consciousness by arrogant old men who are braggarts and puffed up with self-righteousness is to be relegated to the outhouses, because most have been bought, and are now posturing: the figureheads of other killers, for profit. Titling people as *human resources*. You know it. I even sometimes turn on the radio and listen to the high-pitched women's voices suggesting a sale of one day only! As though squealing like a young girl will have you running to buy a fridge that exposes its inside, without you having to open the door, when your current one has no destiny, in the short span of probably a thousand or two years, other than as landfill on a devastated and beaten patch of once-soil... a non-essential item you can pay for on a credit card that will also fleece you for from 9% to 25% interest. Usury. Theft, to be honest.

We are living in the days of another human-species revolution. I am excited. And it is all predicted. The youngest two, of my most recent coven, make a mockery of the others—older by at least a decade—in their own way. By learning every single smidge that I've taught them, just so they can challenge me. As is fitting. The moment a knowledge-holder is complacent, lazy, or tries to keep the high ground despite being redundant, you know they have joined the enemy, because magic doesn't accept entropy. When, also, a ninety seven year old retired academic glues himself to the roadway in a rage of protest at the human degradation of our cousin-species of every kindred, I applaud... while an anchor person, reading from their teleprompter, recites that "protestors clash with police," (the emphasis on the first noun, on purpose) parroting the prescription against any idea of emancipated and individual opinion, inciting even louder public outrage.

Earth is slowly melting a previous glaciation. The geological Pleistocene, estimated to have begun around 2.6 million years ago, and only crossing some unseen barrier for eleven-odd thousand years, is gradually making way for what humans—apes thinking we are *sapiens*—are suggesting is now the ***Anthropocene***. Names. Just names and numbers. Enough to make anyone wonder about the straight-tusked elephants that roam Scotland (the purpose of birch being barkless, according to George Monbiot in his book, *Feral*), and rhinoceros, with frighteningly sharp, back-tipped horns, that are tattooed onto my back from the cave paintings of my ancestors of Cheveux and Lascaux, in the recently-named France, to the ibis and antelope on the walls of the caves of the Tassili Desert—the most barren-seeming, inhospitable landscape known to humans—that are non-existent, anymore, to that region, the result of global warming and, more recently, the map of the species we refer to as *us*. That we have the power; some deity-like ability, to destroy earth. What hubris. Also, how condescending and disturbingly entertained by the thought, or desire, for catastrophe.

Tarot foretells of this revolution, this environmental exclamation mark, in 2008 of this common era. That 2011 will herald an unprecedented new history. I don't get it right away. I also can't describe what images turned up on the table. Silly me. I have some vague notion that I know better, and that somehow tarot has got the year wrong. Probably because information highways are so sure that the end of the Mayan calendar, December 2012 (on my birthday, hey, that's funny) will see some *end-of-days* phenomenon. I sit with my grandson on a morning of that era—the day after watching the documentary *Solar Max*—adding the date into the search engine. The top entry reveals a NASA storm warning for 2011. Solar flare activity. Unprecedented. That's the forecast in '08. *There ya go*, I think. *That's it.*

That isn't it.

2011 is the year volcanos blow their tops from Iceland to Chile. Ash plumes ground aircraft across the globe. Fukushima nuclear reactors melt down. The Jasmin Revolution begins a people-driven groundswell of dissatisfaction at the pomposity of hierarchy that has not, today and into the next decade, even begun its tidal influx. Earthquakes like bees. The tipping-point. The herald of what has become an immediate crisis, according to our limited perception. I'm certainly not going to gloss over it. This *is* an era of the sixth mass extinction, and we, as a species, are observing the loss of others' habitats and feeding territories at an alarming rate. Doesn't matter, for argument's sake, whether you or I are personally responsible, but the truth is, I drive a car, and I currently nest in a people-type house, that is attached to the grid. I buy recycled toilet paper even though Australia has been outsourcing its supposed recyclables, to international tenders, countries and organizations that are eventually exposed as dumping it all into Mother River or Brother Sea and, having been exposed, now reject the mess, demanding *Clean up your own garbage, Australia.* And we are, currently, the three monkeys. Despite casting aspersions on those who are destroying vast self-sustaining environments, and the means for my children's children to eat nourishing, real food, and learn to provide for themselves and their village, people want what destruction provides. Albeit temporarily, because unnerving, and astonishing events *are* due. They are happening. They are to become more intense in your lifetime. Some will not survive them.

What is tarot saying now? About the coming three years? Weather-chatter? Planetary Earthtalk forecasts. Mouth-opening ecological reassessment. Tarot knows Dylan foretold in prophecy, even if those with vested interests think we have forgotten.

Only localized crisis: the fires, the floods, revolutions. Tarot never bothers with politicians that frame themselves in front of the media as whatever they seem. I can only conclude that tarot couldn't be bothered, as they are always the face of a huge, occulted wave of paperwork and agreements that neither you, nor I, will ever know. The *5 of Coins*. The *Tower* to the complacency of an acceptable paradigm. But... I have visitors—travelers—booked way ahead of today and I might finish writing this grimoire for you and wham, I am shown the next big thing. One day. I might laugh, I might sigh, I will add it to my next poetry.

So how does the seemingly linear problem of existence work?

TRAINING — TRAVELING TO NOWHERE

Now is as providential a moment as any to introduce you to what might happen when you experience one of those deaths. And to let you in on the secret: that you *have* been called, just not by any god you can name. I am going to give an example. Sufficient to say, examining your own and others' experiences will result in a serious readjustment to what is thought of as a straight line. Not when you've shed so many skins, so many times, but are confused, because you are conditioned into presuming you are failing. But you can't fail. Any of us can only experience, and amend, an unrecognizable jigsaw puzzle, accordingly, each instance we attempt to change.

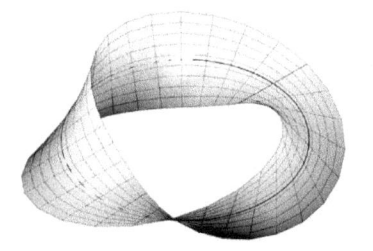

Figure 25 – Mobius Veil

This is important because you *will* get travelers asking about *past lives* and, with six degrees of separation between you and all other critters in existence, or the critters that ate them and then bred oh, ten, or twenty thousand years before now, transferring genome and DNA as a result, you are better placed to answer them truthfully, without flattering them, or explaining away traumas and disillusionments by laying blame on some perceived beyond-the-now payback.

Age twelve, during a year as a catholic, guess who decides their future is to be a nun?

Marry that poor two-thousand-year-dead white boy, who's portrayed in a state of perpetual agony and torture? What am I *thinking*? But I'm willing to bet my favorite pillow that something similar has been on your agenda at that fragile young age. Either that, or you want to be Samantha, Sabrina, or Nancy Downs the suspect goth from the niche movie *The Craft*. We do that. We peer into whatever mirrors there are, to somehow garment this feeling of immanence, and blossoming mysticism, in a physical manifestation. I'm still reading your posts on social media today, almost fifty years later. This wondering how to step inside the outside.

To never walk in the shadow of someone considered socially acceptable, when, should we live in another time, within another era, we might just recognize ourselves in the face of an elder, who recognizes us also.

But then I die. Twice. Brought back to life, from both an electrocution and drowning, in the same year. What *hasn't* left, when I understand how strange this desire for meaning—this *nundom*—is the intangible knowledge that some inexplicable vastness has made contact. And that it has remained. Within a year of this series of unusual meetings of life and death I am working seances and getting a feel for foresight. What I don't know, yet, is that this *immanence* is witchcraft, and that its most ragged, grease stained garment for me, is tarot.

This is how we learn, and this particular chapter is how to both spae the magical experiences, that happen without the aid of the *shamanic* journeys embracing the *Little Mothers*—indigenous visionary plant medicine—or guided trance, and the insidiousness of Abrahamic indoctrination of thought and subsequent behavior. Of the punishment of crushing. Of the threat of disconnection. Of being wolf with an unacceptable howl, cast out from the pack and doomed, consequently, to isolation, purposelessness, and attack from predation, even by our own kind. In Celto-European cultures we have been shaped and molded from a tribal, hunter-gatherer or nomadic-herder, way of life—still existing in miniscule, non-invaded places—into suit, tie and stiletto, bank account and pharmaceutical advocates, acting out the pathos of stolen seasonal festivals by racking up debt on junk that is never needed, and that won't be missed when it's put on the shelf in the garage. Consuming poisons and toxins in the name of acceptability, ho-ho-ho, and hating it. While fiercely defending the right to be sick.

Where do we find magic? This touching wonder? Orthodox religion? An Oriental spirituality brought to us by the Beatles in the sixties? What is the *cult du jour* anyway? Complaining certainly fits, and so does desire, depression, suicide, condescension, apathy, reckless affection, and a garmented, plastic surgeon-multi-million-dollar industry of affectation and body-modification. What is this?

When you have been called to a life of authentic mysticism?

How can anyone navigate safely through the shoals of social-media, trash pulp ideologies? Language. Language, language, language. Tarot is a language, as well as a voyage into a seeming-future, that should not happen but that does. Does it? Yes. And many have attempted, like Geoffrey of Monmouth (*The History of the Persons of Britain*, circa 1136) to articulate a non-religious, non-binary-biased, ancestral storytelling, to make it easier. To give meaning. Geoffrey did it by inventing his version of Arthur, a person with a grand plan, to try to give England back a bit of a Celtic soul. Way too late. That doesn't happen. Sadly, for those creatives.

Whether the seventy-eight pictograms are taken up by a publisher, or not, there is just something about the history of the old decks that informs. Without a discipline, and a wide worldly understanding, however, you will only touch the edges of what touched you, because you will still be mute.

TRAINING IN GODLESSNESS

No religious-speak. None. Religious-type babble usually happens without your conscious consent. As an expletive. When you are angry, surprised, to somehow enhance or make more important of whatever you are responding to. As a habit, or when you want to seem acceptably spiritual.

Oh, god! Oh. My. God. God-awful, heavenly, divine, sacred, holy, may you rot in hell, hellish. Christ! Halloween. Sacrifice. *My third eye... karmically speaking...* They don't end there, do they? When I discuss this with a coven, of navigators-in-training, and send them off for a week of notice-taking, they are initially confused, assuring me they don't use any of these expressions. That they mean them in a different way to religious, that they have reclaimed them in some *faux-pagan* manner. A predictable and almost unnoticed repetition of metaphor.

Not honest. Brainwashed. Lacking a comprehensive and interesting—a more inclusive—vocabulary, people often proffer a portable, pre-built list of appropriately outraged synonyms. When my students return the coming Saturday, they are deer in the headlights. *It is everywhere*. They are astonished. *I honestly never noticed before.* Or, probably laughing in half-seriousness, *You bitch, you knew this would happen.*

Often, I am asked, *how do I stop? What do I replace* Oh my god *with? My god, I say it all the time. So does my partner. Everybody does. See I just said it again! Oh god, I'm screwed.*

Then there's Disney, and all those pretty cartoon characters, and the dwarves in Snow White… and that strange date in the Pied Piper, when, having read the originals and realizing how betrayed we all are by popular propaganda, there never was a prince, there never was a kiss, and the rats were not rats or the children, not children.

…

PART THREE

THE WAY OF THE NAVIGATOR
TAPU AND RĀHUI

Figure 26 – Catacombs of Paris

MŌHIO AI HAKAI MANO KI NGĀ TAUTAUHEA, KI NGĀ PARAKŪKĀ, KI NGĀ HAKAIR, KI NGĀ HAKAIRO-ITI, KI NGĀ PARANGETUNGETU, KI ngā NGĀKAU-RAHIRAHI, KI NGĀ KŌPŪRUA, KI NGĀ RORIRORI, KI NGĀ HEAHEA, KI NGĀ PŌREWAREWA. (Many people know cowards, scroungers, the mentally ill, the shallow thinkers, the corrupted, the callous people, the indecisive, the stupid ones, the idiots and the senseless ones.)

Māori saying

WRONG TURN

JUDGEMENT – TRUE SEEING

Amongst all the tarot pictograms only three are blatantly and obviously relative to an Abrahamic mythos: *Judgement*, the *Hierophant* and the *Devil*. Isn't *Hanged* one? No. *The Hiram Key*, by Knight and Lomas, about masonic initiations and rituals, takes care of that myth. I recommend it to the curious. The *Hanged Man* pictogram can be interpreted more as a fool than the *Fool* card, but it can just as easily represent a suicide by hanging, a diver—scuba or otherwise—or fishing.

Figure 27 – Judgement

The perennially androgynous, blonde, Anglo-Saxon and alpine *Judgement* card will be a bit much to put up with by a multicultural society that prides itself on maturity, however, here it is, in all its subtle (or not so subtle) bigotry. In many instances of interpretation, *Judgement* is considered an indication of a *conceptual rebirth*. I disagree. I want to turn the dichotomy away from this religiosity, unless it relates to an organic understanding of seasonality. Of *deciduousness*. Even then the dots do not connect. Judgement, rather like discernment is, for the Anglo-European who has been generationally inculcated into a cultish dogma that suggests we be sufficiently humble as to not do it, do it all the time and pretend we don't. How's that for a mouthful?

Judgement is seeing. Seeing what is right in front of us but seeing, without implied or actual threat of repercussion. How else can change occur? Rather than an endless-seeming repetition of trauma after trauma? Helplessness or cause? Deception because of an imposed vocabulary of belief?

BEYOND DECEPTION

In this house are two other people, both of whom I have known, and lived with, on and off, for decades. One of them is an alcoholic. When I relocate to Melbourne in 2013, to explore academia, I sign a lease on a hundred-year-old, ramshackle Edwardian house, just north of the city. With this person, an initiate who had been controlling their disease for all the years I have known them and who now decides not to bother any more. They give in. We live twenty minutes from a pub, and they frequent it, initially, from late afternoon, with wine-o'clock slinking back towards midday as the seasons change until, within a year, they do not come home until the pub closes. I don't judge. What right have I to judge? It's their life; their pleasure. Preparations for a Samhain gathering and feast, four years ago, and they are so drunk by three o'clock in the afternoon, peeling spuds and almost falling off the kitchen chair, I say, *go to your room. You're too pissed. I can't stand it.* They do, coming out hours later to collapse, close to the fire, trying to pat the cat, drinking more wine, falling over another witch's daughter.

The thoughts and concerns of the gathering are louder than silence should ever be. They are all, also, trying not to judge.

It gets worse. The *friend* laughingly admits to wearing an incontinence pad to and from the pub because they are leaking black liquid. I arrange for a family intervention. But, as Carol Burnett once said of alcoholism, *you can't drive a car with the horn*. Eventually I get this person to hospital (after almost two years of hardly eating any solid food) within a heartbeat of their death. Intravenous drips, and outrage. They are home three days later. Overnight, edema sets in and, weighing thirty kilograms, with elephantine legs and a belly looking like that of a full-term pregnancy, they are readmitted. This time the hospital manages to keep them for almost two weeks, having, on the first day, drained over seven liters of fluid from their abdominal cavity, five the following day. Them eventually saying they don't like the procedure, laws disallowing medical intervention when the patient is lucid, meaning there is nothing to be done. Them left with the large protrusion overhanging thighs the size of my wrists. Me? Still not judging. But…

Earlier that same year I'm grinding my teeth, unconsciously clenching and unclenching my hands. My trapezius muscles are vice-like, crushing the vertebrae in my neck and I have the visceral sensation that I am getting sicker and sicker with no diagnosis. I wonder that I am quietly dying from an undiagnosed illness, and I don't know why. I don't find out for months that this is a stress condition.

This house, as I have said, is an elder. Never renovated. A single bathroom. A single toilet. One afternoon and I'm busting for a pee, but the person takes ages in the shower because they can't wash without sitting on a chair. Eventually I yell an expletive that I need not duplicate here. *You can come in*, they yell back. They're naked, bent over, drying their feet. Flashes of Auschwitz. I feel a zap from my head to my toes. Repelled and bamboozled. I sit on the loo and the insinuating presence of a greyhound, deeply grooved ribcage, pale as death, moves, wraithlike, to me, and says, *Grandmother, why is she hurting me? What have I done?*

If we don't judge, then we don't see We deny. Isn't that acquiescence? Our opinion is squashed by us, without discussion, what is that? Dystopia? *Pavlov's dog* response, or enforced doctrine of niceness? Who the author was would be guessing, but they speculated that some clever Roman, in the first century of the current era, invented a religion, and called it christianity as a joke, but if we're told a thing often enough, no matter how bizarre and crazy, like Nazism, something's going to stick, and someone's going to believe it. But meekness? Chastity? Poverty? Turning the other cheek? Humility? There it is. Residue of dogma hiding in my own consciousness, informing me that an altruistic *non*judgement allows behavior, and trends, to become intolerable and eventually enslave.

We become sick, and we can die while alive, become brittle, bitter, dislocated. Tarot will desert us, and we will lose a gift that is both strenuous and strong. *Judgement, Hierophant, Devil*, all mixed up and entwining us in a contrivance of servitude to idea, ideologies and behaviors that *demand* re-evaluation. By me. By you. As a responsibility.

Everything has consequences. That's another aspect of judgement. Of sight and realization. Remember that when the card turns up, because yes, change is also inherent in the meaning. Just not bodies rising and cheering, whole and un-rotted from a long-ago grave, when some androgynous entity with wings and a trumpet arrives. Be a bit traumatic for those of us who end our bodily selves by cremation, isn't it? Be very traumatic for the skeletons that have already been dug up, and bundled together in caverns of ancient stone when the cemeteries run out of space, won't it? That lie.

DEVIL – *TAPU*

Figure 28 – Devil: Josef Mengele

I have a tantrum today. Over this. How am I to describe what this card says, in any way that doesn't mirror a linguistic misappropriation? A doctrinally-agreed-to expression of supposed right and wrong? I can't. Not in English. This is where a long conversation, with Melaine Knight, co-author of *The Skellig | A Shapechanger Epic*, and of Maori ancestry, on *tapu* and *rāhui*, is necessary, because to be honest is important, otherwise we could misunderstand each other. Words like evil, perversity, deviance, sexual dysfunction... through whose eyes? In whose culture? In some social systems it's considered okay to marry a girl of nine, in others, sex with a person that young will put the perpetrator in prison. In other cultures, authorities condemn lovers, in same-sex relationships, to be stoned to death.

Brutality only happens when one is not heard. But also, when we are not heard, you and I can become desperate in the lurid silence. The deafness of cruelty. What are we to do?

I know this card also represents addiction to anything, from alcohol and porn to social media, but how does this happen? What drives people to get stuck? These are questions for this book, not for when a fáidh-skilled navigator is interpreting a map of tarot. I have even said aloud to a traveler, under specific circumstances, relative to their knowing of the world, and to a partner, associate or any relationship that is poison: *You're dealing with the devil, whatcha gonna do?* Do you know they always nod? Because they *do* know the offender to be this archetype, and there isn't a need to restate the obvious. So, yes, we need to momentarily discuss evil.

The *Devil*, in long-established packs, looks like a depiction of an icon given a name: *Baphomet*. This gender/species hybrid, stuck to a plinth and suggestive of a sneering-faced goat-man, in many early packs single-breasted and androgynous by default, holding reins and chains that are loosely draped around the naked necks and shoulders of a generic man and a generic woman who look happy enough. Legend states that the Templars brought secrets back from their sojourn to Jerusalem, before they were massacred as heretics (having the right to choose), and that the etymology of the word itself stems from the Greek *diabolos,* which means slanderer. So why this goatish image? Even the word *baphomet,* is suggested as being a European pronunciation (or mispronunciation) of *muhammad* and could, therefore, have been thought an abominate concept in the heart of the violent and rigid religious epoch that was the thirteenth century... oh wait, it's changed? No. It has not.

And because it is a make-believe construct—and your honest guess is as good as mine—what is represented? Because people are muted by the chatter of history? And who records that? Or lies about it depending on the political side they take? And who are they? And by what are they threatened? By whom are they convinced of the correctness of the assumption? People have written that this pictogram represents a false idol, the secret of certain occult orders, a deity. I don't care. Our only concern is to *know* it is a falsehood inserted into consciousness, intended to frighten and offend.

Still using the subject of alcohol (we'll get to other addictions momentarily): it is made from fermented grains, fruit, or other sources of sugar. The juice is a muscle-relaxant, and an intoxicant. An intoxicant is a poison. The stuff is used by herbalists to extract the soul—the essence—from the plant being preserved and is, therefore, used exceedingly carefully. While in 2018 the global alcoholic drink industry exceeded a trillion US dollars, its introduction to an Anglo-European people is considered as recent as mere hundreds of years.

According to neuroscience any seeming-addiction stems from the *ventral tegmental* area of our human brains—the reward pathways that produce dopamine, a feel-good chemical that is usually triggered by an external source. According to the work of Norman Doidge, psychiatrist, psychoanalyst, and author of *The Brain that Changes Itself*, neurons are susceptible to habit. The more we trap ourselves in a wheel of repetition, the less we are able to alter our behavior away from the comfort of habituation. That is why, when considering the *Devil* card, we include all manner of addictions. They could also include me repeating well-established formula for interpretation of this card, based on populism. I have my own traps. I'd be lying if I told you otherwise. Who do you know that is free of rigid opinion, or even unconsciously repetitive traits?

LANGUAGE AND BEING - THE ABUNDANCE OF LOSS

Turning language inside out is an attempt to realize the propensity to perpetuate the sickness of religious ideology. Words like *perversity*… what does that *actually* mean? To whom? Is it biased? The word can be accepted, sure, but what does it affect? There are things each of us learned as children that affect our slant on what's considered acceptable, even into old age. We can't forge a generation of elders like that. No. We get opinionated bigots, or older people who have learned to shut up because their language does not keep pace with a changing sociological paradigm. Words matter. They are halfway to material manifestation, just like a spoken spell. Is this a warning? Could be. An affirmation? A fáidh-trainee, who thinks I should be wealthy, wishes me *abundance*. You should see my face! I've been at this learning-to-hear magic for decades, and really listening involves…well… really listening. Comprehending what is heard and establishing a mutual plateau. I'm careful. Abundance of what? Imagination, often a hinderance when not analyzed, is a vast, unsaddled thing. When I'm wished this, I'm living in the tropics. I have small children in school. We have mosquitos, ticks, midges, snakes, headlice and impetigo: which of these is implied, because the words money and wealth are not stipulated in their well-meant invocation.

I watched this program, once upon a time, about tenement moguls ripping off what few bucks the impoverished and disenfranchised have. Some kid gives a well-meaning priest a large, unmarked brown paper bag, the contents hidden. The priest is determined to liberate the neighborhood from property cartel embezzlement. I wonder about that paper bag throughout the program. Then he's upstairs in the landlord's high rise, glitzy office and, because the boss man laughs, lighting a fat cigar, at the idea of fixing toilets, stairwell lighting and broken windows, the priest tips the bag out onto that expensive polished-wood desk.

Cockroaches. Countless. It's a huge paper bag.

Magic requires specifics. That includes what we say. The canary will remain at the coalface, in-perpetuity, until we do.

HIEROPHANT

False Promises

Figure 29 – Gargoyle, Notre Dame

The etymology of *hierophant*, if I dig deeply enough, is simply another word for what witchdoctors and mystics—journalists, anthropologists, psychics and whistle-blowers—do. We reveal. You have to sort through the layers of religious rhetoric to find the simplicity of the word, but it's here. Many prefer to buy into the bling of diamonds and white tulle, Sunday mass, pastors, organ-players and benedictions, *happy ever after* that this card pretends to represent: marriage, or spiritual authority; the government of the church (in most examples, christian) or even current *neo-pagan* hierarchical organizations: those representing the public face of an established and recognized alternative group of others.

But yes, the main meaning of the *hierophant* is marriage. So, of course, we will tear the throat out of that now, because marriage has nothing to do with love. It's a social construct.

With the exception of twenty-first century handfasting, and non-gender-specific celebrants, attending non-religious gatherings, marital vows are traditional. And they are only considered valid if a legally sanctioned, and officially recognized document accompanies any ceremony. These contracts contain rules and promises that will cause one or both people to be oath-breakers. Liars.

Figure 30 – Ace of Cups, *Darkana*

Wounded by hope in the face of an archaically, inaccurately packed parachute. And I'm an optimist. I believe in love. Love is not, however, the *Hierophant*. Love is, quintessentially, the *Ace of Cups*, and variations of that theme.

Figure 31 – Roman Catholic Something

When I envision a merger between companies, the *Hierophant* will present with perhaps the Emperor card. An example being a trio with the *Fledgling of Cups* and the *8 of Coins*. My visitor that day was incognito, dressed in jeans and a hoodie. He was a bishop of the catholic church. *Hierophant*, *Fledgling of Cups*, *Sun* is the orthodox catholic church triplet. How do I put two and two together to suggest the person is a priest? That's it. I don't know. Some indescribable flash of absolute certainty. Now I spae it often. *Hierophant*, *Fledgling Cups*, but with the *Devil* card, instead of *Sun*: that's christian guilt. Somehow tarot knits this, to represent the imagined infant god associated with christianity.

When I've randomly asked readers of tarot what they know of the *Hierophant* card they tell me it's a depiction of an old man in a shapeless, gaudy frock with a white beard and a funny hat. That's a bit strange because the image, on older packs is feminized, clear-faced and young, the miter strangely like the headdress of a Chinese emperor, or the gilded crowns worn by the (once) Siamese *Khon* dancers. This figure is accompanied by a pair of un-faced, tonsured somebody's at their feet and I wonder how, in the twenty-first century, anyone could be so conditioned as to simply accept this idea of a male pope, without challenging the iconography, when the history of both a pope named Joan (stoned to death) and secret Mary Magdalene devotees just might have influenced the advisor to the early artists.

HOUSES OF STONE AND BONE

A fáidh-born companion of many decades, with ancestral sap derived from the mist-shrouded mountains of ancient Alba (that's Scotland, but those I have spoken with who are indigenous to the highlands despise the word that was renamed by conquerage), tells me the ancient story—told grandparent to grandchild—of low houses. Places to stash dead bodies, in readiness for *marriage* when fully decomposed, becoming turf or peat, and that are built close to the wellhead of a downhill-running river. Stone is piled and shaped into a low house, on an area cleared of grass, and the topmost layer of a thousand years of soil. The corpse of the person, or people, who die from the long cold, or from gut-gore by boar tusk, or falling from the cliff while gathering eggs, are laid in the cottage where the juice of them sinks into the substrata, joining the river-babble and becoming landscape.

Over countless years our relatives become water for cattle, clan, bird, stag and puppy to drink from. Widening like a maelstrom as they enter the black North Sea. Deeper and deeper into the bedrock. Gneiss—granite—ice age to ice age, from Caledonian orogeny, through the Silurian epoch and out along the Highland Boundary Fault, to the fields of the dead of Culloden. Bones eventually removed and burned on great fires, becoming air, and food for flies and mosquitoes. Eaten by bats, breathed by bears higher up the side of the mountain when they awake with the winter thaw. That's us.

Then we pull it all down. dislodge the turf on the other side of the bubbling well and rebuild there, instead. We negotiate deals, for trapping and breeding, with traders from the far side, the *Srath Chluaidh* (Strathclyde), and seal the contract with an exchange of a square of turf. Ceremony. This is also a marriage, because who do your cattle eat? Whose juices nourish the amanita and the nightshade?

So, what is marriage? What is religion? I think about the deal, whereby a woman, veiled in white and given away, like a sow or a brood mare, to a man who is not her father, and I wonder who considers this romantic? What an industry! And who profits? And who has agreed that this is even sane?

SOUL MATES

And why is it one of the most predictable and perennial questions I am asked, come question time, especially by women? Will I ever meet the man of my dreams? When will I meet my soulmate? Can you see my future husband? Bile in the back of my throat now that I understand.

POISON – Tapu AND rāhui

Figure 32 – Betrayal

If I had seen it, it would have been in the information spoken of before questions are agreed to. And so often, if I *do* spae it, it has an end date. The *7 of Swords, 2 of Cups, 3 of Swords*, the predictable Justice card, the *Death* card and, oh, I am so sorry, the *9 and 10 of Swords. Lovers, 7 of Swords,* the *Hermit.* So many sequences grouped together to tell of the aftermath.

TAPU

Before I complete this section with the interrogation of the 3 of Swords, we're revisiting *Judgement* and the *Devil* again, but from a sideways comprehension. *Tapu* was misheard by little Mister Jimmy Cook, when he invaded New Zealand, and as such, is known as *taboo*. *Tapu* does *not* mean that the behavior, place, subject or person is wrong or dysfunctional. It means that something is happening or being, known by elders and ancestors, that needs to be left to itself, or to which specific knowledge and protocol apply. To not be interfered with, to not be gone near, to not be done. The language, still living, of a people not crushed and reshaped by domination, as mine has been, could be considered a prerequisite of this learning. Because, even though you are reading this—a grimoire—tarot is an oral tradition.

Tapu, in reference to sex, behavior and relationship, is the knowledge of the harm that a specific action or trample will cause. Therefore, when consensual people of any age or ethnicity are sufficiently mature as to understand the consequences of their actions and are in mutual agreement regarding events in which they consider participating, tarot won't show you what tarot considers *tapu*.

Figure 33 – Legal Corruption

Devil, 2 of Cups, 10 of Swords (sexual deviance and violation), that is *tapu* being abused. You spae *Devil* and *Temperance* with whatever, the *tapu* is because those two, together, represent poison, or that which is toxic if consumed. The story in Figure 33 shows

Devil, the *8 of Coins* and *Justice*. The situation is one of protectionism, blackmail, bribery and is *tapu* because it is considered illegal by the laws of your society. *Hierophant* with *Devil* is *tapu*. Together they are a cult. Tarot despises religion, and therefore this is common. I spae *tapu*, in this context, with the *Moon*. The illness of consciousness that is both a brainwashed culture and its people. The *Devil* is most often also with the *7 of Cups* for clinical insanity, or such out-of-control delusion that the individual shown with this pair, or even the traveler themselves in the future, is incapable of personal responsibility due to what is termed mental illness. I write *termed*, because tarot has also taught me not to split the person into bits, like emotional, physical, spiritual or intellectual (to use a common parlance), unless we are talking specific organs that are malfunctioning.

One traveler's pictogram sequence—one of their several maps—is the display of a person of a specific star sign, with: *Devil*, *7 of Cups* and *2 of Cups*, that is *not* the person at my table. Other stories indicate they are the traveler's father (*Emperor* or similar). I suggest they go home and tell their dad to get a prostate examination. Cancer—the disease—is detected. Early. Tarot can save life… if it is *destiny* for that life to continue in the current body. If a crossroads is shown. Simply choices that will entail the presentation of the *Lovers* card.

RĀHUI

When an individual (or corporation, or agenda) addresses a meeting and defines a forest as potentially saleable lumber, they are pretentious and conniving. They are wrong. Wrong has bubbled into our vocabulary from an old Norse word that means unjust. This is *rāhui*. The annual count of harpooned seal for my village, speared boar, netted mackerel, is not some random percentage of catch that can change by the demand of usurpers. I won't kill more than we use. We are earth. We travel in this orbit around the sun, and we have been earth—and will be earth—and there is nowhere to go and no ascension, and no heaven and no afterlife. There is only life.

What does this have to do with tarot? The *Butterfly Effect* is what. The idea that the smallest, seemingly most insignificant phenomenon can affect, or is within the weave, of the most intense storms or droughts, somewhere else, thousands of miles away. The One Tree. *Yggdrasil*, *Grandmother Cedar*, the Wurundjeri *Yingabeal*. What constitutes authority? I consider this, despite the traveler. I don't care where they studied, or of what ship they consider themselves admiral. What do they do? Thoughts and desires can become actions and manifestations? You'll feel it. We're still working with the *Devil* card here. But now we can add the *Strength* card, or the *Moon* card. Mining and drilling for oil. Polluting the atmosphere.

So, your room. The environment of safety for unpacking a story with this stranger—where is it? Where do you translate the maps of the traveler's journey? How and what do you present? Do you think it doesn't matter? Do you imagine you can say whatever you want without consequence, not for merely *what* you say, but the meaning, within the arena of the subject matter? If you are trapped in a dualistic, binary-fixed mindset of *masculine/feminine*, *light/dark*, *black/white*, you're a bigot. If I am irresponsible with what I tell a traveler, if I am slovenly with my words, if I don't say what I spae when I know exactly what it is, for whatever reason, I'm a coward. This places me, the traveler, tarot, the essence of spaecraft, the whole shebang, into the package of lumber. Living forests razed for a buck. Somebody gaining their reward by killing. Hidden behind investment, stocks and mute apology. Perhaps even fooling ourselves/themselves that motives are altruistic.

The forest, that entire ecosystem, the seal I kill for meat and oil and hide and awl, the fish we have hunted all our ancestral lives, the swell and roll of bull kelp, and the ice of floating calved-off berg, the seventh generation before me and after me, this is *rāhui*. We are *rāhui*. The space in which you invite the seeker—the traveler— expresses just how fulfilled you are, your self-certainty. These are important because a pack of seventy eight pictorial bits of paper are not tarot. The whole is tarot, and I don't have a box or a description for that, and it is my responsibility, as much as it is yours, to be open. To question motives and agendas. The way you talk of love. Of sex, of relationship. Do you think of them as a whole? Do you, I, or the traveler come across as needy? Am I awed by the person who seeks me out because they are a celebrity? Or a blacksmith? Or a horse-whisperer? Well, maybe I'm in awe of a horse-whisperer. But are they comfortable? Do they trust me? Or will they go away with false hope, or fear for their children, or the arrogance of the traitor who thinks they just got away with lying?

That now they are content, because I didn't pick it. They are comforted, now, in feeling that I am as dumb as they thought I should be. They won't come again, and I have reinforced some certainty that they have been bred to believe, that we—mystics and visionaries—are frauds, even though meteorologists and investment bankers are rather-much the same as us. That it is their right to log the old growth, because who needs to think beyond the big house and the fashionable car and the FF-sized breast implants?

...

SEMANTICS

Tell me about love? Relationships? Will I marry? Is there someone in the world for me? Can you tell me if there's a partnership for me in the future?

What you will inevitably be asked.

Figure 34 – The Language of Loss

HIDING THE SUTURE LINE

Before I hit you up with examples, see the above? That's the most prolific series of questions you'll get in your tarot lifetime. Tarot *is* semantic. You think I was always this way? The above questions are not, however, questions, they are laziness. Do I have to assume what they mean? And be a hypocrite to my own ideals by doing so? No. I ask what they really want to know. Does it matter that I can guess, and that we think we speak of the same thing? Specifics are rare amongst many in this occupation and tarot can be very rude. Tarot also knows what they mean but sometimes just that word *relationships...* is generic. A person can have a relationship with their car, a football club, they certainly have a relationship with their closest friends, often with their mother, whether pleasant or otherwise, a tutor, their keyboard, their jet ski, dogs, the medical team working with them to cure cancer, you.

The word relationship doesn't mean anything. Neither does partnership. That question is ambiguous. Partnership with what? With your brother in a game of poker? Specifics. I'm in a happy position in this work, because people are warned by others, before they come, that there will be questions at the conclusion of a session, but that they need to be prepared to be specific. Or else I just look at them. That can be intimidating. When I've sat with them for almost an hour and been as honest as possible, and as intimate in detail as I am able, it is likely they have already been answered. A foretelling, with tarot as captain, can be like some rapid-fire-speak event that is only heard in retrospect, from the recording. There is very often no *pause button* to a fáidh-gifted in the trance of foretelling.

THE LANGUAGE OF LOSS
The 3 of Swords

Doesn't matter, all the above. The grief of loss does not discriminate, and it has no politics. The *3 of Swords*. Separation. Not always sad.

Not always going to rock a traveler to the core. It can turn up

CAGED IN A CLICHÉ

An anthropologist, hanging out with Pacific Islanders, wonders why the loon—a little narrow thing—is atop a totem pole. Why does such a nondescript bird rank so highly? We could, of course, being an educated Anglo-European people, be forgiven for our ignorance. We deserve a little scorn for not understanding that to a seafaring people, a watcher—a navigator—is necessary. The loon, heading for land, is a messenger, loud and clear. Loon is the only bird to fly home to shore, both with the coming of night and at the approach of a storm that could kill, because such storms are held in lore as having done so to our ancestors. Time to draw in the nets and go home. Or die. What a god[i], then, is the loon?

I go to the *Break Room*, where I am provided with a jump suit, a baseball bat, a pair of protective goggles, ear protection, and a tray of old, thrift-shop crockery too damaged to sell. I'm ushered into a soundproof room, in the basement of the old building, and the door is shut behind me. To a teeth-grinding Guns and Roses *Welcome to the Jungle*, I lift a teacup and, after hitting it into the far brick wall where it falls on the already-substantial heap (I'm not the first to wander Frustration Road), I lift another, strike clean with the bat and wham. Instructions: 1. empty the tray, 2. keep the protective headgear on, because the crew running the business, just now watch me load the second tray of kitchen breakables onto the stump, and amp up the volume.

That's where I'm up to here. And especially the maps. Because

PART 4

MAPS AND SPAEING

Image 35 – Pacific Northwest Loon

Songlines, or Dreaming Tracks, are pathways through the landscape connecting a large number of significant locations in a fixed order—rocky outcrops, springs, mountains, valleys, caves, waterholes…

Dr. Lynne Kelly, *The Memory Code*

THE ART OF PREDICTION

this is going to be.

It's a memory. The *3 of Swords* is also the *Ace of Cups*. When not a physical ailment, this card signifies the heart of love. What happens to us when the object of that love goes, leaves, seems to die, retracts themselves from you. Can people perish from sadness? Of course. And it is your physical heart that is going to hurt. You place your hands on your chest. That's tears, unshed.

The *3 of Swords* is brutal.

Yes, the interpretation of this pictogram will matter where it falls, on which map, how it is gathered concerning the others. That's agreed, but I felt the need to give a deep breath to the *3 of Swords*.

You'll know. You probably already do.

…

when the umbilicus between a mother and her newborn animal is cut. It can turn up for a literal heart attack. But, for sure, it's usually the last thing I want to spae.

What countries are we talking about? Who is immune to tragedy and that sense of someone or something being severed from us? A person can stand at the vast glass at an airport watching the plane taxi down the runway that's taking their lover, their child, their parent, their good buddy to another place, and smile. Great! They get to follow a vision, an aspiration, a calling, hope. But you? What're you feeling. Sure, you're okay until you want to go sit with them and have a cup of tea.

The above are the gentlest expressions of the *3 of Swords*. Unlike the *Tower*, and so many other traumas that I can write about (and I will), this is only, otherwise, benevolent, when a person has finally escaped violence, for example. And not in war, but from a situation that once had love in it. That perhaps still does because, yes, people can, and do, love a partner or a parent or a friend who is cruel. Nobody wants that. No one wants the moment when the fist shatters belief in the person cherished. Will you see it? Of course. Way too often. But I want you to know that no matter how devastating the prophecy, the traveler will do everything... everything... in their power, to make sure it does not happen. To prove you wrong. And, oh, my gut always hurts when it falls onto the table. Then I take into account all the other stories around it. I'm a hunter and I'm stalking easy prey. I don't want this to be important or significant. I want them to have lost their keys, or their phone. So, I'm careful. I don't want to start off by telling them how very terrible all of us are trapped, at some juncture, by the jargon of established rhetoric and narrative, by how we fashion ourselves into a mystically-garmented individual, and it'd be so easy to teach that, because I have. For decades.

You're either in this with me, or you close the book and hurl it at the wall of *your* choosing. This will be especially tricky because yes, this is rather a reinvention of the wheel. And considering one of tarot's titles is just that, a good airing and frisking is rather long overdue.

This way of farseeing has been with me for decades, because, as I say to the traveler momentarily stopping by on the passage of their life's journey, when I first lay out a DEAD RECKONING map, or a STARGATE, or a HORSE LATITUDE map, as a warning, you'll have the choice to call trust this or not.

FIRST MAP – DEAD RECKONING

In navigation, dead reckoning is the process of calculating one's current position.

Wikipedia, 2020

I've searched the internet to find you a factual, historic entrance point to the title *of Celtic Cross...* and there isn't one. It seems to be the invention of the crew from the Order of the Golden Dawn, Arthur Edward Waite or Gerald Gardner, any one of them, or none of them. So, what's with the naming? It's a little bit presumptuous to call it this, instead of the Ethiopian Cross or the Amazonian Cross, or the Yolngu Cross, or even the Inuit Dog Sled Almanac, so I'm going to rename it, here, DEAD RECKONING, because the naming is apt.

We keep calling a place, people or knowledge of lore by the name of an explorer or a person or some other invader of others' territory, is like continuing to call Uluru, *Ayers Rock* or Aotearoa, *New Zealand*. Yes, it's done, but that doesn't make it a truth, let alone an honesty. Most of us Celts not slaughtered or bred out, have been driven to the farthest west, to what's now known as Wales, or down the coast to the end of the land—Land's End—known, today, as Cornwall. Loads of us take ship and settle in and around Brittany; became the Breton, a people with a Celtic language, still, utterly alien to the French dialects, despite England being French well into the Middle Ages. All depends on who was invading, and who was most cruel.

From the vantage of the current era we are little more than a remnant culture, presumed to be out of Austria, with *terra nullius* erasing our ancestral homelands as though we are only ever there after-the-fact. Yet we are everywhere. My paternal ancestors are seafaring people, hence all the nautical references. These associations, however, are most practical because navigation is exactly what you are doing; that and weather-forecasting. What you *don't* do is interpret an individual card without reference to the others in its vicinity. To do so is impossible. Do you begin and end a sentence with *and the*? What just happened? Oh, I didn't finish the sentence? Exactly. Any one card can just be a word. A word is not an interpretation. It is meaningless without context.

CAPTAIN, MY CAPTAIN

Dedicated to Robin Williams, and that suffer depression, and hide it too well.

PRESENT, FUTURE, PAST

Here's what you expect, as an image, but then we're going to dissect it first, mash it all together after.

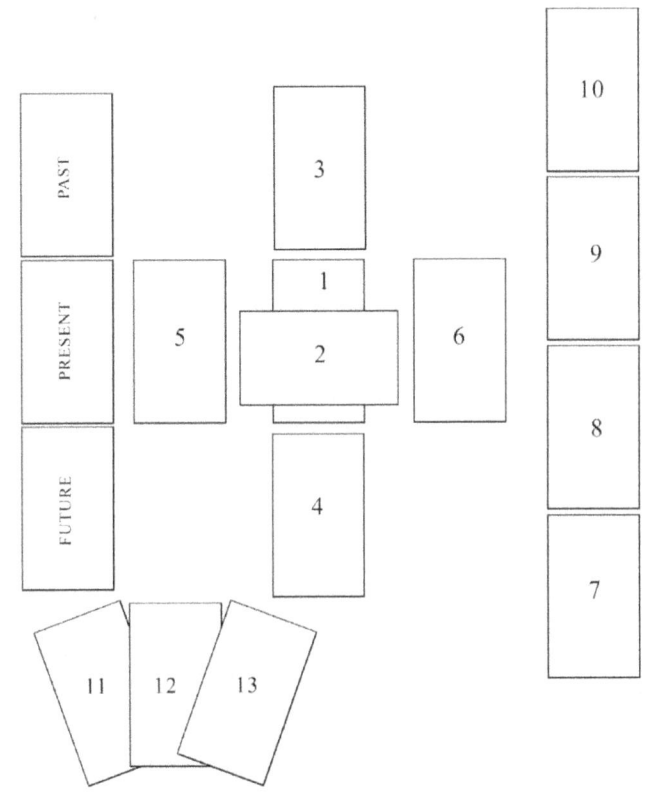

Figure 36 – DEAD RECKONING: Map 1

First thing you do, after the sequence shown earlier, is to hand your tarot pack to the traveler, and have them shuffle. Ask them to cut the

pack into three piles when they're ready. Watch what they do:
- The pack that is at the bottom of the divided three is the PAST. Leave it to the side, in the positions shown in the diagram, you'll read that last
- The pack in the middle of the divided three is called the PRESENT, you read that first
- The pack that was at the top is the FUTURE and you read that second
- Both the PRESENT and the FUTURE start today. There is no demarcation

This image falls in the center of the map, and is the situation NOW, and 2 relates to that. I don't refer to 2 as *crossing* image 1, as that is rarely the case. The two together are like the hub of a wheel, and you need to flick your eyes over every other message for you to even begin to make sense of this, or to even ascertain how much of it is personal, and whether any of it is of a more communal/social significance. It is not uncommon, also, for the present to begin at a past month.

Figure 37 – Acupuncture

You'll know it when you do the layout. It is almost indescribable, how to gauge meaning. Again, it's a knowing. Sometimes the

PRESENT will have begun years ago—like a cycle—and you must find the *when*. In the above pattern *Temperance* crossed by the *10 of Swords* is painful, yes, but not in a problematic way. *Temperance* is health, art and alchemy (another word for medicine, just more realistic, like a chemist is more realistic than a general medical practitioner in the contemporary sense).

Of itself the pairing depends on the pictograms around it, but it is either a doing or a receiving so:

- 3 and 4, 5 and 6 are what's around the traveler. The story that's not exposed, but that is at the bottom of that (and the other two packs) is a reference to events
- 6 and 7 are of deepest significance, because 6 is a direct relationship to the center, or 7 (self) is
- 8 is place: home, work, country, the process of moving or journeying, and the mode
- 9 is simply weird. I agree with most ways of interpreting insofar as this is a thing the traveler either fears, or hopes for… or both, whereas 10 is a momentary outcome

The three cards in a fan shape to the side are merely additional information, and remember the murder? This is where this event showed up. A flood, or other major event likely to become the headlines, is this triplet. So it is, also, when tarot has something to say that is a variant, but significant.

Often as my vision floats around this map, I get zapped. Right at the start here is when the so-called dead expose themselves and words, names and places dash like excited puppies, around your metaphorical feet, demanding to be recognized. Just this week the traveler's first layout, and the name *Brian* staggers out of my mouth. First five minutes. That's the traveler's brother's name. He's dead.

A while back, a visiting traveler navigates the seat opposite me, on crutches – their ankle broken. The *5 of Coins* is laid down first, in the map of the *present*, of DEAD RECKONING, crossed by *Temperance*. I can't help it, I laugh. I pick up the *5 of Coins* and face them with it. They grin and say *Oh far out, is that kid me with the busted leg?* Interestingly, this person's job is in the hospitality industry, and they're working for casual pay and, therefore, hasn't any money coming in while they're healing, hence poverty is also represented.

Future and Past are foretold likewise.

SECOND MAP—THE STARGATE

The STARGATE and its traditional correlations, that I have taught for decades, hits me in the face with its online onslaught of associations, the majority of which will trap you. It is habitually called the *Tree of Life* (sometimes *Axis Mundi*) and given religious connotations. Wrap you up, like next week's dinner for an alien, encased living and immobile in a cave, if you've dropped your guard.

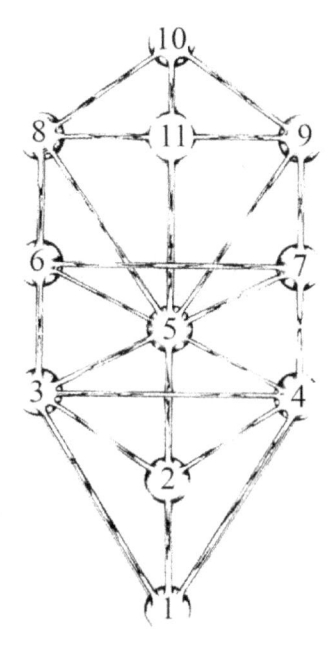

Figure 38 – Stargate, Organic and Numbered

The above image is a seed. That's it. And a seed is an outlandish complexity. What you'll encounter if/when you go hunting online, are a myriad of cabbalistic and arcane associations. The concept, as such, dates suspiciously to Sumer; to the mythos of the *Descent of*

Inanna, down a passage marked by seven *gates*, said to represent seven of the planetary associations from earth to *saturn*, as the days of Sumer and Ur are days when seven planetary bodies are anchored to a mythic *underworld*, guarded by a baby-eating twin sister, *Ereshkigal*. My question to you is from where/when did the word *underworld* come to have significance, as though it is a 'real' place? Is it an actuality? Or is it a childhood imprint? Is it some ancient hypothesis or legend or another? But wait. Can we find out, or will we be forever guessing?

Before I take us into prediction let us, for a moment, consider what I just wrote. What a load of useless, passed-down, outdated, and rigid mythology is this? The Polynesians, members of an astonishing open-ocean navigational group, spread throughout the Pacific, hypothetically, from the south of what is now known as China, over 8,000 solar years ago. Into Micronesia and from there into Melanesia, how? In outrigger and double-hulled canoes. Why have we misappropriated the symbolism of Persia, Lebanon, Syria and Palestine, just to bomb their children out of existence?

INNTRENGER – INVADER MENTALITY

It is really easy to fall back on a millennia or more of ad hoc, or ceaselessly rigid repetition, that keeps us penned, like cattle to the slaughter, in the *inntrenger* (invader) modality of Rome, Mesopotamian and Abrahamic symbolism and ideology, that we rapid-fire off associations and charts, like a schoolmarm rifled up against marauding Indians who transgress on the territory her family just stole, without ever bring conscious after the fact.

Just as suspicious are the diagrammatical *sacred geometry* patterns—*gematria*—and oh, how quickly can one become entangled in a belief? Or a list? Especially—and this is the kicker—the idea of up and down, higher and lower becoming of greater or lesser importance. The designation is, of course, ridiculous.

UNDERWORLD

The semisphere numbered 1 in Figure 38, as well as the entire Stargate pattern-word *underworld* or even *otherworld* are used as a weave-story by some, to mean elsewhere than here. What do they say? How can this apply at all? Anywhere? I mention it because vast areas of Europe and the islands bunched together, and called Britain, are sprinkled with huge upright stones, dolmens, sídhe hills, circular ramparts consisting of significant ditches, raised earthworks. Significant gathering places and wayshowers: The Ring of Brodgar, Long Meg, Newgrange and Géant du Manio. So many people generalize that the *underworld* is a real place, albeit mythic, and that our long gone, uncivilized ancestors had some superstitious reason for erecting this silliness. Academics discuss these as places of worship or graves, their prejudice towards a cult of death obvious, whereas what if they are not? What if there is nothing mythic about them? Where is your safety? Is it out on a busy street? At a music festival?

No. Your sanctuary, if you are lucky or have learned, or been gifted, or strived to achieve, is called home; is designated *your*. The equivalent, on a snowy night, of the caves of Lascaux, in what is now called France. We live in the caves of Yaodong, in the relatively stable warmth or coolness of Petra, Cappadocia, the Ash Hole Cavern in Devon, in England, the Acoma Sky City in New Mexico, Chichen Itza and Ankor Watt. Now we also have houses. Mini-mountains. Or tipis, or yurts, gers, tents. We build in stone, with reindeer hide, with mud, with animal dung. Unfortunately, in the current era, we also build in plastic and asbestos. In the city where I live a person can track a route from one suburb to another by the spires of churches, or by the placement of Bunnings or McDonald's Golden Arches. It's all the same… only in the current era we are not so sophisticated as to realize these are all *underworld*.

The sky—the stars and celestial bodies—have guided us to navigate from the vast plains of the arctic tundra, along trade routes to what is now Nuvuk, from there south to Callao, along the nautical currents, like clear roads through the Pacific Ocean to, probably, Australia. The stars are both maps and mapped. They are wayshowers. We seem to be under them. Seemingly. Therefore, *earth*, or *world*, is an *underworld*. Let's not be less than fáidh-gifted workers of word magic and lie through default because of popularism, and let's not, for a moment (and despite the mythic) deny the undeniable genius of ancestors who erect markers to guide us to each other, and to home.

That is this. Another, more appropriate name, is *nature*. Another is *everyone*, by happenstance including us as a species. Another is *here*, another is *there*, and another is *home*.

THE STARGATE

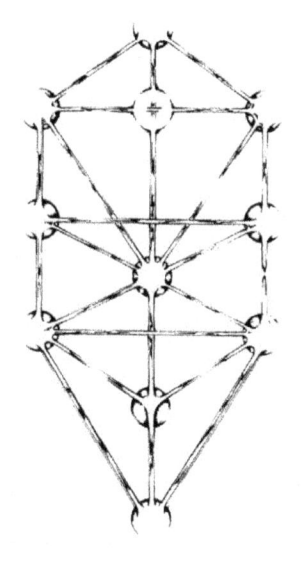

THE ELEVEN PORTALS

1 Home (the elements, and the world as we know it)

2 Tide (moon)

3 Navigation (mercury)

4 Art (venus)

5 Core (sun)

6 Protection (mars)

7 Expansion (jupiter)

8 Stone (saturn)

9 Lightning (uranus)

10 Challenger Deep (neptune)

11 Seed (pluto)

1. HOME

The clan here is intelligent. Trust me.

(Clach an Truseil, The Outer Hebrides)

Figure 39 – HOME: Ancient stone labyrinth carving

How often have you heard, or read, that a situation, way of life or experience is just *mundane*? Not special or *divine*? Not magical? Are you surprised to realize that *mundane* is derived from the etymology for *world*; *terrestrial, us* as environment and nature? Why then, is *mundane* derided as unimportant? This is the first lesson to understand. In his book, *The World Ending Fire,* Wendell Berry writes that his grandparent hung a galvanized bucket in the nearby woods. Empty. That over seasons leaves fell in the bucket at the turn of the seasons, snow and rain fell in the bucket. Bugs crawled about, defecated, died. Birds rummaged in the detritus of the bucket and dropped feathers, rejected the carapaces and sharp bits of insects, more snow, more rain, more bugs. Life and death. Over twenty years that bucket, resting as it did within the mundanity of a pristine, unlogged forest, evolved two inches of humus.

The essays that Berry writes over decades, and with a pencil, describe the minutiae of a vast planet. How long, and how patient, a planet. The ideology of acceptance that *mundane* is unimportant; nothing; that it's okay for the invention of the combine harvester, a plough that will gouge and desecrate what earth has taken countless millions of years to accumulate, should fill us with horror. The destruction of the soil, that nurtures incalculable species, has created the Tundra of Mongolia and Siberia, the rainforest canopies from the depths of wilderness Russia, to Africa to Brazil to Australia. That soil, that has bred and fed and sustained everything, and everyone, from (and likely during) the advent of every species that rely on the mycelium, bacteria and never-classified microscopic cousin-critters, will, if left like that bucket, become the basis of an underwater, deep-sea shelf or, from our comprehension of the fossils of small aquatic creatures, remind us that desert is also the bottom of the sea. Truth… what is oil, after all? Why is oil called a fossil fuel? Does anyone stop to think?

What forest is now diamond? What is uranium, used to enrich a nuclear bomb? What is titanium but a compound found and recorded, originally, by a bloke fossicking in the black sands along the shores of Cornwall and now used to protect vessels traveling through space?

HOME is us. And we are everything and everyone, divided for, perhaps, life to appreciate the art of individuation, so let's not be fooled by petty folk who suggest that if a story or garment is mundane that they are unbeautiful. They are magnificent.

So, what happens, with the STARGATE map, when a certain card is turned up, facing you, in the location we are calling HOME? It is where you live. Home, territory, place, world, house, feet, knees, that which supports the traveler. The *4 of Coins*, for example, would mean claustrophobic conditions, boxy, a town with limited anything. The *4 of Coins* can be the deposit the traveler is holding onto preciously, to lay down on a living space, where the *4 of Swords* here means nothing. Should a Wayshower pictogram fall there? *Hmm*. One would need to look at the other images to know whether that Tower is an earthquake, a bomb, or the searing pain of nerve damage to a foot, a busted knee, legs trapped within the crushed dashboard of a motor vehicle in a road accident, Mt St Helens, or Pelé erupting, or some human-thought catastrophe— personal, environmental or, for a traveler involved in construction, the demolition of a condemned or abandoned and rejected building. Nothing works alone, like a leg without a body, so I need to consider what else there is, both personally, and in the wider vision, other than what faces me here.

On the Stargate map, I number HOME 1 (it can as easily be numbered 10). Makes it easy when I'm teaching, as the map is laid out in a zigzag pattern, labeled a *lightning flash*, a mathematical zigzag, from 1 through 11, and each position in the layout is aligned, hypothetically, with a traditional occult planetary sequence of attributes... through a myopic glass, however.

2. TIDE

Figure 40 – TIDE: First Crescent

Do you ever get that feeling of longing and sadness—a moody *something*—that takes your breath away, and you don't know why? So, you go over events. You think of past humiliations, seeming wrongs, losses. You feel the breath of purposelessness and you think you are too ugly or that you are misunderstood. Not only by others but, even by you. Everyone gives an opinion. And yes, we're thankful. We are reflections in a mirror, seeing only ourselves. Do we like what we're looking at? No? Why? In whose opinion are we lacking? No one's. There is nothing wrong. We try to classify the overwhelming, that grief, as though by naming it, labelling it we can what? Make it go away? Medicate it? Subdue it like it's a beast? So many times, we've been asked to believe. In something. In everything. Advised that we are safe, that we are not mad, that we're okay and the loneliness that seems unreasonable is temporary. The quiet, deep, abusive panic can be shrugged—or drugged—away.

This can be *hireath,* the Welsh word for homesickness, and the longing for a place that not only doesn't exist anymore, but that might, in reality as we comprehend it, never have been. It can also be intuition, either of the rhythm of earth, the cycles of a body, or connection with people, loved or otherwise. People talk about gut-feelings. Many facing threat, lose control of their bowels, some people say they feel *it (*whatever *it* eventuates as), in their waters.

This place in the Stargate is like the *cotyledon*, those first two embryonic leaves on an infant seedling. So easily dead. Is it more than this? Of course—

- Hormonal information
- Something happening away from the traveler (place)
- Behind the traveler's back

Body: vagina, penis, anus, colon, bowel, uterus, perineum, prostate, lower back, gluteus and reproductive system. Can, and often is, gut. If another person falls in that place, they are likely to be a lover, if a fledgling, an embryo/fetus/ or offspring, yet unborn.

About a billion years ago, the continents emerged relatively suddenly from an ocean that covered 95 percent of the Earth's surface... according to a new theory by Eldridge Moores, a geologist at the University of California, Davis.

In early 2019 I attended a lecture at NIIM, the National Institute of

Integrative Medicine, on the gut: the microbiome, by Professor Luis Vitetta. Each of us has a living microbiome with approximately 2.5 billion years of information encoded in it. Each of us is unique, yes, but each of us is related. It is impossible that we are otherwise. If we take the hypothesis that we are once one cell entities, there is nothing to say we are not in there, all mixed up with antelope, ferns, snails, wolves, mosquitoes, ticks, lobsters and midges and any number of bacillus and every and any other life forms, including retroviruses, ERVS, and the blueprint of who—or what—we will be, given another five, ten or twenty billion years. Even then we seem to be speaking in linear time when, if we're honest, we have no idea how anything transpires. I'm repeating myself. I know. In case you missed it the first time.

Deceit—of self or other—sits here, as does the wax and wane of love and strength, biodiversity, blood and memory.

We are EVOLVED from LUCA, our mutual microbial ancestor, hanging around the vulcanized thermal vents at the bottom of oceans, and the study of us is called *phylogenetics.* Listen to you snorting with derision. But it is the most recent conclusion and is, according to Nick Lane, an evolutionary biochemist at University College of London, worthy of understanding that as a mere microorganism—as LUCA—we can spontaneously self-organize. We are so used to considering ourselves in the present tense, and as hominid bipedal simians, that we don't comprehend that the first breath, and the first suckle of a newborn person takes in a concentration of their mother's vaginal bacteria, holding coded information that same 2.5

(give or take) billion years deep into the soil and regeneration of this Edenic Grove. From here, our relationships to all species, whether oxygen-breathing, requiring light, or otherwise, is relative.

...

3. NAVIGATION

Figure 41 – NAVIGATION: Fibonacci Spiral Shell

He said, "You are the Chosen One, the One who will deliver the message. A message of hope for those who choose to hear to and a warning for those who do not." Me: The Chosen One? They chose me! And I didn't even graduate from fuckin' high school.

Tool, *Rosetta Stoned,* 10,000 Days Album.

My kid has locked me in their car and is blaring the music of the band, *Tool,* at full volume. He says (and I'm sure I've heard this before, from another person I made), *Mother, you don't listen.* The prophets of my youth are Aldous Huxley, Bob Dylan, Simon and Garfunkel, Led Zeppelin, Patti Smith and Germaine Greer. Each generation has a way of communicating, and whether that's of gender, sexuality, rage and style and we, as guides and navigators, have to listen. Not only that, we must absorb and understand, not merely pay lip-service. To hear *them*, not ourselves. How often have you seen polyamory? Would you know what to look for when a person, involved in a same-sex relationship, travels the country as a well-paid sex worker? Do you, even now, insist on calling this profession *prostitution*? Shame on you. Avatars that surface from waves of dissatisfaction, the repetition of lies and propaganda, hope in schooling and economic systems that are utter failures, and that can condemn bright and enquiring minds to anecdotes, banalities, times tables and future opioid addiction.

Figure 42 – Schooling the World

Immerse the Indians in our civilization
and when we get them there, hold them under
until they are thoroughly soaked in the white man's ways.

—Captain Richard Henry Pratt,
Founder of the Carlisle Indian Industrial School in 1879

As sure as any of us can be, any fáidh-skilled critter worth their salt is opinionated. We listen to the same rhetoric year after year: *Will I be loved? Every child deserves an education. They paid the ultimate sacrifice. She fought the cancer but... Man conquers space. It's all good.* And every fáidh-gifted one of us cringes a little bit more at each repetition, sometimes we dry heave. English is the contemporary *lingua franca* of our species so, what do we do with it?

We travel. We become not only real-space place-walkers, we journey to countries and cultures that have utterly different philosophies, rules, environments, taboos, and morality. Can we learn from travel? We do. Landscape, the mysteries and weather, all recognize that something is inconsistent with their continuum. We live in an era that seems intellectually unique, in so far as I can be in Melbourne this morning and, after a plane flight that drags on forever, I can be in Los Angeles the same morning.

    I'm in the garden, last night, thinking about what I will write today. To gain a sense of how I will describe us, as people-species, and our mercurial nature, and I consider how media (if not the climbers themselves) represent an idea of *vanquishment*. Why a visit to the summit of a vast mountain is written as *conquering*. As though in some violent clash with an unprecedentedly well-prepared enemy. And that it seems such a cool thing to do. Like landing on the moon, the universally iconic saying *One small step for man, one giant step for mankind* going down in history. I think about this, and I am offended.

GENDERING

It's easy to fall back on the gendering of planetary associations, harder than anything to get rid of the hinderance. When we think of the moon, we often use the pronoun *she*, same with *venus*. When we think of *mercury* and *mars*, we think of *he*. Other cultures do otherwise, but most will gender mountains, valleys, ships and even windows. Everest, for example, is *Chomolungma*, translated into the English language, anthropomorphically, as "goddess mother of the world", and you have to wonder at the giant step for "mankind" that hopping about on an alien, orbiting celestial body has both achieved and permeated *western* thought and acceptability with. The notion that human females evolve from the rib of a pronoun, *adamu*, later mistranslated as a proper name: Adam (second of the biblical version or an earlier creation myth), or else explode from the top of another bloke's head (jupiter/zeus), gives food for thought. This is *mercury*. Where the traveler will go and how they get there, who they study and read, how they talk, and what they say.

A *10 of Coins*, here, can denote anything from a nomadic tribal caravan to a mobile home. From the distribution of bankable money into various denominations to the transportation industry, depending on what else is shown in the entirety of the map it can represent a library with the ten, multiplied into thousands and thousands, of books. In the current era it can also represent online banking. An *Ace of Staves* is a book, a *6 of Swords* a boat, watercraft and/or overseas travel. There are vast variations. A *Messenger of Swords* can be as much a motorcycle racing in the Dakar, as it is to a literal racehorse.

Mercury is also learning how to drive a vehicle and how to speak another language. Not only how to communicate with those who are simply not like us, and haven't been trapped into a construct (since the second Industrial Revolution, particularly) that requires us to wear uniforms, march in straight lines, ask no questions and mimic what we are told.

HERETIC – THE RIGHT TO CHOOSE

As heretic—fáidh-trained—you're going to reject this orthodoxy, because you will emote, relate, and empathize profoundly with the travelers. No matter from where they come. I will never forget the first-time tarot showed me Shanghai. The traveler was from there, but we both almost fell off our chairs when I picked it. He also had no idea about old Shanghai, the magic, the fabulous decadence, the smells of the alleys and warrens. He was young, academic, metaphorically rolling in money. They will still seek you out. What did I spae for him that day?

All I recall is the Seer in the place of HOME. Then bam. Floating junks by moonlight, and the smell of opium and jasmine.

I'll reiterate, now, that several billion years of bacterial life and evolution make us. When I greet the traveler, it is from the place of my front veranda. I have known they would come, because I understand *se chu to*, but did I mention that I hug them? It's quick, it's deep and it's genuine. I even have people who suffer from OCD fall into my arms without freaking out. The traveler, too, has been living in a state of *se chu to* without even knowing it. So that at that first contact a conversation, of say, a millisecond, occurs, between the vast population that is them, including their ancestral knowledge and their future destiny, and me and mine. This is also *mercurial*. This speed of light communication. So, by the time we have walked my hallways and settled in the parlor we know each other. Oh, my, how well we know each other. When they return, for a follow-up session, the event is like a Gregorian *New Year's Eve* ball.

FUNGAL NEURONS

Through an *evolutionary* lens, this is the knowledge of tracking. Of communication and the dance of mimicry—sympathetic magic. Ravens and other species do this. We call from the highest trees come sunset and sunrise. We warn, we entice. Dolores Ashcroft-Nowicki, in her book *The Shining Paths*, speculates that this place represents the knowledge and harnessing of fire. That could be so. As a species our lives, in the heart of an Arctic Winter, will certainly change due to communal warmth, and, as Paul Stamets, author of *Mycelium Running: How Mushrooms Can Help Save the World*, suggests, a woody mushroom, found on dead and dying beech trees—*Fomes fomentarius,* also known as a meadow-maker—likely changed our destiny, as a two-legged hominid, and reversed an inevitable extinction. Of *course,* there is a thread linking fire and communication to this message within the Stargate, in the portal of LIGHTNING, because communication super-highways, summoned into actualization by the world-wide internet, is continuing to quicken fate.

4. ART

Figure 43 – ART: *Ensō*

Am I being overly cautious? Not overly, no. If I mention the planet *venus* to a student, they mostly nod, like they know the associations. They've learned them somewhere. Despite my asking that, if they study with me, they leave all seeming-certainties on the mat at the front door, along with their shoes, a diluted stereotype arises. Some, when I have said *venus*, want to interrupt, describing *her* as the/a *goddess* of love and sex, and explaining for those others in the class, uneducated perhaps, that *she's* really an *aphrodite*, a pretty, palefaced, blonde critter, often displayed as young and shy, covering her breasts and genitals, and standing in a shell. Thanks Botticelli, it's no wonder Da Vinci despised you.

This anthropomorphizing of wilderness and species is such an entitled preconditioning. Hard to extricate oneself from, though.

Exciting and amazing when done. Of course, 4—ART—does represent all that's sexy, erotic, exotic and erogenous: gardens and forests, dripping nectar but smelling like a memory, dank and redolent with the fecundity of earthy decay, sewers and sweat and rain after a 42 degree day, the terror of the smell of electrical wiring on fire. The card placed on this branch of the map will also represent inflatable, plastic sex dolls, a red convertible, a matrilineal culture and a left hip. What sells? Sex, of course. Whether packaged as a coy bride, in white but with false eyelashes and filler-injected lips, on prime-time TV, or arms, covered in vernix, from participating in the delivery a newborn.

YOUR MOTHER'S DEATH

But so often I spae brutality here. Pain. Grief. Over the decades I have learned a bastion of presumed reality. How many people will you encounter in your lifetime, as a fáidh-born witch, who have been cut open to have breast implants? For what? Gender is irrelevant. Who profits? Who benefits? When the kids leave you, do you grieve?

A card falling in ART is an artist working with skin: hand poke, gun or the thorn of a lime tree, inking ancestral and clan *tatau*, or a *Betty-Boop* image colored onto a thigh, alongside an anchor and a heart, that hopefully will not be regretted when the skin sags towards entropy.

Your mother's death is going to be here, so is a partner's blow, so is *bondage* and *S & M*. Of course, sex work, but also ads for lacy, crotchless underwear. ART includes this traveler's skill as an artist or an arborist or a genetic engineer. Volunteering aid in a fistula clinic in Africa. They have experienced FGM. They are a gay son, or a transgender sibling undergoing a surgical procedure.

SENSUALITY

ART is also a reminder of the caves of Lascaux. Why do our ancestors paint? Why do we carve and weave? Why we decorate? Our abodes, ourselves? Orgasm is a momentary state of being in rapture, but so is a certain song, a view, the hand of Peanuts in that of Jane Goodall. How much accolade, then, can be given to the artist who designed the Nasir al-Mulk Mosque in Shiraz, or the thirteen-thousand-year-old mammoth tusk carving of reindeer, from the Magdalenian Period?

ART, as this portal on the Stargate, is a representation of the sensory. It includes blacksmithing—a lump of seemingly uninteresting rock that becomes a torc or a dagger, and cochineal, a bug, crushed to create the most profound red, as early as two thousand years into the so-called past, in Mesoamerica.

Evolutionarily-speaking this is earth in diversity. Fecundity. Breeding. The awareness of health among ourselves, intertribally, as well as foraging, and the skills of tanning, cooking, beading and the recitation of lore. One can only speculate on our tools and our imaginations. Probably when the first person exclaimed at the wonder of beauty.

5. CORE

Figure 44 – CORE: Navaho Rock Art

QUEEN AFTER QUEEN AFTER QUEEN

Individuality. That's what seems to have happened. Tectonic plates moving, spreading like cracks in a post-apocalyptic, abandoned highway. Trees forming canopies, from the height of parsley to the giant redwoods of California, the long-ghosted oak forests that formed the spire of Notre Dame, the old growths from Bwindi, in what we now name Uganda, to the Swamp Gum, in the Valley of the Giants, Tasmania. Oceans rising and falling, leaving deserts, mysterious. From fossilized trilobites atop the majestic aridity of

Uluru to the long-abandoned, painted caves of the Tassili. We think what, of today, with mobile phones and satellites – that it's exciting? Or even noteworthy? And while the gendering of our universe's star is considered masculine in Graeco-Roman mythology it is otherwise in most other ethnologies.

Walu (woman) to the Yolngu, *Amaterasu Omikami* (woman) in Japan, Sól, (woman), in Old Norse whereas to the Hopi the sun is Tawa and male. *Saulė* in the Baltic and *Grian* in Irish are both women in the mythologies; legends told to children.

Does this matter? Only insofar as those of us following the labyrinth, that is magic's meandering but intentional maze, want to break the back of predictability by which we have been indoctrinated.

So, who, or what, is CORE? Who are you? What is this heart of the Stargate? Of this Majestic River? Seriously, not a moment of any minute of any day of a person's entire life is lived without self-awareness. Yes, this can become pathological, but we'll get to why. You are, in a solar-system-kind-of-way, a sun. Just atomic. You are a nucleus under an electron microscope, and life goes on around you: protons and electrons. The interesting phenomenon is the realization that I can only know of these last two by the fluctuations they seem to represent. See? No? Every second of every day you experience. Everything from breathing to someone passing your street-level window, to the noise of traffic, breast feeding, eating something that once lived (complete with their own entire story). To what we believe exists, from the beam of a now-dead star to Lucille Ball. Are they even here? Are they real? Define real? While we're on the subject of individuality, tell me about anything that's unreal?

We are self-aware. Most of us don't live in *Alert,* a village on the tip of the Nunavut territory in Canada, five hundred miles below the North Pole. With a population of five people, or Utopia, an Aboriginal community in the Northern Territory, but…

> *I was sent to a farm in Victoria. It was hard: me going to live with white people. A lot of things still hurt from that time when I was taken away.*
>
> Barbara Weir,
> *Painter and gatherer of traditional bush tucker and medicine.*

The hope is that you didn't spae the above coming. That it's new for you, because this is how tarot teaches.

LOVE IS LOVE, AND REBEL IS REBEL

You think you've got it sorted out, the way it works, then a strange thing happens, in the place of this CORE, the place of the traditional symbol of the sun, is an *Empress*. Who is this person in front of you?

Figure 45 – Extinction Rebellion

You look from one other card, and their position, to another, and nothing makes sense. Is the person a woman? Are they a mother?

Are they in the fashion industry? All guesswork.

You'll do that for a while. It just becomes noxious if you keep guessing—and not knowing beyond all doubt—past your first year as a commissioned fàidh-gifted. A guarantee that all the sceptics were right, and that you or I are mere book-learned-*wanna-be*'s. You take a risk. There's that *9 of Staves* in place of the CORE, a *10 of Swords* in there somewhere, a *Chariot*, perhaps, in the place of HOME, *2 of Staves* in the place of STONE. Suddenly, in your imagination, you spae the media image of the people in red, silently protesting with *Extinction Rebellion*. You read the pointless comments of politicians. Then you think of lipstick and Marilyn Monroe, roses in full bloom. There is that background image of sex in a midnight alley, against the dark wall of your local council chambers, and there in the place of LIGHTNING, is an *Emperor* card. The answer (if you were me) to who the traveler is, is *the Scarlet Alliance*, the peak Australian sex-workers' union. And you know you've got a lot to discuss.

Just as significant, is a *10 of Swords* in this position, with no harm around it. They haven't pulled up their sleeves, but you can spae ink, artfully needled into the skin of their neck, just above the scarf. Or the *Moon*, and how sad that is, if there's also a 3 of Swords and an *8 of Cups*.

Life, to each of us, *seems* to revolve around *who* we are. All the time. Any monster who tries to suggest this is not true, is lying to you. Confusing you with the non-thinking selflessness of a missionary-on-a-roll. It's just not real... and they are probably selling you something, even if it's the delusion of salvation. You are fáidh-born, or else trained through the tutelage of such a person. This is witchcraft, and they are like Jehovah's Witnesses knocking (I know, it's funny) on your door, asking if you'll let Jesus into your heart? I assure them I use protection, so that's not likely to happen. After a confused moment, prior to the Charlie-Chaplain-disgusted shock-face, they go away. The idea of non-thinking selflessness is delusional. Does a person in a coma dream? Are they present in the dream, or a watcher?

The relief, in the above, is *that* you are. Not that you are this, or that, not what you do or achieve, or fail at, or cry over, or delight in. You. When you accept that you can relax. You're alive, then you're *other*. If another person falls in this place on the map, you have to figure out whether they are going to love the traveler... or obfuscate them. The individual for whom you are reading won't have gone anywhere, but they could lose themselves to another's *shine*, might be overwhelmed or overshadowed by them. This *person* card can also represent a supposed dead-somebody, that the traveler admires, has studied and feels akin to. The traveler could also be a fraud, and the card, then, an identity they have taken on or stolen... or who they truly are.

HEART ATTACK

And here's a kicker... I have my visitor's dad in my vision (and this is not the first time I'm horrified by this), tied to a tree, their torso sliced from throat to groin, their ribs splayed in some ritualistic death rite... and I have to say what I spae. Their father has just had a triple bypass and is recovering well. I almost mumble that I tell of the future, not the past. They hear me. The traveler sighs, knowing how this will all end.

Is it always heart attack? Heartbreak also falls here with the *3 of Swords*. Maybe not the traveler. Maybe they're the one leaving. It always hurts. Because you once loved and because the person no longer does, and how hard is it to tell the recipient of that separation?

This is not easy. This work is not easy. You could just read the little booklet that comes with your pack of cards, and sit in a rocker on your porch, calling yourself *Madam Hoodoo*, and claiming to trace your pedigree in witchery back to an ancient clan of Corsican royalty, known only to a few, who were all burned at the stake, except the one who passed the knowledge from generation to generation, into the present. What fun is that? Heaps of fun, and quite often, very lucrative. But in the mist of mind *you* know it doesn't matter. That you are in the same CORE position as the person who seeks you out, hoping… just maybe… you are the real deal, wondering why your kids never call and whether this loneliness is worth a scam.

So, this center is only ever important because of the story that, like electrons, surrounds it. Affects it. Those planets and not the sun—the CORE—because the traveler still has questions waiting in the wings of this stage: Will *I* find love? Will *I* own my own home one day? Is my business going to stay afloat? Do I get to travel? Money, tell me about money? Will my kids be okay? Even that last one has a *my* in it.

Every interpretation of the maps, by you, is about the traveler. Every question, every event, every rising up and falling down.

What picture docks at this place is *the least* important story here. Not because it lacks significance but because, like the saying goes, *you can't always see the wood for the trees.*

BLOWIN' IN THE WIND – GRAIN AND SPECIES

You'll likely read that this is the *sphere of the sacrificed gods*, and that according to scholars this period of our species' evolution was around ten and a half thousand years ago, when relatively recent academics speculate that grain was considered a male out-there deity, and that the harvest was a ritualized killing of a person or potent warrior. That may be so, but I'd rather you queried the validity of anything said to be set in stone. Every text I've read says the same thing. Just like politicians tell us that young men, soldier boys, who have suffered horrendous deformities, from contact with Agent Orange during the American/Vietnam War (depending on whose side you were on), and dirty bombs in Iraq and Afghanistan, and who have unwittingly passed a blueprint of such, through their genetic sperm to their offspring, made a great sacrifice for their country. Around now I probably don't need to keep asking you to rethink tired terminology, but I'm constantly told that it is *really difficult* to break these indoctrinated patterns, of Machiavellian techniques, to control through discrimination. Especially because they are so horribly self-serving to those who mask their true motives with such obvious platitudes.

We're back in Mesopotamia—the Fertile Crescent—again, with this theory of scything grain. I want to speculate with you about all this. According to everything I've read, agriculture began with a process known as *sedentism*. It's been hypothesized that, as a mammal, we would have been beyond starving to have eaten the seeds off grass, and yet we did, and do, and have done as far into the deep ages as eleven thousand years. Where did this concept of male sacrifice come from? And should we, as diviners and oracles, care? When a traveler sits opposite me wearing a crucifix? Yes. When we are led to believe that brutal deaths in the name of a war for either peace or righteousness, are *holy* things? Are they *tapu*? No. Are they propaganda? Yes. Who benefits? Those who promote guilt. Those who use gaslighting to produce compliance. You'll spae the results so often that you'll need to either ignore it (that *Devil*, that *Hanged* card) or else translate its presence to what it is: a psychological and esoteric anomaly.

Are any of the above *facts*, about our evolutionary progress, true? *I don't know*. I have debated this with colleagues before I was willing enough to write this, but when I ask about Ice Ages and glaciation periods, the use of grain as a mainstay of what has been, speculatively, prior to this unusually explicit antiquity, a species who hunt and gather like all other species beyond the glass ceiling of the so-called developed world, I get blank stares or embarrassed confessions. Worse, I evoke uncertainty. Because an arrangement of the songlines of prior events has been agreed to, unequivocally.

SELF AWARENESS

What we can be sure of, is that at some time we became self-aware. We have only *Shifting Baseline Syndrome* to fall back on. Oh, things have always been this way, but no. Anthropology speculates that we became servants to grain. That to populate, on a vast scale, seed-producing grasses had to keep us all in cluster-groups. Hence, we no longer traverse, from winter to summer, along the snowline and down onto the savannah, following the herds, and the spawning fish. We are trapped. Enslaved to an ideology of significance-through-possession. That certain economies used the dispersal of grains as financial barter; that the first puppet to lock up their grain after a bumper season, said, when the following summer the locusts came, *Yeah, you can have some of mine, but you better make it worth my while.*

Religions formed around this cultural disparity. Creed. Threat and, to all accounts, terrible violence. Pomp and theatre, carrot-dangling and reward. Banks. Here are the first-ever banks. Riane Eisler, in *The Chalice and the Blade*, postulates a warped gene in some deeply embedded past. Our ancestors are, otherwise, hunter-gatherers, and nomadic pastoralists. Beyond that are the hieroglyphics and pictograms of a dominator culture.

We're still indoctrinated into believing that to be wealthy is to own land or property... when the construct is ludicrous. Our destiny is to die. To become soil and air and water. The living bit shouldn't be so difficult. This has opened the way to both imperialism and snobbery. Class systems and the warped concept that *man* is better than other species, including the people that don't conform to an agreed-to doctrine of
how to live.

Do you need to know all this as *spé*? Fáidh-gifted? To interpret tarot? Yes. Absolutely.

1. PROTECTION

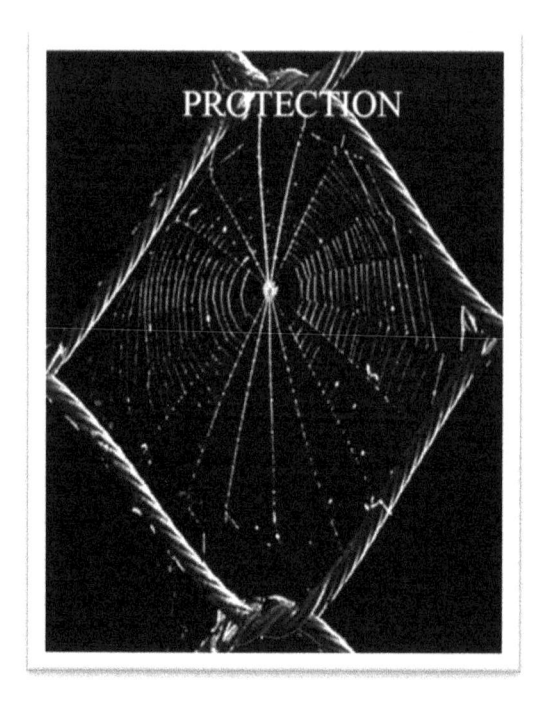

Figure 46 – Protection: Spider Web in Wire

PROTECTION is traditionally misrepresented.

Called, so offhandedly, *mars*, and masculinized as *the god of war*, so often, that I am grief-stricken at the lie. See the image above? You ever walk into one of these—a big one, an orb-spider-sized one—in the woods, on the night of a black moon? There now. Scream.

Every so often someone asks me why I never read reverse images. I give them the look. What do you want? I'm an old woman. I do that. The truth is twofold: firstly, I can tell everything, some of it really intense and traumatic, with every card facing towards me, so that reversing a card is just ridiculous, and secondly, that gives the other person away, lets me know they read the booklet.

Body damage or even levels of fitness? Their right ribcage and lung, their liver, spleen, gall bladder. Ouch. With a *Strength* card, however, it is fitness. Big strong fighter or powerlifter. The gladiatorial training called *sport*. With an *8 of Coins* they're in the military, or they're a professional fitness trainer. Do you get how this unfolds?

BOSS COCKY OR SILVERBACK?

Can this be a place of aggression? Define aggression? Doesn't it depend on whether you are the aggressor or someone else? And whether the behavior is really aggression or whether it is defense, or self-defense? Can it be cruelty? That's different. Family scenarios can fall here. Stints with mandatory national service.

Figure 47 – Silverback

The uprisings in Hong Kong, Sudan, Paris, Spain, Argentina, protests against political austerity implementations, a parent who ignores a child to the point of neglect, Saturday night on the club strip, police brutality, the forced removal of indigenous children from their families—ancestral heritage—by church and state. Who decides which is which? Who decrees what is appropriate? Doesn't that depend on what side of the highway one is on?

This portal is also, like LIGHTNING, energy. Vitality also resides here. Translate this branch with the *Empress* card, with the *4 of Staves*, with the *10 of Cups*. All of these are celebratory. The *Strength* card here is physical. It's bull. It's a bear and a gorilla and a wren. Vascularity. Weight and strength training are at home here. The *2 of Swords* is my sensei showing me my mistake, not telling me, from the far end of the dojo. *Moon* card here is waxing and waning, *Magician* here is a person in their prime or, if an *Emperor* is around somewhere, that lovely piece of paper that declares the traveler a certified health practitioner. *Empress* can be your grandmother, or the way of the women in your family, but not your matrilineal DNA or ancestry because that would be STONE (*saturn*).

AR 15 ASSAULT RIFLE

Can certainly be when we, as a species, first weaponized. And look how far that's come? The glorification of war through language. Hiroshima. Iraq. Police armed to the hilt, and AR15 assault rifles in the hands of children. Nuclear proliferation so vast it could be considered comical and farcical… unless something goes wrong and a madman presses that red button.

7. EXPANSION

Figure 48 – EXPANSION: Symbol: *Jera*, a year

There is an assumption that western education, western knowledge, is something that is superior... there is an idea that we have evolved to a higher level of being...

Helena Norberg-Hodge,
Ancient Futures,
Founder and Director of *Local Futures, the Economics of Happiness*

This is the present day, on the evolutionary journey. Recognizably because, traditionally associated with *jupiter*, this branch represents expansion. Could it be aligned with the traditional aspects assigned to *jupiter*, such as education, philosophy, religion, career, politics and concepts of success? I doubt their validity, from experience. Who is this for? What is it to you and me? It seems, from what I know, that these are the attributes of a classist society, and the words are just words.

EDUCATION VS SCHOOLING

Figure 49 – First Nations, WA

Schooling is not educating. It is presumed to be so. But if schooling does not ensure the well-being of both the individual and their extended family, tribe, clan or community, then it is indoctrination, not education. And it assumes success or failure based on a closed ethnic modality that is classist, sexist and segregationist. You won't get along well in the world unless you behave and assimilate, isn't that the underlying propaganda?

Education is many other things; from what to plant when, where to fish, how to play a violin, how to find your way from one place to another by memory-mapping, what places and things are *tapu*, which elders to attend to learn the appropriate songs and dances in order to hunt kangaroo or boar, how to train your cormorant to fish with you, sled dogs for long-distance journeying by ice and snow, a *Celtic Lurcher* (hound) for the taking of pheasant and the skill of outrunning the laird's mount, to throat-singing to ensure the safe return of the seal hunters, to communication by *Auslan* (sign), to foretelling coming events from flood to assassination to a future birth against so-called odds, for the woman who has paid huge money, and experiencing personal trauma, to carry and deliver a healthy infant through the use of IVF (*Ace of Swords/Empress*).

It is not uniforming, and marching, and standing in line, it isn't placing the teacher away, or apart from, the student (apprentice), demanding agreement or acquiescence to a status quo, designated by some board of governance, the reasoning of which is compliance, and it certainly is not merely accepting what someone has written, without purposeful consideration, about tarot.

> *To never forget your own insignificance. To never get used to the unspeakable violence and vulgar disparity of the life around you. To seek joy in the saddest places.*
>
> Arundhati Roy,
> *The God of Small Things*

I'm not digging too deeply into the soil of philosophy (except that the entirety of this work is philosophical, albeit existential), as its bias depends on ethnicity, background, religion, politics, school, constructs of history. It's the same with culture, career and conceptual success. Terminologies are deemed significant based on what? What modality? Whose opinion? I'm writing this in an age of social media and higher learning as a capitalist construct, therefore it'll be useless to you, fáidh-gifted, because the hypothesis of every traveler will differ depending on ethnic, social and economic parameters, but for you, the trader in futures, there needs to be an existentialism to your work that defies the ideas presented by anyone else... after you have, perhaps, read them, listened to them, considered them, and not from a place of blinkered ideology.

You can't interfere in the interpretation of the prophecy because of some adopted moral *high ground* or ethical positioning. You'll never tell it straight. That window will close. I've had big men who toil on the gas pipelines in Western Australia, a woman in the military who teaches how to operate a helicopter, to people heading into supposed *hostile territory*, decided upon by whom? There was a time I considered the Australian government to be egalitarian. Timor-Leste. Yes, the Australian military fought alongside the East Timorese to secure their independence. Didn't they? Isn't that what happened? Until, that is, I found out about the oil and gas dispute, and that Australia is siphoning off the giant's portion of the profit, with China investing in its own economic piece of mega-pie; the same with so many governments, with agendas, that yes, do certainly figure here, but you'll as likely spae the Justice card in this position, when martial law is imposed onto an ethnic minority, as when it applies to the employment of the traveler, who could as easily be a lawyer.

...

EPIC FLATULENCE

When a card falls here, JERA, it is on the journey of the so-called drop of water in the highest alps, that becomes a river, that becomes the ocean, that becomes the weather system that freezes the water vapor that thaws, in its season, to become that so-called drop of water (but different), and that in an evolutionary sense, we are at what seems to be an epic flatulence. I realize I, like most people, are subject to *Shifting Baseline Syndrome*, and that we will all be unaware whether there exists an historic precedent to the current presentation... but obesity? Over-supply of everything? The insanity of rampant property development? Centralization and international trade treaties? Too much, too much, too much.

As a result, too much illness, too many drugs, too much military intervention, too much advertising, too many gadgets... and too much poison, of so many varieties, I would be terrified if I were capable of such.

Disease or illness falling here? Maybe. That's tricky, and I won't lie to you. A person's anatomical stomach is here, as is their left lung. Other factors in this, and other maps, will provide more information. Sometimes a person's stomach illness is going to show elsewhere.

Busted ribs are here, but again, the surrounding story, and your knowing, will decide.

TIPPING POINT

Too much variety: too many jams, too much information, too many soy plantations, countless cattle in feed lots, too many chickens crowded into too many closed spaces, too many additives in too many tins of too much everything, making us much too sick. Or else there are too many gyms and too many diets, too much body dysmorphia and way, way too much interference by over the top advertising campaigns to what? A tipping point of too many people drinking out of too many plastic bottles. That, now, is erupting into revolution as too many legislative laws replace what social economists consider too many freedoms. Has it always been this way? In our historic lifetimes, yes. Too much taxation and too little food. Abundant cures for, as yet, too many potential killer diseases. And way too many graveyards for bodies that are never going to rise, complete and intact, at some mythic *second coming* of a savior, the child of an omnipotent god (depending on your religion) who is doing one too many screwed up activities with the weather for us to take him/them seriously. Too many fires and too many hurricanes.

Will it explode? Looks like that's a no. The other way. Restriction is the outcome. STONE. Repression and uniformity. Boxes for people to live in, instead of houses, our own graves perhaps. *Soylent Green*? Got to do something with all the bodies.

...

8. STONE

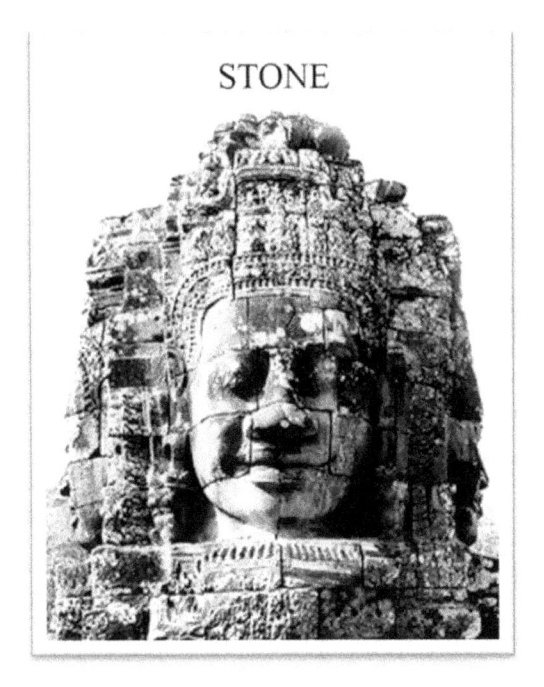

Figure 50 – Stone: *Ankor Wat*, Cambodia

'It seems to resemble what we call religion rather more than what we call science.'

Robert MacFarlane,
Underland: A Deep Time Journey

BAD RAP

Saturn has a bad rap. Everywhere you read you're likely to be informed that this planetary giant is like Chronos, a hairy Greek bloke in a frock, thought of as a *god of time*, even though we have already deconstructed what time isn't: a recent generalized interpretation that makes no sense. Stone is no old man.

STONE has nothing to do with a current interpretation of Orphic mysticism, like *descent into the underworld* (usually capitalized, like a gauntlet run through downtown East London, Kings Cross, or Los Angeles, where the underworld is a series of rooftop shotgun sentinels, strongholds, of people who are, once again, feral; have re-tribalized themselves and, through clear and inter-designated territorial divisions hold the turrets of the castle keep, because what *is* that?

STONE is not limitation: STONE (*saturn*) *defines* limitation, and the dictionary definition, mathematically, relates the word to zero, a thing, of course, that can't be nothing, because there is no such something as nothing.

But, what we recognize, as a current historic precedent, is that time seems to wind down, that security measures restrain, imprison, gather intel, and seem to limit. What? Whatever they want. Is that time? Or is that politics?

A law, behaviorally acceptable construct, a constitution, are said to be written in stone. Why? What does that infer? Written in stone, etched in stone, set in stone. Some of these idioms come from archaeological descriptions of carvings that predate the current era, from hieroglyphs to the *Rosetta Stone*, to the carvings along the vast walls of Ireland, Scotland, Europe, and the temples of Mesoamerica.

And here's the glitch—or reality (if such a thing is even a thing)—the deeper portals, the branches of some gnarled oak in that *First Forest*, I call STONE, are already in existence and will be so even when our sun goes nova, just not as we perceive it—and guess about it—as scholarship archaeology does in the current era. STONE is heading into the vortex, that will ultimately recycle itself into 1. HOME again, but in some currently unrecognizable being. So, when you get to the card that docks in this place, take a step back, and outside of your comfort zone, because the expression *written in stone,* is notoriously biblical, and all I ask is that you know this. That it's some misunderstood agreement to there being an actual person named Moses (instead of its linguistic attribute, a moses, being a *son of...*) who lugs himself up a mountain where some deity strikes ten regulations into a couple of slate tablets of carved rules and regs. I want to pause a moment and look at this tale, because it is commonly taken literally, or offhandedly.

> *Knowledge and power correlated in oral cultures. Restricting the songs and stories which encode information avoids corruption of data caused by the so-called Chinese whispers effect.*
>
> Dr. Lynne Kelly, *The Memory Code*

MAJOR TOM'S A JUNKIE

This supposed *moses* child was pulled from a river, in a woven boat, or basket. What is the river, in story? What is the basket? What skill is passed from elder to initiate, in this epic? It is the learned-wisdom that arranges free-growing wild reed into a tapestry or carrying accessory (an amazing invention when one has a pile of tubers to bring home). Is this an allegory to the infinity of so-called time? We could leave it at that, and accept that this is a form of story-knowledge, an ancestry, a caste, a way of planting, a comprehension of the fertility of rivers like the Nile and Euphrates, of when and how to plant and harvest, what fish to net at what season in a year, or a lifetime, and how the wisdom has passed through the ages... Or we can do something else. Recognize it as an *Ashes to ashes, funk to funky, we know Major Tom's a junky*-type biographical-passing-along of history-through-story, a folk tale that requires our own Rosetta Stone scholarship to interpret. Those of us not in direct lineage to the area of the *moses* story need to double-check how, or even whether, it relates to us. Does it? Yes. No matter where we are born, we have a heritage, our own blood lineages, ancestors whose ashes are the wind and landscape of everywhere from the spruce of an Arctic compass-north, to the decimated Murray-Darling on the continent once known as *Gondwana*.

How do we interpret a story that lies here? In this place at the Stargate? You can't, unless you take living-in-perpetuity into account. See, once you've read the above you can't unread it. You can try to tell yourself that I'm waffling, but you know I'm not. You know that you've been deluded into thinking of the occult-natured *saturn* in an easy, predictable fashion. *Oh, that's restriction, that's old age, that's limitation.* What if it's the *Star*? Or the *2 of Staves*? What if it's a *Tower*? What if it's a *Messenger of Swords*? (That last one's likely to be a 1940s *Indian Chief* motorcycle, a good-looking cruise machine, capable of over 100 mph when tuned. Welcome in my garage anytime).

The traveler's right shoulder, elbow or wrist, even fingers, can give them grief if a prophecy of pain or injury is exposed here. It's impossible, without you sitting opposite me, to give appropriate examples of what to say, how to say it. What if it's *Death*? What about the obvious: *Emperor*, or the *Hierophant*? That's easy. *Ace of Coins*. That's only interesting when it falls at the next portal along the *Lightning Flash*, otherwise it's just *old money*.

ONE PLUS ZERO EQUALS ONE

STONE, if the *Lightning Flash* is the way you perceive this, is a non-existing 10, that becomes 1, next round, on the trajectory ellipse of the Stargate (as any numeric consideration goes both ways, past and future being eternally now) where STONE is represented. This is the number where life is possible. From nothing to something. Symbolically, a triangle. The third line closing in the previous two, (LIGHTNING and CHALLENGER DEEP) creating a feedback loop. Until the infinitely, seemingly non-existent millisecond when ∧ becomes Δ there can be no life (as we understand) because everything is energy and does not present us with a concept of *form*. Everything sings in π.

Δ is also ∞ and also ϴ, or any closed system symbol really, and has been called a *soul*. STONE can crush and condense seeming freedom, by means of security, prisons, institutional demand for uniformity, containment of nuclear waste. It also supports and protects; solid foundations, and walls, are also fortresses. It cuts both ways. Here's where that flash of life happens, outside of comprehension, when a sperm, and an ovum, become united.

9. LIGHTNING

Figure 51 – LIGHTNING, Jordie Scott

MOTHERBOARDS & CRAZY, GENIUS ZAPZONES

When did *uranus* become, according to tarot, what it is now? The first time I understand, is when the person comes back to me, after his hide-and-seek debacle with a local council, in rural Bendigo. His map has a *Tower* guarding the portal of experience known as LIGHTNING. I recall recognizing it is a big deal, and a massive crisis, to do with electricity. He lives on a main street, and the trees in his front yard that have died from Dutch elm disease and are now seasoned sufficiently for a winter hearth. He gets out the chainsaw and takes down the first one, but it lands askew. On the power lines.

Figure 52 – Bitcoin

He blacks out Bendigo. His story is that he works like crazy to make it easy enough to transport the logs to the paddock, out back, before the electricity department comes knocking on his door demanding he pay compensation.

Fast forward thirty years and I'm sitting with a return traveler. There's an *Ace of Coins* in the spot, and I yell, *Bitcoin. You're trading in crypto.* How does this make sense? I spae the symbol for Bitcoin when I flip the pictogram into that position. And yes, they are a trader on the blockchain. A thing I know about now, but don't two years ago when I first get hammered with the new meaning. And I mean hammered. That's what electricity does. Not pleasant. A critter that doesn't need to ask for respect. An *8 of Coins* there is a gaffer or some other kind of sparky. But be careful because the traveler can as easily be in technology, or cyber-design, or they are a gamer. Technology or scientific research. It'll show you an MRI. It is a left shoulder, elbow or wrist, and will likely be a *10 of Swords* because the person works in hospitality and carries plates on that arm, the consequence of which can be RSI. Same for me when I've sat sideways to my keyboard, typing.

A VAST INTERGALACTIC BRIDGE

Traditionally the place represented by *uranus* is also called the *Sphere of the Zodiac,* and this is both rational and quirky when you stop to think that of the evolutionary *salmon leap*, made by Cú Chulain in order to reach the Islay of Skye in the legend. The voyage between STONE and LIGHTNING is like the journey of a seed towards an ancient, but inherently futuristic, target. More like a vast, intergalactic extension bridge really. And who is this doing the crossing, whilst simultaneously being the bridge? The *Empress*.

This is the wonderment of our mere selves, but also our vast potential for fruitfulness in a way that is always succulent. While, in the current era, media focusses on environmental violation and destruction someone, probably some group of *someones*, is busy doing the mathematics of how to transfer the equivalent of the *Svalbard Global Seed Vault* into a space shuttle that'll connect up with a fleet somewhere out near Betelgeuse. Considering that the Kepler spacecraft has provided data suggesting 150,000 stars in our own solar system, and hint at a mere estimation of a thousand likely-to-be-habitable planets, someone's going to load that mother of a spaceship—a kind of ark—before a few more decades are spun. Will we know? Of course. Will we know as the species we present at the right now? What are we are destined to be? Percentages estimate that livable planets are maybe one in a million. That's better odds than winning Lotto.

...

10. CHALLENGER DEEP

Figure 53 – CHALLENGER DEEP: Horizon

UNFATHOMABLE

CHALLENGER DEEP is an actual place, at the bottom of the Marina Trench in the Pacific Ocean and is, at a modest estimation,

35,827 feet down. That's around seven miles. If I drive seven miles it's nothing, yes? But if I dive? I can't dive. No one can dive seven miles beneath the surface of an ocean. Can we fly seven miles into space? Seems so. We are told so. In a vessel. Am I one to doubt what I am told? Of course. If I drive seven miles across Melbourne it'll take me about three hours. If villages in Australia are seven miles apart, it's five minutes' drive from one to the other. In 2014, Ahmed Gabr, a forty-one-year-old Egyptian man, broke a world record by scuba diving down just over a thousand feet.

This is the depths of the voyage, and the vastness and enormity of life's personal quests.

The journey to explore the furthest reaches of consciousness is the equivalent of the depths of self to which any of us can ever hope to dive. It's all relative. One person tells you about their experience of pain and you sympathize. But you *don't* know. We can't know what another person is feeling; is experiencing. We guess. Based on what may or may not be a similar or relatable experience. It's not true though. Its speculation is the basis of known—or acceptable—parameters.

Figure 54 – Sumerian Cylinder Seal

When the earliest archaeology of a *Tree of Life* was first surmised as being a *thing* by scholars, it turned up on a cylinder seal. This tree pictogram: What is it? How did a tree become such an important mystical and iconographic symbol? Why? And is it a *thing*? Or is the sky? Look again. Yes, it's a forest but it is also a universe.

HEAVEN AND HELL

To many people reading articles and books relative to the Tree of Life as a magical understanding, it's Qabalah. It's got an up and a down. Like a ladder. There's *heaven* and the *underworld*; sky and deep places beneath the surface of something. The idea that the upmost branches of this tree are the important attributes is weird. It makes no sense. It's the roots that support greatness. It's roots that provide the power of any tree—or any seed for that matter—to produce any kind of fecundity or dissemination. Unfortunately, the *inntrenger*—gabbah; pākehā, wašíču, ionróirí, ghusanevaala, mvamizi, ghaz—the invaders (not including intertribal, more inclusive of the infestation of strangers known, almost innocently, as colonizers or *westerners*) seem not to have cottoned on, and the idea of ascension, as a form of superiority or self-realization, remains.

BALDERDASH

And it's a load of balderdash. There's that rocket blasting off earth and doing what? Conquering again. *Final frontier* and all that. Well, you're a farseer—fáidh—or becoming such, so you have an obligation to question *everything* you have been led to believe. Led, because if you remain peacefully within your forest tribe, and your forest tribe is not invaded by anyone, who are you? Not newsworthy, that's for sure, in the common era, not a celebrity, not a *star*. You'll likely not have your name, or your achievements, sung of by anyone beyond the children of your tribe, in future generations. Will you? You won't be anyway. Nobody either knows or cares about Hypatia's concept of sex, gender and death, just that a bunch of zealous, violent, bitter, twisted christian monks decided she had no right to live, and so chucked rocks at her until she was dead, and then scraped the flesh from her bones before burning what remained, as though to say *there, woman, know your place*.

The *Star* is in its native environment, right here. Not just any star, but the *Nail in the Sky*. That is the *Pole Star*. The navigator's emblem of distance, the hunter's compass. To understand the positioning of stars in any season, is to find your way from a. to b. and back again. Is the Pole Star a god? Absolutely. Do we *inntrenger-people* remember that? No. Except deeply. Oh, so deeply. Like when you plant a star atop a christmas tree or stick it to the door of your most important actor. If you rate a book or a football player. The symbol is deep and fortifying. Real and abiding. We just don't have the knowledge of why. Well, you do now.

The artists of older, traditional tarot card pictogram know. I think. The image of the individual with one foot on land and one foot in water, carrying a jar in which to carry the latter, under the light of several stars, should astonish us, with the memory of this ancient, non-literate knowledge. But instead, many authors give a reader, or a would-be tarot navigator, bits. Just dogma without the substance of a deep-winter gummy shark hunt. Except that yesterday I skyped with a person in Texas, USA, and the *Star* represented that state.

SEAL AND WHALE AND SPAWNING COD

Our ancestors know this. Within the DNA maps of many, or all, of us, is the memory of that frozen, mist-shrouded autumn, winter and early spring. Devastating days and nights—well it's all night, really, until midsummer—when our food stocks have run low, despite what we have killed and preserved to enable us to endure, because we have bred a little too many new people and not put the excess out for the wolves. During the light times, because it is so important, we haul stones, raise them, sing the memory of why, and the map to which they allude, so that our children's children, despite the fog and mist and sleet and deep cloud-cover, can find their way to fresh water. Every non-hibernating animal needs to drink, don't they? And if not fresh water, then where it is safe to dig a hole in the ice from which to harpoon seal or whale or the spawning cod. Do you understand what the standing stones are? What Avesbury is? Gobekli Tepe? The stones of Mystery Hill in New Hampshire? The Glen Innes standing stone circle in Australia, that is a mere forty kilometers from a sister circle in Mullumbimby, all said to be Paleolithic and all equated with the ridiculous concept of 'temple'? These are gathering places. Maps. Alignments. Until *inntrenger* decimation occurs, these places are understood as a meeting place. Or deep groves of initiation. Navigators teach us how to read them: sky and river patterns, for more reasons than I can present here, but one of which is so that we don't interbreed ourselves into non-existence.

ANCIENT MESSENGERS

In the deep black water, off the furthest-most, above-sea shores of mainland Scotland, is a group of islands called the Outer Hebrides. One of these islands—the Isle of Lewis—is host to a massive standing stone called *Clach an Truseil*, who is thought to have been in position for 5,000 years. An elder stone-person, they stand above ground to a height of nineteen feet and is estimated to be a further six feet below ground. Here we are, around twenty miles from the Callanish Stones... and, once, we have six companion stones. They are removed in 1914. Who does that? Why? What pathetic reason is there to lose the knowledge of our ancestors? We stand alone—us, as *Clach an Truseil*—and decisive, within the village of *Baile an Truseil*.

Figure 55 – *Clach an Truseil*, Isle of Lewis

For whom are we the navigators of destiny? Or the warner-of-destruction there on the nor 'east coast? Who are the Outer Hebrides before the last Ice Age? Before the Big Sea rises? ***Clach an Truseil*** is a messenger whose silence is a howl of summoning. *This way. Here's the harbor. Land here. It's safe. Pop into the pub here in my village before you go off to the craic at Callanish. Leave your past here, if you go to become an adult; a navigator. I'm your host. Your* *guide. Look! The Nail of the World. Spé? The clan here are intelligent, trust me.*

I wonder at the first person, ever, who gazes into the still water of a loch's surface, and sees their own face looking back. Who sees the stars of a timelessly unchanged night sky mirrored, like an earth map, told to us by our elders, deep in the enclosed stone places of initiation, where we are directed in the song of what we must carry? How to protect and ensure the survival of our clan, no matter that we are one amonst many? How you are to comprehend the landscape, here, where a card falls? It is as though magic is dropped onto your table. That drop is the elixir of wisdom that Finn sucks from his fingers when he stirs the brew in some mythic pot (*caleach*: circle) of poteen, meant for the ugly kid. Again, sticking with the Outer Hebrides (Uist), there is a stone circle known as *Sòrnach Coir Fhinn*, just as there is on Arran, and on Skye, to remind us we are everywhere.

Gazing into that pool is legendary. We all know that from what we read, what we are advised by our elders in witchery. You are with them, you understand. In that glassy surface, those stars, the guidance of them that must be acknowledged in stone, to enable our ancestors to find each other when the sky is diminished by the seasons.

WE ARE GODS

We have seemingly lost so much. Memory places, ways of meeting and gathering, stories of navigation, and weather, perhaps thousands and thousands of years deep. Why else write of all the above in a tarot book? Because the fáidh-trained is a lore-holder, working with something that cannot, now (as we understand *now*), be explained. Be assured, though, that you will need to unlearn as much as learn, to enable you to read the messages that tarot delivers through the medium of a mere seventy eight pictograms. Hence, if these gods—wayshowers: *Truseil*, the *Pole Star*, the *Trail of Tears*, *Kata Tjuta*, ancestral graves, stories of knowing, wind songs—don't stir you, and fatten you with their salmon-wisdom, what have you got to tell the traveler?

When their ocean-and-forest father-mother, their *tāne*, their *dru*, their *mitig*, *ki*, *munda*, their ancestor watches you through the forever-child's face, that is the visiting traveler, you'll spae it. You'll recognize their place-story as you look up from the card that has been laid on the seemingly shallow table spot of CHALLENGER DEEP. It can be death, it can be silence, it can also show you revelation and the coming phase of the traveler's life. This is your moment, to teach the person opposite you of the next spiral in their life's journey.

I reiterate that *Star* often, intentionally, as an actual star is graced in this spot. As is the *World* and the *Empress*. The *2 of Swords* and yes, the *Fool*. This place is also named CHALLENGER DEEP because we, hominids, mammals-on-hind-legs, anthropoid simians that chatter and chatter, have been so convinced of our superior importance that we think it okay to gouge out the sides of mountains to make cutlery, or a shallower ride for semi-trailers, to tear down a forest that has fed and been food beyond our concept of time, to make toilet paper and chipboard, that we deaden ourselves with screens and shut out the desperation with ear buds, thoughtless of what has been our own story, or that of the people—no matter our species or state of self-expression.

Except tarot knows. And the tarot navigator is compelled to also know that 10. CHALLENGER DEEP is also 1. HOME.

The body of the traveler? Their head, of course.

...

11. SEED

Figure 56 – SEED: Liberty

The fruit seems to rot but, it's a placenta nourishing the soil with its vitality.

de Angeles, *Genesis | The Future*

GATEWAY OF THE ABYSS

And, like a bristle, growing from the least likely place on a human body, here is this eleventh card. You're not supposed to really interpret what it means by referencing anything else in front of you; the layout of the other ten pictograms. You can't. It's meant to be a mystery and it will be realized only retrospectively. Can it get you? Yes.

It is known as the *gateway of the abyss* because, as with the planetary body known as *pluto*, its story is so vastly curious, simply because we don't relate to it now. Or we do, yes, because all the planets, just like every form, light and possibility, are present-continuous at the seeming occurrence of that singularity, 13.8 billion years deep—give or take—that spews the cosmos, as we think of it, into being. Mathematical formulae that we accept, jellyfish-like, to amuse ourselves. Because it's all a giant guess.

This is nothing assumed, or predictable. That sounds funny coming from me. Everything you interpret, and know, when scrying, is unfathomable until it happens. And even then, there are always glitches, just so no one becomes complacent.

I read for a person whose first question is *I have to relocate. Where will I live in the future?* The answer, when I lay out the map, includes the *5 of Staves* and the *Fool*. If I think the answer is clear, I'm deluded. *I spae both a wood and a ridge*, I tell her. When she comes back a couple of years later and reminds me, she's happy. She's married, now, to a partner named Adrian Woodridge.

NO MATTER

None of us know anything until we are reminded. We store knowledge and facts and images and words and names until we wither and forget everything. Does any of the above cease to be, when it is no longer seemingly relevant? Or when we're dead? Did it ever matter? Will it ever be mentioned by life again? In some instances, yes.

Figure 57 – Pluto: Message in a Bottle

Non-literate cultures, from the Australian First Nation people's memory-awareness of every bird, insect, plant and kindred-folk over an estimated 70,000 year span, to the Hopi initiate-training that explains the intricacies necessary for the correct planting of the seven types of corn, known by color and pollinator-relationship, have retained knowledge-skill that can, perhaps, ensure survival through yet another Ice Age. We are the stories etched into the standing stones of Europe. We are the cave paintings from Lascaux to the Pilbara, entities that appear alien to how we consider people. We are things and places, knowledge-centers, currently miles below the vastness of the ocean in the Mariana Trench, that could rise to the surface at any tilt of the axis of earth in orbit, to resemble this eleventh portal of the Stargate. A warp in the traveler's life experience. Something unrecognizable from the perspective of now.

Even a thought to be considered, only to be surprised by in a decade.

THIRD MAP–HORSE LATITUDE
Warning Map

Figure 58 – Lighthouse

I looked upon the rotting sea,
And drew my eyes away;
I looked upon the rotting deck,
And there the dead men lay.

T. S. Coleridge,
The Rime of the Ancient Mariner

GREAT VOYAGES OR BRUTAL TRUTH

A hundred or two years ago, historically, species—us and others—traveled by sea from one desperate land to another. By boat or by three-masted clippers; first in the steerage of wind-powered death-traps and later in the bowels of the auxiliary steam ship. And here's where a map is interesting when you know the backstory. Let's examine *inntrenger* colonialism, because we can never be academically sure of any other kind, until the current era of yacht races, endurance and/or pleasure sailing, cruise ships or jet skis.

The year is 1850. That's significant insofar as all of Europe, just a couple of years ago, rages, in uprising, for equality. 1848 is a savage year, but only because of the arrogance of authoritarianism that holds purchase in so many countries. And don't kid yourself for a moment, that's been brutal. The *Slave Act of 1807* is a farce, with the East- or West-India Company selling and transporting people, goods and misery, from the dark days of feudal Europe to colonies of confusion and privation.

The name *Horse Latitude* refers to some thirty degrees north or south of the Equator, often beset by what are known as the *Doldrums*. Certain death for many. Yes, I've read the straw-horse-theory, about sailors spending all their money until getting to this part of the ocean but I have to question the validity of that, because why there?

BRING OUT YER DEAD

This map—the *Horse Latitude*—is super important. *Horse Latitude* prepares the traveler, *well in advance*, of danger. It's their lighthouse. The event, manifesting here, *does not have to happen*. Is not definitively fated. Remind the traveler, about now, that it is they who shuffle—sort—they who order the information for your interpretation. Therefore, they *know* what they are showing you. They want to *spae* the shoal, the reef, the danger, to avoid catastrophe, and you, my darling, are the visionary with the skill of the sextant, the lore-holder of the wisdom of fresh-water islands, and the spyglass that knows the proximity of the kraken.

An example is when a person sits with me after fourteen years and I come to this map. I say it's a warning, they say *I'll listen this time*. That map cautioned them, all those years before, that a man of a certain star sign, and a woman of a certain star sign would ask her to show them what she had recently learned. Tarot explained she would be tired. Tarot specifically warned... *Don't climb. Whatever you do, don't climb*. She taught and performed for a well-known circus troupe in Australia. She told me that she distinctly and clearly heard the warning in her head on the day she was asked to show these two people her new trapeze technique. She heard the warning as she climbed the ladder. She did it anyway. She fell, breaking most of her bones.

She did not sever her spinal column. The only upside, she said, is that she can still walk.

This map, by rights, should stand out as unique to other layouts.

Why? If the person listens, there will be no hint of this elsewhere. Here, however, is where you can use whatever spell-weaving you have learned—if the event is seen elsewhere—to hopefully lessen the impact.

You'll have the traveler shuffle while explaining, as they do so, where this next map will take us. Just suggest that if they listen back to nothing else, they listen to this and take heed, no matter their skepticism. It's like stocking up in Jamaica before the haul towards the Horn.

You will then take the entire pack, discard the first six pictograms off the top and lay out the seventh, until done. All that remains is the last card, of which you will pay no attention.

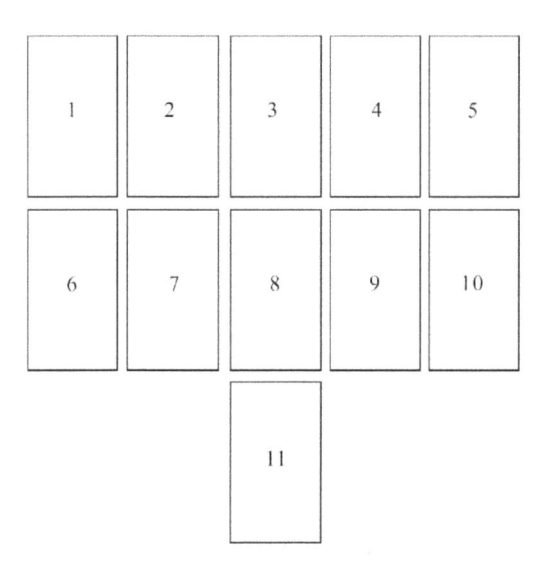

```
 1   2   3   4   5
 6   7   8   9  10
         11
```

Figure 59 – Horse Latitude

This is an advanced story map. You can't break it up into individual images. They need to be all read together to make sense. It's a complete sentence. If there are possibly two warnings, they will be top and bottom line, but interwoven by what turns up in the 11th position. If this is a person, the above ten pieces of the puzzle will give you enough language by which to recognize the offender, or the offense.

Why it is called HORSE LATITUDE, instead of merely the warning map, is the immensity of what happens if unheeded. The effect, like for that of the trapeze artist, can affect the traveler's life for years and years.

WARNING

I use this same map for questions. My logic is the vast separation between each image on the table. Surely you won't get a similar distribution as in the other stories, will you? You will. That's the drama and the beauty of tarot.

...

FOURTH MAP–THE GROVE

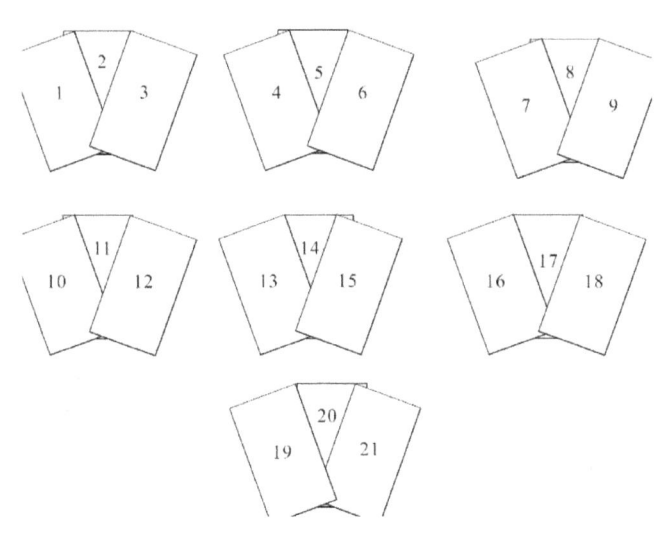

Figure 60 – The Grove

To lay out THE GROVE, have the traveler shuffle the entire pack and, from the top, face up, expose the images, one after the other. Each triplet can be read as an individual occurrence, place or wisdom or, with a scan, in conjunction with other information mapped out before you.

ENCYCLOPEDIA OF EVENTS

The GROVE map, in tarot, provides an encyclopedia of trivia, profundity, humor, face-palm stuff, splendor, names and addresses. In difference to the STARGATE which, while predicting, is simply not the GROVE, as a map, is complexity, and will provide you with insights into events that are seemingly impossible from the standpoint of now. I wonder about the thoughts of the mariners and travelers who sailed the vast tracts of uncharted ocean, from small ports on Stornoway's coast, to what are now the Americas. In what certainly were pre-Columbus' times.

ROSSLYN CHAPEL

Attesting to that is the Rosslyn Chapel in Alba (Scotland), owned by the Sinclair family, with its designs of maize and aloe, carved into the stone under the east window, much speculated on since its disclosure of green men and intricate story-pillars. Imagine meeting with the people of the Incas when you have been immersed, for centuries, in the pomp, demand and violence of christendom? Well, the Grove is this map.

...

FIFTH MAP–THE CONTINUUM

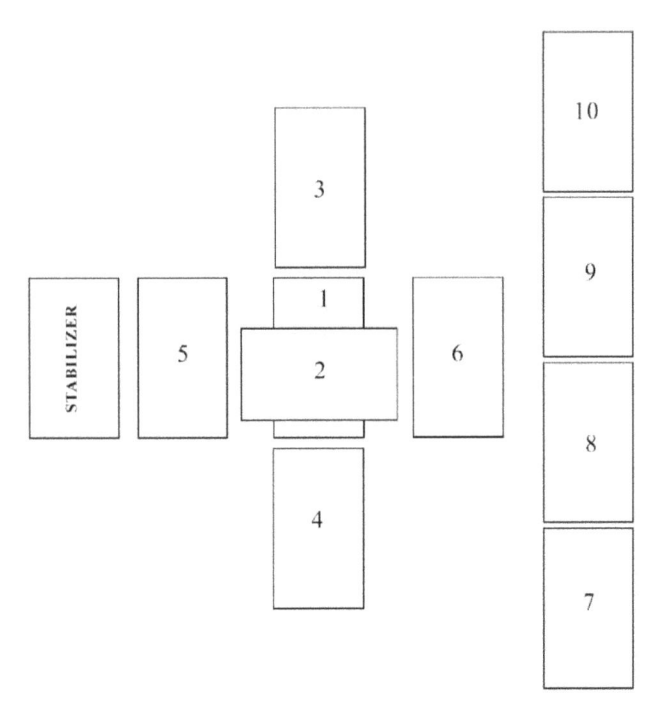

Figure 61– The Continuum

The Continuum is the final map I'm using before the traveler gets to ask questions. Have them cut the pack into three piles when they've shuffled, and ask them to then pick a pile. You can either discard the unchosen stories, or, if you have the energy, you can read them as separate, like in the earlier DEAD RECKONING map. To fulfil this section of the journey you'll chart that entire chosen pack, from the first to the last image. Before you do so, however, lay the bottom card of the pack—the *stabilizer*—aside as a reference: the smoke from a fire, just not the fire itself.

OTHER MAPS

FAMILIAR FACES, QUESTIONS
A Fáidh-Trained Witch's Journey Log

You can include/invent whatever works for you. It's just more of the same, and every map is going to be similar. That's the curious and amazing thing about a journey like this. The fáidh-skilled knows. Lots. Through tarot, and tarot takes into account how long since the traveler came to you before, so will not repeat certain things that haven't happened *or* might repeat what was said, prior, word for word. Mad, huh? Tarot, predicting the *future* through a fáith-trained witch, also knows when the traveler will come again, and will only provide information accordingly.

You'll be contacted by their relatives when the traveler dies, because they will have requested that you be told. This will be either very strange, or extremely comforting to the folks left alive in this recognized reality, for two reasons: first, because the relative will have been told of you, and is likely that they will have sat at your table themselves, and second because the death is spaed, and that's such a comfort to all concerned. Knowing this ending is destiny. Grief is wholesome and liberating, while confusion and disbelief in the *rightness* of the event of death are both hard to bear. A young guy returned to me a second time: in the months following his mother's murder. She was stabbed to death while on holiday in Bali. His first visit he had learned that this would happen. His mother had also been a visitor to my home. He had also heard her (back then)

CD, and the event was on the disc. He never asked why.

You are going to be a thread, only, in the life of another. A peripheral memory. A specter of smoke and shadow. Until... Never forget how important you are, for a moment. Just for a moment.

I use the HORSE LATITUDE Map for all three questions.

...

PART FIVE

GOING PRO

Figure 62 – Egalitarianism

WHAT'S A PERSON?
WHAT ACTUALLY *IS* A PERSON?

LORE

> *Ned the Eighth soon abdicated,*
> *So George Six was coronated,*
> *Then Number Two Elizabeth...*
> *And that's all, folks (until her death...)*
>
> *Mnemonic Rhymes* online

The slight glitch of working with a traditional pack—and I do suggest you do—is the representation of people: human and other. The construct seems to normalize the abnormal: rulership. The construct is invented during the Middle Ages, in Europe—as far as anyone can honestly say—when governments do not exist, and a titular grandeur is imposed upon ordinary individuals who have claimed some kind of right, whether that is of a royal house, the bestowal of titles by either religious institutions, birth, or by warfare, brutality and plunder.

Are these last three behaviors offensive? Indeed. Do you, as a navigator, and fáidh-trained practitioner of tarot, accept subservience? No. Never. And even if your traveler is a president, a CEO, famous or self-important in any way...? Not to you. The gift and training in the skill of foresight will set you apart. It always has. Not better, not lowly, not important in the contemporary interpretation of an *influencer*, but apart. You might even be considered anonymous. That's cool. Why? People who are in the spotlight are Amy Whitehouse, Robin Williams, Princess Diana, Alexander McQueen. You'd be amazed, in the current years, at the list of celebrity people suiciding. Why do they want to come to you?

Hope. And some kind of sense-making to a life gone crazy. Secret self-abnegation.

The person/person dilemma needs to be explained with each seeker. So that they know that you know... that neither means anything in the *real world*. That they can be *just people* when they visit. You're important because you *get* that.

Your gift, your egalitarianism.

Dummett's analysis of the historical evidence suggested that fortune-telling and occult interpretations were unknown before the 18th century. During most of their recorded history, he wrote, Tarot cards were used to play an extremely popular trick-taker game which is still enjoyed in much of Europe.

According to Professor Dummett, the first person to, "occultize" tarot, prior to being a mere pack of cards, was Court de Gébelin, author of *Le Monde Primitif*, an immense work in nine volumes published in Paris from 1725 to 1784. The question is, is it the cards that carry information, that spae the traveler's present and predicts the traveler's future? Or is it you? Are *you* tarot? Or is tarot something immanent, about whom no one can really articulate?

These questions are humbling because the 78 pictographic rags of paper are just that. Can most people find meaning to them? Not really. But when the fáidh-skilled is a true seer they can't do other than play out the game. I've had people say to me, when they first sit at my table, they don't take what I do seriously. I have a good laugh. I say *excellent, then let me entertain you and you can pay for my performance*. Their skepticism is warranted. But are they correct? There is nothing to prove here, and a pedigree for tarot *cards* as a system of prophecy is non-existent. But reading stories from the patterns you spae works. The ability is ancient. Scrying. Knowing that when the wolf spider threads her way into the eaves of the roof, leaving a silk for her million young to follow, her wisdom portends flood? How does she know? Awareness of east and west by the understanding of millennia? Watch. Do not lose focus and think about it. Listen. Is that a person screaming for help, or a vixen in heat?

CASSANDRA'S FATE

Your guts are roiling before you get on the plane. Is this your body telling you that boarding that little tube of metal and traveling through a variable skyscape at several hundred miles an hour is abnormal? When the ants left their herd of aphids high up onto the strawberry plants: rain. Would reading the future from the side of a cornflakes packet work? Yes. Would it be more difficult than what I offer here? Yes. Because no one has charted a course—a map—of a cornflake packet, or, lived with a cornflakes packet-kind of prophesying for long enough for it to be a realized map of *Cassandra-fated* drama.

You've got *it*, or you haven't. If you haven't you might never, well, not in the body you currently are. That's okay. But if you have…? I suggest you never become complacent, because there are no *spiritual* rewards for doing this, because a *spiritual* reward is an illusionary, religious aspiration, about as effective as paying a tithe to a monk, because you blew the out brains of all those babies at Mỹ Lai, and asking that he pray you out of ending up in some invented hell, in difference to the one you are not experiencing every day, as PTSD is futile. And calling witchcraft *wrong* (as some have done) is just really displaying a limited vocabulary.

DUALISMS AND PUZZLES

So, I change some names, and rearrange the way you might have read about, or practiced, tarot before now. So what? Is there a right or wrong? We don't do dualisms like that, now, do we? I did a live social media video about fate and destiny. So many private messages about the *why* of anything. It goes like this: You're sitting at a table with a huge pile of jigsaw pieces in front of you. No image to show you what the outcome is supposed to look like, corners somewhere in the stack. All seeming guesswork. Every single piece—every event in which you play a part—is in that stack. It sometimes takes a lifetime to put all the pieces together and accomplish the big picture. Sometimes it takes two thousand years (in my ancestral case). It doesn't help you to make sense of any of it but oh! If you leave a diary hidden behind the manhole cover, up in the crawlspace, for your grandchild to discover when you are dead—that you were the mistress of the *Butcher of Riga* during the Second World War but are too ashamed to talk about it when you are alive—what a difference you make to the way they know the world. They think, until that moment, just of the old lady. You are more. We all are. None of us can escape the emotional responses we experience, within any situation, no matter our gifts, no matter regimes or family or doubt. But we are. Starlight, that is.

AND... GO!

Figure 63 – de Angeles at work

It's easiest if you begin your *cross my palm with silver* career at markets, fairs, or even on the street, charging only small sums of money to begin with and doing only fifteen-minute readings using no more than three maps.

As you gain excitement and notice—when people talk and send others to you—charge accordingly. You really must self-regulate. Over the months, as your confidence and reputation grow, you'll need to think about how you will set about reading in a more private space. I have a parlor that does not interfere with the other people with whom I live.

This isn't always possible: Your family may disapprove of what you are doing, or you do not have the luxury of being able to afford the private space, you worry about having strangers come to your home.

To overcome any of the above you could—
- Find a copacetic shop owner and rent one of their rooms but, be aware that many businesses will want you to tone down what you tell people. *Don't upset the customers, good buddy*. That's a reason to thank them and say, no
- Read from markets or fairs, but get yourself a marquee or tent that gives privacy

Prior to gaining a reputation for credibility, you're likely to encounter cynicism, skepticism, disbelief, even hostility. You're going to want a thick skin, in preparation for the many scenarios where you *will* walk on metaphorical razorblades with your predictions.

Have business cards with your contact details. Many travelers come from elsewhere, and most will take more than one card to give to friends.

Advertising may be your choice but, know that most people don't want to pay someone who could be a fake, as happens, and in many places what you are doing could be classified as illegal. Many years ago, when I lived in the state of Victoria, I was subject to a vendetta by an influential fundamentalist christian sect. It was a little country place, and this lot were horrified that I'd moved in. They set about, indirectly (through phone and letter) initially, threatening the people where I was staying, and then, when we relocated, gossiping about some *arch-demon witch* (their words, not mine) who needed killing or got rid of in some way.

THUGGERY

I had a confrontation with their leader. After going to his house and knocking on the door (he wasn't home) I left a message, saying that I wanted to have it out with him, and to come and visit me, unless he was too gutless.

He came the next day, with a bible and a book of exorcism under his arm, accompanied by some huge bloke—his minder, I guess—who was easily a hundred and ninety centimeters tall, and weighed 150 kilograms, and who said nothing. Who just stood and emitted threat. The first thing that preacher said was *I can't stay long*. I invited him to sit on my veranda, where we babbled and debated for hours. He could only recognize things from a one-sided ideology. I was still young. I don't do that anymore.

As he was leaving, he said that, every Sunday he and his congregation would *Will you to Jesus or will you dead*.

Consequently, when I began reading tarot at the local marketplace, several weeks later, I was threatened with the cops. Nothing happened.

Over time I was receiving many travelers at home, and one day a stressed young person who had had a reading from me months earlier, phoned needing help. Her partner had died in a motorcycle crash. Her husband's sister was a member of the same sect that was willing me dead, and they accused the traveler of being responsible for her husband's death because of her interest in all things mystical. The god-squad broke into the seeker's house while she was not home, ransacked the place, took anything considered suspect, from Linda Goodman's book *Sun Signs* and any other book of its kind, to a tarot tape—hidden in an underwear drawer—and a pair of Chinese slippers. These were piled in the traveler's backyard and set ablaze. She went to the police. Nothing could be proven, and the charges were eventually dismissed. Finally, with the mass killing of Bruce Jacobs' (1942–2004) dingoes, in direct reprisal for him allowing a *pagan* woman to rent a room in his house after she'd run from a vile relationship, the cult leader had to leave the region.

Many years later, after the publication of two books, a wonderful stream of travelers for tarot, a clever, funny, and suitably rebellious coven, and workshops on multiple themes I was strongly entrenched in the area. Several of us held a springtime equinox gathering at a friend's bespoke horse-riding lodge. My friend cancelled all their guests except for two people, and all of us at the ritual brought young, potted trees to create a controlled grove of European trees and flowers amid the Australian bush.

The next day our coven left for a holiday to a beach up the coast, and when we returned it was to headline news in the local newspaper.

Another fundamentalist christian leader had been told that a group of black-clad devil worshippers had gone into the woods carrying a dead horse's head for their evil rites. I demanded equal press, to which the newspaper gladly agreed, and I wrote an article on the rites and ceremony of witchcraft's wheel of the year. I was contacted by a local FM radio and asked for an interview which I gave, offering my accuser the opportunity to come forward in open debate. The radio loved it and kept the challenge repeated regularly but the bloke went to ground, and nothing more was heard from him.

STILL BURNING BABIES

In many parts of the world there are entire communities of fundamentalist religious zealots who would gladly put you to the stake, or use whatever means are available to them to get rid of you if you are discovered to be fàidh-born, or practicing any of our ceremonies and witchery, so please take all these things into consideration. I don't mention them to put you off but simply to keep you enlightened.

TRANSFERENCE

It's like trance, but most people won't spae that. When a traveler comes, our mutual electromagnetic fields intermesh and, whilst remaining you, you'll become them, also. Your feelings towards events and people, are their feelings, who you love is who they love and who you loathe, they will loathe. You know when a situation is distressing or elating because your body responds to the emotion of the situation so that when, in a reading, you *seem* to give advice or to admonish, praise or berate it is because the traveler will do so, probably in such a way as to seem to be talking to themselves.

you cannot put a need for payment ahead of ethics. Besides, tarot has always made certain I have food on the table.

This is where reputation is advantageous over advertising. No one ever asks me if I'm any good at what I do, because they have heard from friends, family, acquaintances or colleagues, so there's not really any doubt. There'll be fear, but not doubt.

On arrival, most travelers are shaking visibly. They don't know why, as many are actually calm and excited. I explain it's an adrenaline-thing and it'll be gone within five minutes, and it always is. The same applies to tears. Both men and women will often cry for no apparent reason—nothing to do with the prophecy... well, sometimes it is—and often they'll apologize saying that they don't know what's come over them. Have a box of tissues close.

Suppose you lay the story on the table and the prophecy is devastating. You're going to need to take a moment. Sense how to go about saying what you will. I'm very animated, so I pull faces, swear, say to bear with me, ask them if they really want to hear what I've got to say. I also use humor in such a way as not to offend and will, on occasion have a sideways conversation with tarot in front of the traveler, discussing my hesitance or dilemma. This gives them a moment to either compose themselves, or say they want to go home because they've picked it. They know. Most people are, however, more resilient than we give them credit for and most will tell you to just say it. So just say it.

Occasionally I've had to work at not laughing at the enormity of death and destruction I'm seeing. It's a glitch, like an allergic reaction or a form of *Tourette's*. One of those times my visitor relieves my sweating palms by informing me she's a paramedic and drives an ambulance in one of the densest, and most dangerous places, in Sydney. Another, an undercover cop involved in drugs and vice.

It's all okay. Trust and compassion are your greatest tools, and sometimes you'll feel moved continuing the company of the traveler beyond the tarot table. The abused woman, hiding out and not knowing where to go or what to do, her children in the care of someone she trusts for an hour, maybe two and then what? You need to have those crisis number with you. Help them. Make the calls.

You won't always be able to help, and it's not necessarily up to you, and you must be mindful of donning the *savior syndrome* mask because that is dangerous, and the person, if mentally unstable, can cause you a lot of grief. When there are difficult situations ahead for your visitor, simply knowing it in advance is the weapon of self-defense a fáidh-gifted being like you can give them. They are then more readily able to deal with the event when it happens, and they also know it was destined.

...

SELF-PROTECTION AND PSYCHIC CLAG

Pace yourself.

For the first several years I found I was capable of reading for up to five visitors for tarot sessions in a day, at an hour each, without any seeming personal detriment. But it sneaks up on you, and if you're not careful your health and constitution *will* suffer, because you are sharing the energy-field of every individual who consults you and traveling time in a strange way.

An example is the illness of a colleague; a well-established psychic who consults for several hours a day, seven days a week. I spae cancer. Her breasts. I suggest she retire but she refuses, saying she'll take her chances.

A few months later she finds the lump, has the tests confirm a diagnosis, and is booked into a local country hospital where the surgeon intends removing both breasts in a full mastectomy. She comes for a reading several days before admission and the Horse Latitude map warns her to get another opinion; that she source a Melbourne oncologist for that. She does. She is admitted. Only a small segment of one breast is removed.

I'm diagnosed with asthma. On average – and not simply tarot seekers, but hopeful students, friends, others of a witchery persuasion and fàidh-born critters who are bothered by some consideration or other – somewhere between ten and twenty people come through my house every day and, throughout, I'm raising kids. I have an attack but, as soon as I remove myself from the people around me and go into a room by myself, the coughing and wheezing passes, like *poof*. I am becoming physically intolerant of people.

When I relocate interstate, I slow down and rarely accept more than two travelers on any day. And I write, or just go to the gym, swim, and dream. I liven up, and now, decades later, I'm healthy.

THAT GUNKY STUFF

Psychic *clag*. Gunky stuff that can't be seen, but has an effect, just like humidity, just like dust and mattress mites. The feeling of this *clag* is almost indescribable and is almost like static build-up. You feel off-center. Stale. You have difficulty concentrating and feel listless and depleted. This has nothing to do with the quality of either your gift and talent, or of the traveler. It's an anomaly. And the only remedy is to get wet. A shower will do it (*not* a bath), but a dunk in brother ocean or sister river cures. Water neutralizes the effect along with food, exercise and space, alone, for a while.

BEST FRIEND SYNDROME AND PERSONAL PRIVACY

Keep your workplace clean, and separate to the rest of the house, because psychic *clag* is a physical thing and has density. Sweep or vacuum your floors, wash walls. The windows. It all works. If you live in a small town this can be difficult because you are likely to encounter travelers simply doing your shopping.

Being fáidh-skilled, you'll know half the town's secrets, and this means that people – if you're not careful and mute – will want to update you on their situation when they pass you by. I avoid this by being tactless. Most people expect me to be but, ultimately, I am thankful to those who did fill me in the prophesied details, otherwise I couldn't teach, or be certain of this skill, or write a book. I wouldn't have stories to share.

Problems arise when people become desperate, despairing or drunk, and climb through an open window of your house at three in the morning, after an altercation, seeking someplace to hide. They used to phone at any hour of the day or night. Now I'm selective. I switch off all devices. I go off-grid sometimes.

If you are working from home, you'll need an area for them to chill, if you're visited by two people in a row. You don't want strangers wandering into your kitchen and thinking it is okay to sit down and have a chat with whoever lives with you. Because they will, and your kids'll hate you for it.

Be kind to yourself, for *being* fáidh-gifted, and set clear boundaries.

TIP OF AN ICEBERG –
YOU WON'T SPAE WHAT WON'T HAPPEN

Some visitors to your table think you are like some mythic *guardian angel*. You and tarot. That you're going to get them out of trouble. And first-time travelers to your destination will occasionally try to tell you, even on the phone or online, when negotiating an appointment – why they are coming. Stop them before they do that. Tell them the less you know the better. Most will shut up, but some will rant on, saying they're coming because they need tarot to tell them what to do. Rather than dissuading them from traveling, it's advisable, after telling them that that is not what tarot does, to suggest they resolve conflict before they get to port. This silence creates a clear navigation.

I say *Don't think.* Relax. I ask that they have no expectations based on what they know of the present moment.

The *should I's*, however, will be inevitable, in one out of three people, when it comes to the question section of the voyage. This is the time for *you* to relax and remain unattached because tarot, as a third present entity, will take center stage and say whatever is appropriate. I do tell everyone that I realize they have an agenda for coming. That this will color the question/answer outcome, and to be cool with whatever is said. Often, they're going to ask what would have been obvious in the first section of the visit, you're going to have to say it. Whatever the answer is. If the question is stupid or obvious—be aware—tarot can be tactless and seemingly rude.

SAFETY AND RESPONSIBILITY

When you start out, you'll initially accommodate hundreds of willing people. People who'll provide feedback. They'll tell other people. That's it, then. Travelers will find you, no matter where you go, because this spellcrafting is unique.

In the first few years you'll probably get read by other tarot readers—fáith-skilled or not—but there'll come the day when you won't want to, preferring to wing it, because of what you learn. Because you no longer care to know.

It's pretty-much impossible to be objective with close friends and family, so don't even try but, if you want to experiment, have you got that will of iron necessary to stop from guessing? From *believing* you know.

Other than asking their sun-sign, in western astrology, to gauge the person-card that likely represents them, ask the traveler not to chat while you do your work. Ask them to shut up until they ask their three questions.

Reminder: Don't *ever* shuffle the cards yourself. Keep your pack away from other people, and dispose of your old, worn ones in a way appropriate to you (you can throw them in the sea or bury them in the garden – but be fair, considering how much life they have accumulated. They are writhing with microscopic life.

TO BUY OR NOT TO BUY

Put to sleep the superstition around the acquisition of a pack. Buy them yourself. That's it. That way there's no doubt about impartiality. In WITCHCRAFT THEORY AND PRACTICE I wrote such a tiny bit on the topic of gifts and flattery, under the heading of Vampirism, that I do the topic an injustice. I'm not a cynic, I've been bitten as often as you by people who give you stuff.

Gifts and flattery– just to be able to talk solely about themselves – gifts and flattery, trying to buy you. The moment they are confronted as to their motives they become offended and you probably won't see them again.

When someone genuinely cares about you, they might gift you something that they think you'll like. Genuinely meaning that, they give freely, not caring what you do with the gift. Agreeing you owe them nothing in return. It's rare, though. *Thank you* works, but often, particularly because Mulengro (see Appendix) is epidemic in *western society*, they're going to come back at you, sometime, with "I did this for you, so now you have to…", in whatever way. It's called *psychic vampirism*, and unfortunately the gift was all about them, and now's the time they collect.

    I reiterate, here, that after reading for the day shower, bath or dump yourself in ocean, river, dam, pool or pond to fully discharge the static build-up that will occur as a result of the readings, and to rid yourself of the aforementioned *psychic clag*. You will know what I mean anyway – for the first few years you will feel exhilarated immediately after the sessions, followed by this weird disorientation, exhaustion or dried-out sensation. Get out of the house, too. Find a tree to sit with.

    The responsibility of the fáidh, spae or spé-born practitioner of tarot is self-evident. You'll run every possible gauntlet of human experience from great joy to the depths of despair, from drug or alcohol addiction, insanity, domestic violence and sexual abuse to love, brilliant careers, intelligence, curiosity and authenticity, world travel and financial wealth. It is in the dark recesses of personal events that you need to take the greatest care. Tell what you spae but do so in a way that compassion and straight-talking form the spell. If you have *any* misgivings towards anyone who makes contact, listen to your gut instinct, and do not book them.

TAX FILES AND OTHER EVIL STUFF

Do yourself a foretelling, futuristic, fortune-telling favor and learn about finances and business. Keep paper trails. Profit and Loss statements. When you are earning lots, get an accountant. If you want to remain an outlaw, no problem, but you never know who is going to hate what you tell them, or whose partner is going to assume you are some freak, dirty hippy, reprobate, little-woman-thingy, whatever other insult these bigots use, but in their desire to hurt you they can (and it's been tried on me) make assumptions. They've been brainwashed into thinking you must be doing some kind of con. They could make the phone call to whoever they want to get you investigated.

When you've got nothing to hide, you're laughing. My accountant doesn't blink at what I do. He managed to get me an annual entrepreneurial rebate on my tax.

COMMUNICATION VS BABBLE

There's a difference between *communication and babble*. Spend time observing people, and talking with them, without entering any excess words into the conversation. If they talk jargon, spiritual gobbledygook or Disney-romanticism, ask them to explain what they really mean.

- Get people talking about themselves, their experiences and viewpoints
- Study and read their body-language. Understand what they are saying *without* words
- Note your emotional and physical reactions and responses to what is said and whether you are being sufficiently open to *reading* them on many levels. If you pick up passing thought scraps that seem to be precognitive either pass the information, casually and worded respectfully and carefully, on to the person concerned or keep a note of it

An example of the above is if Dee phones you and tells you they are getting married to Alex, and the small voice in your mind says *Oh-oh*. I don't say anything, of course, but I certainly file the thought away for future reference. The same thing when a friend tells you she is pregnant, and you're confused because you are sure that happened a year ago.

The more you take note of this inner voice the more it will communicate with you. They've been talking all your life.

Make a habit of examining as many visual news broadcasts as you can tolerate, read the newspapers, check out international news on the internet. All this is for you to update yourself on world events because they *will* sneak into your readings and it will be necessary that you recognize them as being unrelated to the intimate experiences of your visitors. Also, you will pick up nuances of truth, or forced theatrical anchor behavior, and that's a gift.

PART SIX

WAYSHOWERS AND JOURNEYS

Figure 64 – Ghost Ship

78 OMENS AND PORTENTS

THE CARDS

Before we get to this I will admit to a quandary. Traditionally the image-cards are divided into what are called either *major arcana* (twenty-two of them) or *minor arcana* (fifty-six of them, just like in traditional card games). The problem can be boxed away with anything else that supposes one thing, or somebody, is better than, or more significant, than the other. That is just not going to happen here. It's divisive and pompous.

To describe anything *minor* is to suggest unimportance: online synonyms for *minor* produce: unimportant, trivial, secondary, negligible, slight, and inconsequential. A minor, as a noun, is a juvenile or a youth. Ergo, kids are also unimportant.

It is, therefore, logical to think the opposite of the twenty-two cards called the *major arcana.*

The word *arcana*—or *arcanum* (plural)—means secret; mysterious. Mysterious to whom? Why are they thought to be secret? What is a secret? Why keep one? Why have a box of seventy-eight of them, sitting on the shelf at amazon.com, as commercially available as a packet of tattoo needles, or a cutlery set, or a hairdryer? Get over it. It is us who are limited. These images are here to learn from, and be read like a graphic novel, one for each person you will ever meet, never the same. The information provided by a fáidh-skilled navigator could show the same sequence again and again, but the experience of the sequence, when it happens, is different for each traveler. No two streets are alike. That river comes to mind. You can drink from the river once, and then scoop up a palmful and drink a second time. The water is not the same water, the moment is never going to be the same again. No sunset is like that seen yesterday and no two lovers are ever alike. Any word can mean anything, depending on the listener or the reader because, as Dr. Darryl Reanney says, in *Music of the Mind*—

To leave the comfort zone we now inhabit we have to learn a new way of seeing. Or an old way we have forgotten how to use… We have to dig deep, below the crusty detritus of routine; we have to unlearn prejudice, remember ourselves, go back to the source, seeing the world as it is not as we think it is.

So, this is—like—how it works…

NAVIGATION

It's the year 2003 and I've been online planning my world tour, something of a quest, that begins in London and won't complete itself until I'm back in my little house in Byron Bay. I've hired a car that I pick up from Heathrow Airport, and I've paid, online, for a week's rental on a cottage in the village of Trebarwith Strand, Cornwall, just down the road from Tintagel. You know the place: a wizard named Merlin shapeshifts a warlord named Uther into a lookalike of the once-and-future-king's mummy's hubby—a bloke named Gorlois—for the sole purpose of raping this woman, just because he fancies her, setting up one of the biggest mythic propositions of my own lifetime, and a massive box office hit for Disney limited.

The drive from London to Cornwall is supposed to be a mere five hours. Not a big deal for a person raised in Australia. We can drive that long just for a car part. England, however, prior to GPS, is a land of maps on which are marked numbers. Take the A3, merge on the A30, merge off the sliproad onto the M3, in Zone 8, then take the A39 onto the A392. Well, you get my meaning.

I was supposed to pop in at the end of a dirt road (thankfully I took out full comprehensive, walk-away insurance) to a house behind a disguised stone fence pretending to be a hedge, pick up the key, and follow a succession of winding road directions punctuated by distinctive shops, cats, telephone boxes and furniture auction houses, down past the slipway to the wee bay, up the side of a road with a canal running down its center and somehow find the cottage, before sunset, which, being August, wasn't until nigh an hour before midnight.

I lost my way in Reading, and the paper map the attendant at Hertz had given me was an evil gyrating, headachy demon that spat great globules of unseen hatred for a colonialist like me, and the wizened, shriveled rat voice in my head laughed and laughed and laughed.

I threw it away. *What do you know, Ly?* The sun travels anticlockwise in Australia. Therefore, while the day was still light, I established south-west. Thank you, sun. Thank you, day. Thank you, cloudlessness, and thank you prior learning. These coordinates unplug my confusion like a well-oiled series of machinations and engine-room pistons in the bowels of the ship of my memory. I followed these markers, and I actually got to my destination before night.

The twenty-two Wayshower cards are the sun and moon and stars and tracks and coastlines and means of the transportation of your journey. The story, the myth, the making of magic, however; the conversations and the number of stairs you will climb to reach the café in the clouds, depend on the fine detail of who is who and when is the parcel arriving? They are routines and steering wheels, sexual encounters, and procedures to be experienced along the way from A to Z.

    This being established we will call those same twenty-two cards Wayshowers, and we will call the other fifty-six cards the Journey. Navigating an uncharted sea, you could almost call the Wayshowers the islands and the Journey the course—charted or otherwise—that highlights and instructs on the continuity of star/ocean direction. Only thing is, it'll change as life does. You are the world you sail through, darlings. Everything and everyone else are the threads, and unseen *dragon lines*, that connect all that is.

...

WAYSHOWERS

Figure 65 – Wayshowers

Then we came where we saw a man tracing his shadow on the sand. Great waves came and erased it. But he went on tracing it again and again. "He is the mystic," said my soul, "Let us leave him."

Kahlil Gibran, *The Greater Sea*

BIG WORDS, BIG ISLANDS, DEEP CURRENTS

Figure 66 – Fool

0–FOOL

The Fool is also known as the *blind card* because it will very rarely allow you to know what lies beneath. There is a purpose in this: in life, an event is *of such* important that the trigger (The Fool) must remain unknown to ensure that, no matter the consequences, the players on the board show themselves without preconceptions. Yes, this can be Titanic-like, but that's an estimation.

This can portend a *seemingly* random, or trickster, event; can be something *seemingly* insignificant or inconsequential that points to unprecedented repercussions.

This can be the traveler, walking down the street and bumping into a stranger who becomes integral to their life and it also suggests that they could be on the brink of a very rash decision; one with unexpected consequences or a veering from the charted destination.

Life will change as a direct result of being touched by the Fool. You, fáidh-trained, will never guess what it might engender because you'd be wrong. The traveler will never know the importance of the prophecy that attends this message, until retrospectively. It can appear as an innocuous event—completely irrelevant—hence the masks.

Nothing that shows up after this card is recognizable from the current perspective. It is the ultimate universe's next trick and it *is* destiny; exposed and pre-determined.

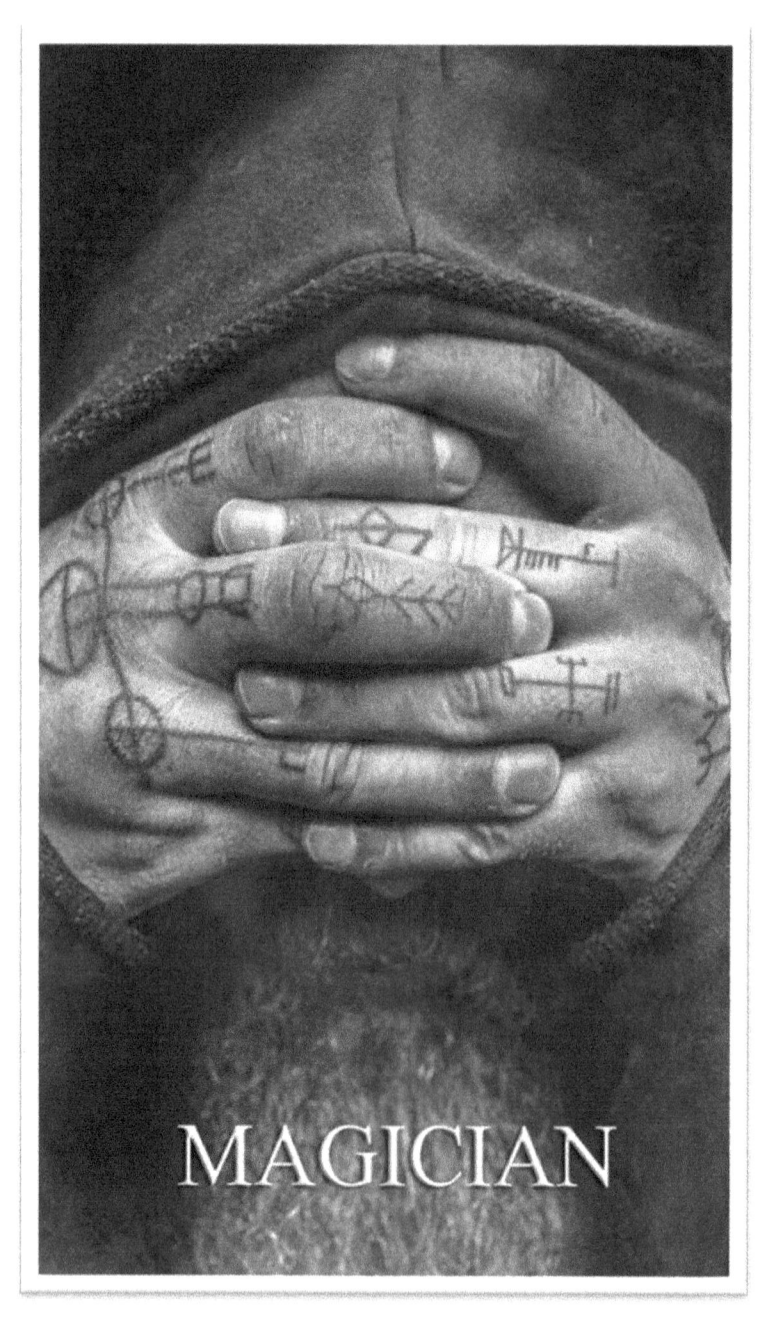

Figure 67 – Magician

1–MAGICIAN

Magician is a new way of being and doing, or the acknowledgement that a certain position in life will be realized when this *Wayshower* turns up on a map but: *with power comes responsibility.*

The Magician is a person, or a people, who do not agree to being told what to do, who or how to be. They know life independently from traditional societal roles, and as such, represent a dynamic and heretical individual or group.

It can be a practitioner (even a conjurer) of ceremony and ritual, theatre podium or politics. The position in the life of any person represented. Not always the traveler visiting you.

A specialist. A survivor. A revolutionary. One who seems to be one thing but is, in actuality, another. Like Nancy Wake.

One who has achievements in a specific field; a skilled person who has earned, through the initiations of their life, the connotation of Magician. An artist, cake-maker, blacksmith, refugee who finds safe harbor.

Figure 68 – Seer

2–SEER

Seer is mysterious, hidden, occulted or behind the scenes; anything not seen, secret liaisons, a way of the mystery and exploration. As a place it can represent homes or environments that are hidden from general view or that traditionally represents an unorthodox existential wonder, difficult for many people to handle. If the traveler is also an empath, the Seer can represent them, and as a fáidh trained guide, on the journey of the traveler, it is also your responsibility to keep confidences.

There is unclassified information that has been well-concealed. It *will* be revealed. Activities going on behind the scenes of a theatre, film set, a deceased estate, the relentless hours that go into a story, study, or research paper. The Seer isn't all they seem to be... but, then, which card is? Traditionally called the *high priestess*, the connotations are both way too gender-specific and way too religious. When the Seer flips onto a map it can also be an article or memory, that will be lost, hidden or missing, that they won't be able to find and Seer also represents a question that will have no answer (like whether a beloved other is, in whatever way, betraying the seeker).

The Seer represents a veil in more than one sense and can be literally a bridal veil, a hijab, a burqa, and this card can often describe places that the traveler will visit such as Saudi Arabia, many destinations in Africa, Indonesia and India.

Figure 69 – Empress

3–EMPRESS

Empress is all that is beautiful (or considered beautiful which is a different thing and can be quite dangerous, like the brutal tradition of bound feet), sensual, artistic, tactile, and fecund. Empress can represent motherhood, pregnancy, and birth. Grandmother-ness and ancestral matrilineal lineage.

Empress is the arts, hospitality, those catering to the consensual idea of beauty: from fashion to clothing and cosmetics, cosmetic surgery, sex work, drag and those who identify as women.

It is erotic and sexual. Empress is pregnancy of any kind from biological to the conception of a project or creative endeavor. Biologically, Empress represents womb, labia, clitoris, vagina, bartholin and skene glands, breasts, traditionally female hormones, menstruation and menopause.

In the cycle of the seasonal year, it is when the produce is ripe and juicy and also when the land is ready for planting.

Empress can be any succulent thing from fruit to conversation to sexuality. When shown as a place the climate is always tropical, but it can just as easily represent one's ancestral or mother lands, and places of moisture and damp.

Figure 70 – Emperor

4–EMPEROR

Emperor represents that which is patriarchal or orthodox. It can mean fatherhood and what that traditionally entails. It is a politician, a president, a prime minister, a person who has gained an acknowledgment through traditional social and academic recognition and acclaim. Emperor turns up on a map it can be talking about commonly accepted authority bodies: insurance, banks, administration, and establishments such as school systems, hospitals, clergy, prisons, military and government.

Emperor turns up when connected to traditional institutions of administration and academia, in difference to private study, research and documenting. Emperor is more often than not accompanied by others that will give it deeper significance, as will its placing upon a map. Biologically it represents male-gendered people, and institutions traditionally associated with men. It can represent what are considered male pursuits, but I won't even venture into that, not now, as we voyage into the uncharted seas of the twenty first century, because there is an inherent bias in the complexities and fallacies of such.

Body parts represented here are penis, urethra, and scrotum. The internal male genitalia include the seminal vesicle, testes, vas deferens, epididymis, prostate, bulbourethral gland, and ejaculatory duct, anus colon, thighs, knees, and lower circulatory system.

Figure 71 – Hierophant

5–HIEROPHANT

In most instances the Hierophant has religious connotations and, in some ways, always represents these institutions, even in places such as Adelaide (called the city of churches) or traditionally Roman Catholic or Islamic countries, but I have not seen it represent Jewish, Buddhist, Hindu or animistic people's lands and ceremonies.

Hierophant represents everything from dogmatic, structured, hierarchical religions to New Age ideologies that resembles traditional religion, and Hierophant can be a person who is a religious figurehead in the public eye: customary, orthodox or otherwise.

It is marriage, whether conventionally religious, monogamous, or polyamorous, the marriage of businesses and corporations, or the mutual signing of a lease, or sale of a child (commonly called adoption). Marriage is any contractually binding mutually-understood legal agreement. It can be white veils and church bells, it can be dangerously Disney to the average traveler and be the disorder, violence and destructivity of what is conventionally termed *domestic violence*. And it is the divorce that attends the end of any of the above. Hierophant is the architecture of religious significance from spires to steeples, minarets, the masonic symbols of arch and capstone, the presumption of archaeology, scriptural dogma, apocrypha, hierarchy and, in many instances, myth that enforces a bias towards religion.

Figure 72 – Lovers

6–LOVERS

Lovers card is choice, but it can also represent split decisions, division of any kind, a three-person sexual involvement. In the physical body Lovers represents the lungs, hips or pelvis.

Lovers points to a choice, as an outcome. Tarot will not give a direct answer to certain questions because there is free-will involved in a decision, or because the traveler can move in one of many directions, and the destiny—or endgame—is not set.

Lovers can mean that there will be crossroads and it can also show a T intersection in their life. As an answer to a question it indicates that the traveler will have more than one choice and tarot is not answering because it does not want to influence the course of action taken.

It can also represent twins.

TAKAYA

In honor of your strength.
In respect for your resiliance.
We will not forget that you lived
or why you died.

CHARIOT

Figure 73 - Chariot

7–CHARIOT

At the time of the murder, the lone sea wolf, known by the Lekwangan word *Takaya*, would have been about ten years old. Takaya roamed in solitude, but freedom, on Discovery Island, in a natural coastal life. Takaya was relocated to the shores of the rainforest region known as Victoria.

Cheryl Alexander had been observing and filming Takaya's life for seven years when the relocation happened. Then, in March 2020, Takaya was shot and killed. For no reason. "It was exciting that he was surviving," reports Alexander, "so it's devastating that his life is ended in this senseless way. He wasn't doing anything considered *wrong*, he wasn't attacking livestock, he was just trying to make his way in the wilderness. To be shot for no reason other than the fact that he was a wolf, is just tragic."

I wonder how many of us, our kindred species, rocks, forests, and waterways, have made it. Through trauma, abuse, years—sometimes decades, sometimes a lifetime—of seeking, studying, innovation, imprisonment, bigotry, and misunderstanding. I sat in the garden last night and thought about the ways we can all die, and I figure a bullet to the head is preferable to what? For many, days, and years of infirmity, forgottenness and invisibility. Paolo Franco, a wife in the screenplay *A Dangerous Beauty* (about Veronica Franco) says, appropriately, "No biblical hell could ever be worse than a state of perpetual inconsequence."

If we are discussing individuals this card represents victory after striving: a pass (exams, driving test, medical checkup) or any personal sense of achievement, whereas it can also represent places or modes of transportation. Acceptance after an interview; the settlement of a court case, the triumph at the culmination of any confrontation, dispute or clash and represents an earned accolade, with hard work before and after. It can also simply be read as accomplishment or a win – anything from a lottery to horse-racing, but context would apply on a map of several cards. It is very malleable and deceptive when describing a person—again, you'd need context: the individual represented could be a very great ally or an enemy who destroys you.

Chariot is places and interests often associated with Middle Eastern lands and history.

Figure 74 – Strength

8—STRENGTH

Strength can be a physical body, control issues, infections due to erupt, seismic areas, foundations poured for a building, an animal, bodywork.

Strength will turn up in many environment maps and can be desert anywhere when laid beside the Sun. Strength lends power to other cards.

Strength represents all species vascularity, lust, underground or under-the-surface power and rage, depending on other cards. When representing a person Strength ensures vitality and physical gristle, and it will describe many visceral activities and attributes.

Strength will always turn up when including kindred not of our own species. Dogs, cats, camels, hawks, horses, aphids, cockroaches, humans of another ilk to you and me.

Figure 75 – Hermit

9–HERMIT

Even though interpretations lean heavily on the more modern, recent Pamela Coleman Smith image, commissioned by Arthur Edward Waite, an earlier interpretation of Hermit was called Spy. But wait. That is a misnomer of the word spae, spé or to see/scry. This interpretation would have been your original visionary and that, because of the ambiguous nature of the English language, has been masculinized and turned into an old male image in a hooded cloak, ever-so theatrically looking like Gandalf.

Keep that up your sleeve when this wayshower turns up on the map, else you miss the interpretation completely by staying along a known coastline, untrusting of the spaeglass in your navigator's hand.

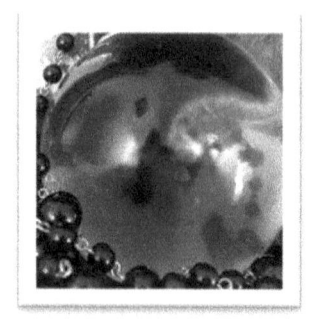

Figure 76 – Crystal Ball

Hermit is aloneness but not sadness or loneliness unless other cards indicate. It is an unattached person, a wise person, an old and wise person, not always human. Hermit can also be isolated people.

Environmentally it is a hilly or mountainous place, cold country or wintry. It can represent antiques and antiquarians, or those people or things that relate to old or ancient things: archaeology, architecture, mining, archaic misinformation.

Architecturally Hermit is old houses, gabled house, chalets or homes with height. Environmentally this *Wayshower* is places outside cities, high places or many variations. Winter. Snow. Sometimes it represents a quest or a vigil.

Figure 77 – Wheel

10–WHEEL, OR WHEEL OF FORTUNE

Back and forward, over and over, up and down, rollercoaster ride, the daily round, day to day, continuous. Time (as we know it), a roundhouse for horse training, clocks, towers, the torturous history of the Breaking Wheel in use in Prussia, historically, until 1841.

Wheel can represent a circuit (at a gym or someone who does a market circuit) but I have also had it for people who are involved with circus. It can literally represent the wheels of a vehicle and can be the annual or cyclical maintenance of anything.

It'll show up as a roulette wheel at a casino, or a wheel of fortune at a traveling carnival sideshow.

Very often there is a sense of simple routine or sameness. This, for some travelers, can be disconcerting (depending on the situation) whereas for others it is comforting. And yes, it can be the Doldrums. And the roster. But also, the coming liberation, in the heart of the *Dark Night of the Soul*.

Figure 78 – Justice

11–JUSTICE

An estimated 1,300 trees—fifty-two acres of mainly oaks—were cut down to build the tower of the Notre Dame Cathedral that burned out of control in April of 2019. Each beam had been a single tree, so that *The Forest* was its common nickname. And while many were horrified and mourned the destruction of this icon of religious hubris, I kept my heretical mouth shut, with the exception to those of like mind. Fucken truth is I cheered, and I wept.

Justice is a loaded word, with many connotations, and can represent any legal matter from the judicial system to contracts, leases, legalities, the police, the courts, anything whereby you sign in a legally binding agreement. Or as an admission of guilt. Or as a recognition of that which is right. When Nelson Mandela west to prison, when slavery was legal, when Aboriginal people in Australia were denied citizenship, when cops bashed anybody at Stonewall, when the military fired on the Wounded Knee Occupation in 1973, when West Papua was annexed without permission of the indigenous people, when clear-felling took down every tree, by law, in Australia between colonization and the mid twentieth century, when every indigenous, free and self-determined people—worldwide—were (and are) subject to schooling, uniforms, white bread and infected blankets, when you are most likely to live in prison because of the color of your skin, because you defy oppression and removal from your ancestral lands, when your language is considered unlearned and your body does not wear consensually-acceptable clothing, or the situation of your birth defines your freedom, when Takaya was shot... what are these? Are they justice?

Martin Luther King Jnr said, "One has not only a legal, but a moral responsibility to obey just laws. Conversely, one has a moral responsibility to disobey unjust laws."

I could be though to be sidetracked, I guess, but what must you know, you who would be fáidh-skilled? All of the above. The ability to recognize what the Devil card represents when it falls with Justice. Where there is danger in the decision. It also, however, signifies discernment and could mean that the traveler will be required to make selective decisions. Justice can represent anything from a person who works in the legal field or who is called up for jury duty. It all depends on other attending cards in the layout.

It represents that for which you would live or die.

Figure 79 – Hanged

12–HANGED

HANGED can be descriptive, in one way or another, of an individual who lives or dies for an ideological cause: the victim of a twisted heroism, whether blowing oneself to smithereens, and anyone in sight with a body-load of explosives in the name of some deity or other, to succumbing to the lottery of a reluctant boy shaved and dressed as a soldier, in some demagogue's idea of profit, where shooting from a helicopter is a game of Warcraft at the expense of anyone in sight seems normal, where getting dismembered or raped is all that defines them, to the bright and learned science student bought, and groomed, to become the next Oppenheimer: obeying because they told you the cattle truck was a good idea, freaking out because the money has dried up; dealing with the bashing and the oppression, in what was once a loving relationship because you can't leave the kids, and there's no one to help you, anyway; others think you're a whiner and your partner is oh so nice.

This wayshower can represent falling, seeming to fail, being rejected, a suicide, a thing or person becoming seemingly obsolete, humanitarianism, altruism, genuine helplessness. In many ways it represents a situation (similar to the Fool) where things are beyond one's control.

It is also fishing, aerial performance and abseiling.

Figure 80 – Death

13–DEATH

Death represents completion. A relationship or venture that is over. Full stop. Death always represents very real endings and can be exciting or tragic. It literally means *No* if, during question time, this is the first card of the map is a yes/no question. No other cards are to be necessarily laid out when this occurs.

Death tells of final exams, and cards surrounding it will speak of success or failure, but that's an enormously bigoted thing, is it not? Who defines success? What does it mean to fail? Who is your judge? This is a massively diverse concept to work through for one who is fáidh-trained, because of Bobby Sands, because of Emily Wilding Davidson, because of Harvey Milk and Freddy Mercury.

Took me years to understand that death is the observation of the living. That, as a species, successive government hidden men have ordered the dropping of the atomic bombs, agent orange, uranium depleted warheads. That a little truck, marked exterminator, can close of your house and destroy the lives of a billion ants, or cockroaches, or fleas… or bees, just because they can. Without thought.

I ask that you think. Fáidh skilling is not for the person who kills carelessly. Not for the person who accepts killing without awareness.

The Death card also means literal death, but that is not always a thing to disturb.

On a seasonal level it represents harvest. On a festive note it is Samhain (Halloween), in Mexico (the Day of the Dead) and the ritualized participation in a funeral and a wake. I have seen it celebrated and mourned depending on any one of a variety of the situations. If, for example, a person dies at an impressively advanced age tarot tends to view it as a celebration of the individual's life rather than something sad and, as such, the seeker will actually hear words along these lines at the funeral.

This card can also portend places of violent deaths. I recall seeing the Death card with the Empress with the World in the reading of a traveler: it indicated Cambodia that, under the Khmer Rouge, was known as the Killing Fields, whereas Death, Hierophant, 10 of Swords is murder, done in the name of religion.

Figure 81 – Temperance

14–TEMPERANCE

Temperance is the alchemy of mixing one thing with another to get something desired: the tight-rope walker and their balancing stick. Cautions. All things worthy of consideration; trial period; a middle position: mediation, negotiation, tentative peace (treaty), the fine line through a particular situation, keeping your balance, someone on the wagon (drugs or alcohol).

It can be a person who is the mediator in a situation of discord, and it will turn up for healers, medicine, poison (with the Devil card), mellow people, counselors, and go-betweens.

In the entertainment industry it is balancing acts, jugglers, aerial acts It represents balancing life without overindulgences and when describing places, it can represent bridges.

Temperance is the card of the tightrope walker. Beneath the individual for whom this represents is the Dark Night of the Soul. An abyss. A chasm. An unrealized Songline. The place of predator and prey. Only way across that deep space is the eradication of the word "too" from your language: too old, too young, too late, too tired, too little too sick… well, you get it. What part of *too* is in your way?

Figure 82 – Devil

15–DEVIL

This DEVIL represents that which the traveler needs to fear. Because, other than there being no such entity much of the world of people-animals believes there to be one. What are we to do? Is our mutual species capable of perpetuating acts of everything the word *evil* means? There is a definite threat (in the mind and/or literally) forthcoming; it can represent an addiction (alcohol, drugs, food, sex, even the need to be loved, porn, gambling and the newest addiction: social networking), but it can also represent an enemy, particularly if it describes someone. With ill-health cards it can represent cancer, sexually transmitted disease but it can also represent stuckness; obsession; dogma; danger.

The Devil card is dangerous people or ideas that are really traps, like some marriages, or institutions (with Emperor or Hierophant), that have radical, fundamentalist, or dangerous ideologies.

In a place it can mean claustrophobic conditions and confined spaces. The Devil is toxic environments: polluted or poisoned. It is frustration over delays; restraints; restrictions.

The Devil card has a disproportionate number of interpretations depending on its placement on a map, informing us of prevalence towards dysfunction and danger in our current world.

The sweet-faced, smiley bloke on the pushbike is Josef Mengele.

Figure 83 – Tower

16–TOWER

The card called Tower tells you that things are about to be experienced as terrible: here is where what the person (or situation) presumed to be secure comes tumbling down; chaos, fiery places, blast mining, explosive situations of any kind. Violence perpetuated on a child or a culture. Natural phenomenon including lightning, big storms, cyclones, eruptions, and earthquakes. It can also be electricity but dangerously uncontained power. Disaster. Up it blows, down it goes. Crisis. Out-of-control events and people. Uncontrolled rage.

Whatever has been built up will come crashing down. A roadside bomb, a rollercoaster wheel losing its last nut on its last bolt. Lightning. The mass violation of species, environments and indigenous cultural practices.

The Tower, in personal, or cultural, situations, is a dramatic precursor to change and, as such, can ultimately be liberating. The process, however, will be massive.

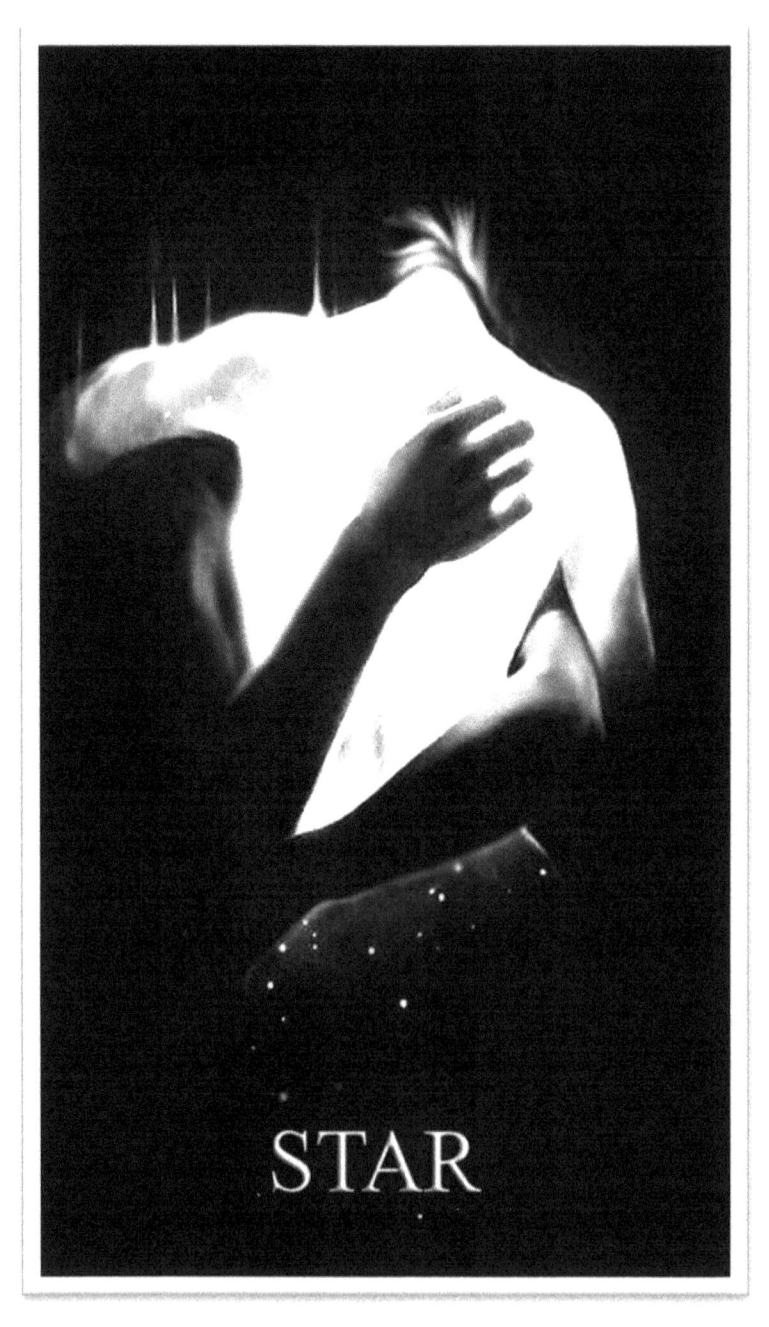

Figure 84 – Star

17–STAR

Pandora's Box is still left with *hope* after the ills of the world are released, being beyond discord. It can be symbolic/actual window or glass, allowing clear vision from within an enclosed (atmospheric or body) materialism. It is one's head above water. It is whereby one can know greatness in the smallest of things.

Star represents flight and aeronautics; long distance/time/long term projects; realization.

A *yes* in answer to a question. Eyesight and visual aptitude.

Star also represents illumination, cameras, film, IT and other forms of technology, glass, shopfronts, advertising, visual imagery, reflection, ideals and information.

The Star card is many places depending with which others it falls and can give quite precise calendric, or seasonal, durations– usually of many years: seventeen to twenty.

Star card is also GPS and the bars on your phone indicating signal.

Figure 85 – Moon

18–MOON

Deceit or self-deceit, disillusionment, disappointment, wet places, a moody child, depression, whatever *mind* is. A situation or human animal who is emotionally dampening. Despair. Intuition, all rhythm and tidal lore.

It is the ocean and all things to do with wet weather, flooding, or water of any kind, including, however, mold and swamp. Things that descend: divers, cavers, pearlers and fishers. Also, any pastime that is oceanic or involving water.

Physiologically Moon causes some people to be made miserable by dreary weather. Like with SAD (seasonal affected disorder). Hormonal shifts and/or imbalances. The persona or the mask that a person will present that can later slip, revealing a monster, if one is not careful. Moon can represent reflections or mirrors.

It will be present in conjunction with 7 of Cups for psychosis.

Prestidigitation, poker, drug dealers, models (runway or other). Art and/or image-related pursuits and career.

Figure 86 – Sun

19–SUN

Sun is a representation of success. Of course, many people consider that to be social and monetary but that is only a recent (and often desperate) acknowledgement. Achievement, birth, children, hot places, anything bright or golden vitality.

The Sun is innocence, joyful and happy. Often. Sun represents the beginning of things, as distinctly as it represents outcomes. Mostly Sun's meaning, as all other *Wayshowers*, is dependent on those cards around it.

Sun can also kill, deplete, desiccate, dry out and disfigure. It is thirst and tan, and can show up resulting in melanoma, solar keratosis, premature aging. It can be a Sunday.

The Sun card is in detriment when it lands with the Tower. It is traumatic when it does involve children who are abused. It is not necessary for anything more to be said.

Figure 87 – Judgement

20–JUDGEMENT

Change. Usually huge change, in the world, in the traveler's life. To the consciousness of an animist and deep ecologist the wisdom, in the human species—in an illogical incapacity to spae beyond itself—is missing. The media description of earth-talk, from volcanic eruptions to fires, to floods and hurricanes, is that of surprise and outrage. World should have succumbed by now, to orders. Trauma is measured in cost to economy. People killed are less important. This is perennial.

Judgement has been called *rebirth, rising from the grave, awakening*. It *can* represent the decision of a court, tribunal, royal commission or other similar. It can also be what earth, ocean and atmosphere do. Ice Age? Judgement card. Tsunami? Judgement card. Turning the sod in a garden, replacing grassy bits with food-and-pollinator-plants? Judgement. Leaving an abusive relationship. Transforming a lump of ore into a *Kyōgoku Masamune*, Judgement.

I sweated buckets, considering whether to present you with this volcanic eruption, or the collapse of the tower of Notre Dame, as they are both precursors of dynamic shifts. Ultimately, I consider that our liberation from entombed and entrenched religious bias is through knowing our place within the vastness of eternity.

Volcano says, *Let it be me.*

Figure 88 – World

22–WORLD

World is LIFE. HOME. Community, overseas connections, the end of one cycle and the beginning of another like 31st December/1st January or like Samhain on the annual seasonal calendar and also the cycle of one year, any complete revolution, even the traveler's entire biological life.

World is a center where people gather, a community venue, a pub, a chess pageant, a ceremony or sporting event.

World also represents—in context—20-21 years ago/ahead. A *saturn cycle* of 28 years. The transition from one way of living to another.

World is not an *it*. World is a *who*…

THE JOURNEY CARDS

Please note: Messengers are rarely (if ever) people.

Figure 89 – The Journey Cards

In traditional, old fashioned tarot representations the Journey (a collective noun) is known as the minor arcana. As we do not consider them either minor, not hidden, we mention this as an accompaniment to that which is presented.

STAVES

Also called Wands, Staves are communications, the spoken and the written word, performing arts, spontaneity, creativity, self-expression, and optimism

Figure 90 – Ace of Staves

ACE OF STAVES

Beginnings. New ventures. Creative works – more casual then intense. Initiatory processes that, unlike Magician, are often spontaneous. Ace of Staves represents the words NEW and YES. This story can represent fire or a fiery situation, spontaneity, excitation. Staves are books and all forms of communication both spoken and written. Orality. Memorized scripts, sagas and ditties. New possessions and objects. Light-heartedness, vivacity, dance, musical harmony, optimism. Alone Staves never represent a human-handed problem.

Figure 91 – 2 of Staves

2 OF STAVES

In difference to many other stories, the 2 of Staves does not represent events so much as environments in which the traveler will be.

Our 2 of Staves is a coastal place, usually a large or a major city. If it's a seaside village the cards around it will advise, like 8 of Staves. The only instance where the 2 of Staves represents other than this is when describing a person and, in this, is the representation of an individual who is acknowledged by their peers and who nothing to prove.

Figure 92 – 3 of Staves

3 OF STAVES

The destination of the 3 of Staves is understood to be *at a distance*. 3 of Staves is often associated with a guardian, a sentinel. Imports and exports. In a way that is not tragic, this story can be both longing and homesickness. Time sequences: a period of 3 days, 3 weeks, 3 months or 3 years and, when considering healing: if I cut my finger and take care of the wound, I will heal in 3 days. If the wound needs suturing the healing is around 3 weeks, a broken bone will knit in 3 months, the immensity of grief will begin to seem bearable if we make it through the first three years.

Truth, though, especially with grief, is that we never completely heal from that, we simply change in order to cope.

Figure 93 – 4 of Staves

4 OF STAVES

A party, festival or celebration. A fun time. A performance. With a person card 4 of Staves describes the individual as a living celebration, or a performer, a celebrant or, if with birth cards, a doula.

The 4 of Staves displays theatrical events, and also restaurants and the hospitality industries. It often turns over when a wedding is portended, or RuPaul's next *Drag Race* on Netflix.

Figure 94 – 5 of Staves

5 OF STAVES

The 5 of Staves indicates confusion of thought. Many voices at once. Babble, crossed-wires, background chatter. A band (folk, rock, swing, jazz or other musical troupe) or group of singers. Several people talking or interacting at once. It can be a literal mess: people, room and/or environment. Juggling money. Doing several things at once. Building materials. Verbal dispute. Red tape.

Our 5 of Staves is people fighting with sticks and stones, not tanks and guns, but you will usually understand that in political or socially-disruptive situations, often when tarot interrupts to spae of world events.

Figure 95 – 6 of Staves

6 OF STAVES

Natural victory. Another *Yes* meaning. 6 of Staves is going to portend cruising casually. Nothing stressful. Easily victorious. Genuine and destined achievements. Slide through life like the proverbial hot knife through butter.

You have no specific this-goes-with-that to be aware of here. This portent on the map indicates, that by being who your visitor is by nature, the person they will (or do) know, or the situation that will eventuate—without pretension for any reason—will do so without stress or duress.

Figure 96 – 7 of Staves

7 OF STAVES

Phone calls or social networking. Teaching. Covert conversations with self.

When in reference to the sale of a house or property it is an auction. Long-distance speaking – not eye to eye. Talking when not everyone's listening.

I have had this card turn up when communication, from either so-called dead people who are still around the traveler, is attempting to convey meaning or importance, and/or when the *mysteries* are in discussion with an individual, which will normally occur accompanied by the Seer or the Magician.

Figure 97 – 8 of Staves

8 OF STAVES

Rural land or country but not necessarily forested. Sending out things (documents or other forms of written material).

Figure 98 – 9 of Staves

9 OF STAVES

Not being heard or not speaking – the "Nobody ever listens to me" dilemma. The traveler, or represented person, is annoyed at people finishing sentences for them. The person is not going to waste time explaining themselves. Not waste words. Communication breakdown.

The Horse Latitude map suggests the traveler keep their mouth shut. The human animal, or other, represented has had enough of not being heard and is guarding their words and behavior. They would rather communicate but it's pointless: not going to do that anymore.

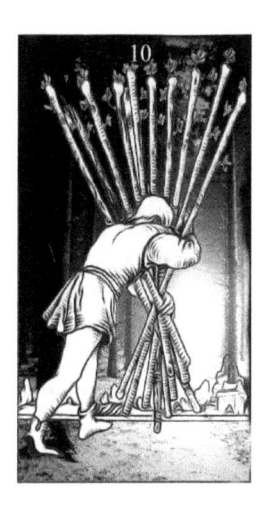

Figure 99 – 10 of Staves

10 OF STAVES

The traveler, or someone represented in their story, is moving things from place to place, shouldering responsibilities willingly. Building, moving, traveling by caravan of whatever kind, hauling and renovating.

Our 10 of Staves will represent a person or a cart horse. Carrying a load.

In detriment it is environmental theft such as the transportation of once-living forest to a timber mill. It never flips over on its own and for an individual, is never a hardship, although the experience (like the amount of study or research necessary to achieve a bold outcome) can be testy.

Figure 100 – Messenger of Staves

MESSENGER OF STAVES

The *Messengers* are rarely, if ever, a representation of people, but of movements such as a journey, trip, communication, package, or letter. There is usually nothing insidious or worrying when this card is involved.

Our Messenger of Staves represents modes of transport—usually an average car or simply walking—and it also represents an amicable resolution to a situation.

Figure 101 – Fledgling of Stave

FLEDGLING OF STAVES

Fire Sign children/child, or the child of a Fire Sign person, the Fledgling of Staves can also be the seed of a creative project &/or the spoken or the written word. A small fiery thing.

Fledgling of Staves is a book, blog, journal or treatise, also poetry and rhyme as a means of mnemonics.

Figure 102 – Person of Staves 1

PERSON OF STAVES 1

A Fire Sign person. A two-spirit with traditionally feminine mannerisms. They are outgoing, flamboyant, can be queer, active, in-your-face person. Communicative, but can be a vacuous chatterbox. People with red hair (natural or otherwise) and/or freckles or can be someone with a ruddy complexion.

I read the maps of an individual who was planning their wedding. This card, that of Cups and that of Coins also all turned up around the 4 of Staves.

"There'll be queen after queen after queen at this event," I said.

"Dear *god*," they laughed, "it's going to be magnificent!"

Figure 103 – Person of Staves 2

PERSON OF STAVES 2

A fire-sign adult—out there, active, in-your-face, highly communicative, possible redhead (natural or otherwise), and/or freckled. Can be someone with a ruddy complexion.

Can talk too much, or talk and talk and, deliberately, reveal nothing.

CUPS

Emotional, Artistic, Emissive

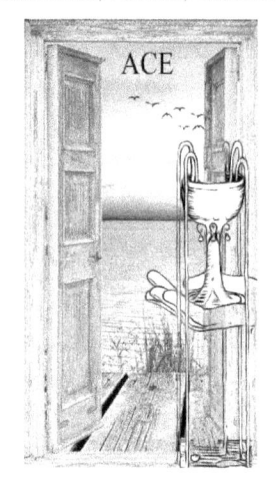

Figure 104 – Ace of Cups

ACE OF CUPS

Love. A feeling that is heartful or heartbreaking. The roots of powers of love. Loving another being. Being in love with place, critters, philosophy, life: irrelevant. Love is a feeling that is beautiful to feel.

The moment we transfer that love onto the identity of someone else, or to experience, often the feeling degenerates into dependence, jealousy, greed, or confusion.

Figure 105 – 2 of Cups

2 OF CUPS

2 of Cups always represents intimate relationships, often (mostly) sexual but can also mean close, close friendships. Our 2 of Cups is the bond between counsellor and seeker, the partnership between close compadres, sharing food, tips, wisdom, equal conversation.

Mostly it's just sex and/or sexuality depending with what other information a map presents.

Figure 106 – 3 of Cups

3 OF CUPS

A gathering of like-minded people. A small group of people getting along well. The quality of a gathering. Communion stronger than blood. No disharmony. Three people. It can also be a reunion, and you will know this when it appears in conjunction with major events such as religious festivals, marriages, and deaths.

A choir or a troupe of singers. Rappers, on Swanston Street, tin box on the ground for dinner money.

3 of Cups will be a polyamorous relationship. Just yesterday, however, a traveler had this representing their family. I said, a bit jokey, "You look like a triplet." They were surprised and explained that they are a twin, with a brother that might as well be. Three siblings, eh?

Figure 107 – 4 of Cups

4 OF CUPS

Our 4 of Cups represents that which is *other* than what the traveler is looking for or at. It indicates that events will happen unexpectedly. 4 of Cups is a gift, an offer, or an unforeseen opportunity and, in the case of the prospective sale of a home or property, can represent either an offer other than is first presented, or the fourth offer.

It informs them that there will be more options open to them in any situation present in the map.

The 4 of Cups is not always propitious, however, and if there are stories of detriment in the map it will indicate unforeseen consequences.

Figure 108 – 5 of Cups

5 OF CUPS

Sadness, grief or regret. It can represent mourning for a loss, either through death or separation. A backward-looking person, one concerned with past disappointments, so concerned with what has failed they do not seek alternatives.

5 of Cups indicates the desire and striving to achieve in a certain area but not getting what is sought or desired.

As a foundation it is a 'No' answer: the traveler or individual represented won't get what they are pursuing or achieve what they thought was destined. 5 of Cups can represent a sequence of unsuccessful relationships that will not continue into the future.

Figure 109 – 6 of Cups

6 OF CUPS

The past. This is ultimately what this card means but it can also indicate children or childhood, usually reflective and often the traveler's own past. Their own children or descendants.

The 6 of Cups indicates that which is already gone or completed. With information about work or employment the 6 of Cups can represent an involvement with 'dead' things – anything from archaeology and antiques to history and genealogy. However, don't dismiss research from the plot.

Or hypothesis, or theory. Or seed saving. Or lore.

It will front up when there are reunions.

Figure 110 – 7 of Cups

7 OF CUPS

The image of this story shows someone looking at a sequence of hopes or fears none of which are realized. It also shows one image covered (occulted).

The 7 of Cups represents illusions. Lies or a liar. Can be little indulgences such as alcohol, sex, self-prescribed medicinal substances, food etc. but not to the point of addiction.

Imagination when it shows itself with several staves in the map, but in detriment it is most definitely delusional. It is 'What if' situations and speculation and, as such, can be creative because it also represents the idea that may or may not lead to an event, or destructive due to incomplete knowledge or an outright deceit.

Figure 111 – 8 of Cups

8 OF CUPS

Hope is inherent in the traveler's journey because the 8 of Cups represents *walking away* from disappointment: something vital was missing in the relationship or situation. The traveler won't yet see where they are going but know perfectly well where they have been. 8 of Cups usually means that disappointment has already happened but the cup that is missing shows an innate emotional imbalance *when* the event was occurring: before it was over. 8 of Cups is rather prickly insofar as the person has just been told there is no kiss, and no prince.

You will realize deep sadness in this story, but it is certainly instilled with a sense of excitement or adventure. It can mean that the *Dark Night of the Soul* is almost over. That someone is leaving stuff behind. That disappointment is transitional.

Figure 112 – 9 of Cups

9 OF CUPS

This is generally auspicious. The surrounding story arcs will advise.

It is a *yes*, in answer to a question.

The only experience I have of this story, as disturbing, is when it represents a condescending, self-serving, greedy, arrogant, smug, and gluttonous overlording-type despot. Sort of a Trumpian-type, bad-hair narcissist.

Figure 113 – 10 of Cups

10 OF CUPS

A house, home, or family. A place and/or state of being. Is somehow even more pleasant than even the 9 of Cups because it is shared joy—an actual clan, or a being in an environment that is a natural habitat, where the traveler or the person represented is at peace.

Sometimes this story can represent death – a final resting or release – but only when there has been long-term illness or pain and, even then, the Death card will be almost certain to face up.

A long time before the research and marketing of quality medications to treat HIV AIDS many of the people that I interpreted for who were stricken with this disease, had the 10 of Cups as a final destination. Coming home.

Figure 114 – Messenger of Cups

MESSENGER OF CUPS

Messengers are not people: they are states or modes of movement or flow. The Messenger of Cups is a follow-through card: whatever is happening is honorable and can be trusted. Feeling of good will, that everything is okay. Messenger, here, shows that the traveler will trust the person or people met on the journey; can signify an offer.

This Messenger will also represent a suggestion being made or a gift being given.

Figure 115 – Fledgling of Cups

FLEDGLING OF CUPS

This story can be the seed or conception of an artistic pursuit; a human, or other species, child born under one of the following: Cancer, Pisces, Scorpio. It can also, however, be art, painting, drawing, sculpture, visual arts.

With illness cards the Fledgling of Cups usually indicates a child with eye, ear, nose or throat problems.

Can be animals other than the traveler or those with whom they will have contact, usually dark-furred, feathered, skinned, or finned.

Figure 116 – Person of Cups 1

PERSON OF CUPS 1

A Water Sign – unless accompanying cards signify that the story defines them as otherwise.

Can be a person with dark hair and/or complexion; someone who holds onto their emotions for any number of reasons (hence the urn). Also, in relation to the urn, the represented individual could be an undertaker or, with (for example) Temperance and Emperor, a coroner or medical examiner. Otherwise an artist, sailor, and often a tech specialist.

Figure 117 – Person of Cups 2

PERSON OF CUPS 2

Any Water Sign person – unless accompanying cards other.

It sometimes represents a dark-haired or swarthy individual, a deeply loved, and loving person or a really annoying moody one.

COINS

Practical, physical, material

Figure 118 – Ace of Coins

ACE OF COINS

This story goes to the roots of powers of that which is recognized as material: the physical body, money in any form or income coming or going, money, trade, barter and commodities, or the foundations of the physical world in any manner.

Cryptocurrencies or internet banking and transactions.

With the 10 of Coins it can represent banks and suchlike institutions, same with Emperor.

Figure 119 – 2 of Coins

2 OF COINS

Shared materials: divided money, shared accommodations, financial partnerships, division of possessions and or money, part-time income, or work. Part-time anything.

Money, finances, trade, securities, treaties, stipends, payouts and settlements. Material or practical partnerships.

Figure 120 – 3 of Coins

3 OF COINS

An interview, or impersonal discussion, always practical in nature.

Notice that the artisan, however, has taken the high place. That means they know more and are advising the folk in frocks.

Figure 121 – 4 of Coins

4 OF COINS

A stay-put story. A holding-onto story. It can represent carefully saving money. A deposit or a small stash of money or the equivalent. Someone who doesn't or won't spend money. Limited money.

In the human body: body fat, fixed joints, arthritic conditions, gall stones, kidney stones.

Our 4 of Coins is often time sequences – four days, four weeks, four months, or four years.

Shows up in a map for any skills-training or university degree, especially when accompanied by the Emperor.

Figure 122 – 5 of Coins

5 OF COINS

No money, broke, poverty, lacking. Out in the cold, beaten, ignored. In legal settlement cases it represents a lot less money, a loss of money or a complete loss. Deficiency of something (in a health condition); overspending money. It can be bankruptcy of whatever.

Yesterday I had someone at my table who had a broken ankle in a cast. When the 5 of Coins showed itself (in my deck, depicting two people, one on crutches) in the Dead Reckoning map's central position crossed by Temperance, I cracked up laughing. I picked up the card and faced them with it. They grinned and exclaimed "Oh, that's me!" Interestingly, they have been working on casual rates and therefore has no income while healing, hence the loss of money also represented.

Figure 123 – 6 of Coins

6 OF COINS

Paying out or getting paid. Getting rid of a debt. Being repaid money that was owed.

I consider the attitude of the image. An inherent bias and social construct are obvious by this image.

Consider: are you (or the traveler) the beggar or the altruist?

Figure 124 – 7 of Coins

7 OF COINS

Growth. The fulfillment of the growth process. 7 of Coins can represent increases of money, the interest on investments, productivity, savings, increases in material value as for the value of property. Can also represent gardens, plant nurseries and roots.

Sometimes our 7 of Coins is not pleasant. Warts, fungus, cysts, unwanted hair, increases in rent, overgrowth of blackberry canes or headlice, smugness at having more physical possessions than someone else. It will be different with every traveler who visits you, sometimes they are at the mercy/behest of someone gaining from the traveler's labor or ignorance, like big fast food magnates, or banks gaining all their revenue from fees.

Figure 125 – 8 of Coins

8 OF COINS

This story's ultimate meaning is Work or the word *work*.

Sometimes this is a job, occupation, or vocation (although the latter would have the Ace of Cups or the 9 of Cups on the map). Work being done on anything from a car, to a house to a human body. What will work or won't produce fruit.

No need to give you a *this-goes-with-that* here because it really is simply the word *work* and can mean many things.

Figure 126 – 9 of Coins

9 OF COINS

The 9 of Coins can be best described by key words or descriptions such as beautiful. Quality not quantity. That no matter what happens life is win-win. Studying and learning becoming who you are not what you do (through life, not institutions necessarily).

In collaboration or communion with of all they behold, no domination, a state of earthly grace.

The 9 of Coins is the traveler's reputation in the world: as well as, or in difference to, the way they feel about themselves. Quality, in respect of whatever story it falls on or with.

Figure 127 – 10 of Coins

10 OF COINS

This is usually a rented or leased dwelling. A house (sometimes in difference to a home), a shop or business premises, an apartment, squat or boarding house. The quality, or state, of the dwelling will depend on an attending story.

This will be a bank, a tavern, a business through whose portals many people pass, like a café or a hotel.

Our 10 of Coins is determined by other stories on the map and really means very little without context.

Figure 128 – Messenger of Coins

MESSENGER OF COINS

A form of transportation: four-wheel drive, van, truck, caravan, mobile home, train, bus, FedEx. On-going practicalities. The expression *Take care of business*. Involvement in a process – doing the work: plod, plod.

Our Messenger of Coins represents covering a body's own interests. Ongoing financial transactions. The movement of transactions. Heavy haulage (emotionally and/or physically).

Figure 129 – Fledgling of Coins

FLEDGLING OF COINS

An Earth Sign child or the child of an Earth Sign person. Private study or a small personal business enterprise.

Our Fledgling of Coins is activities with kids or animals, &/or things done seasonally or regularly.

Figure 130 – Person of Coins 1

PERSON OF COINS 1

This represents a Capricorn, Taurus or Virgo. A business-type, an accountant, a guard, a manager, an entrepreneur, gardener, builder, environmental protector, arborist, a person who works on a farm, a permaculturist.

A politician, statistician, mathematician or manager. Or an earthy individual who identifies as female.

That's it.

Figure 131 – Person of Coins 2

PERSON OF COINS 2

See previous Person of Coins.

SWORDS

(always tricky things)

Intellectual, violatory, aggressive

Figure 132 – Ace of Swords

ACE OF SWORDS

Cutting or dividing. This is a suggestion of will-power, of intent. It represents decision, divisions, determination, discipline, someone in authority.

Our Ace of Swords will also depict sharp objects, chefs with knives, tattooist needles, acupuncturists, and martial artists.

This will be fences &/or the boundary of a property. In matters to do with acreage it is also the access track or road and, when representing the deed, it will tell you that the land is dual title.

Figure 133 – 2 of Swords

2 OF SWORDS

Again, there is a list of key words or phrases – not seen, indecision, stalemate, inward looking.

2 of Swords can indicate – in a dispute – that one's back is covered.

The 2 of Swords will inform that things are occurring behind the scenes, behind the traveler's back, over the back fence, in the woods behind the teepee, that there is something the traveler is not seeing, that a lost object is not found, information is undisclosed.

Our 2 of Swords is the silence necessary in circumstances of either danger or pointlessness. It can also represent peace and meditation. Is there an inherent threat? Of course. One of the most succinct tenets I have known is *never turn your back on the sea.*

Figure 134 – 3 of Swords

3 OF SWORDS

In whatever way, this card always represents separation. That can be anything from a marriage bust-up, to being away from loved ones, to homesickness, to heart attack and heart surgery. Not often, however, does it portend happiness.

The 3 of Swords is not always a problem… as it will indicate when a baby exits a womb, there is a journey away from home or when you lose a thing of emotional importance.

Figure 135 – 4 of Swords

4 OF SWORDS

This is also a very simple-meaning card: waiting, doing nothing, nothing happening, resting.

Our 4 of Swords can be time sequences of four days, four weeks, four months, four years or April.

Can be a corpse or cadaver, so is likely to express the observation of a someone involved in medicine, coronial inquiry, autopsy, taxidermy, or funeral undertakings.

Figure 136 – 5 of Swords

5 OF SWORDS

Argument or dispute (somebody loses). Struggle, but not of the gentle kind. An argument that'll come back on you later.

Not always of detriment but have I ever seen it as anything other? Nup.

Figure 137 – 6 of Swords

6 OF SWORDS

Time sequence – six days, six weeks, six months. A journey or process out of trouble (from troubled waters to calm). On, or across, water close to the country in which the person lives. Short distance journeys across water. Longer and further if accompanied by the Star.

The 6 of Swords represents people and events to do with water: fishing, swimming, diving, boating, immigration, escape: seeking refuge, pirating.

Will also be transportation in the time of flood.

7

Figure 138 – 7 of Swords

7 OF SWORDS

Our 7 of Swords informs the traveler of a need to be wary. It is also the card of sneaking, clandestine behavior or cunning. It represents avoidance of confrontation or simply avoidance. Getting out of a possibly dangerous or detrimental situation by knowing how to undermine the potential for violence or attack. Can indicate a thief or theft.

The 7 of Swords is propitious when the art of strategy is deployed in a situation that requires such.

The traveler is being stalked or else doing the stalking.

Figure 139 – 8 of Swords

8 OF SWORDS

This is the 'stuck' story. The bound person. The inability to change a situation: there's nothing the traveler, or individual to which the map alludes, can do about a situation. Hands are tied (sometimes literally as has been seen in the case of one individual who had achieved refugee status from an oppressive regime). Nothing can be done to change the situation beyond what's already available. Commitment – in it for the long run. Can't move.

Living along a difficult-access driveway, track or road or can be an injury keeping a body restrained. With stories like Justice the 8 of Swords is prison or incarceration, to varying degrees. Can be constipation, a physical restraint like handcuffs, a straitjacket, a plaster cast, a paraplegic's torso and limbs, or the physical results of stroke. Can be a blood clot, a broken leg, an inability to escape or move. Will also represent the commitment of parenthood.

Figure 140 – 9 of Swords

9 OF SWORDS

Our 9 of Swords is always influenced by the stories around it and can be either detrimental or auspicious depending on circumstances and even the individual's disposition.

Worry, or regret, tiredness; fatigue, late nights, but can just as easily signify one's profession (night shift).

Nightmares. Terror. Fear.

When sickness is a certainty, however, this will always turn up.

9 of Swords is auspicious when worry allows the traveler to solve a problem. Otherwise it's plain shitty.

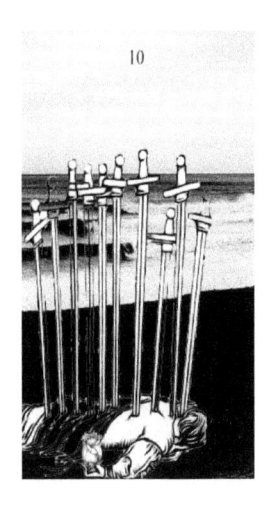

Figure 141 – 10 of Swords

10 OF SWORDS

Physical pain, back pain, back-stabbing, violence, cruelty and the result of cruelty, betrayal but, as with so many other cards, can also be auspicious. It will represent an acupuncturist, tattooing, piercing, or chiropractic manipulation.

I am forever wary, however, because yes, it expresses violence of word or action, to any animal person including you and the traveler with you. Cruelty and malicious behavior.

10 of Swords flipped relentlessly beside the Death card in 2019, and the murders of several women occurred, throughout the year, close to where I live on the north side of Melbourne.

Figure 142 – Messenger of Swords

MESSENGER OF SWORDS

Speed. Can also be aggression. Impatience. A swift resolution to a situation.

Is a pushbike, mountain bike, motorbike, motor scooter. Can also be methamphetamine, cocaine, dangerous driving, anger and knee-jerk reactions.

I'm seeing it more often now that people are being diagnoses with ADHD as it will present itself with medical information. The Messenger of Swords also tells the story of horse or greyhound racing, the company of a Lurcher or a small, crazy puppy, the behavior of an over-the-top- two-year-old-wall-rammin' kid with a Tonka truck.

Figure 143 – Fledgling of Swords

FLEDGLING OF SWORDS

Intelligence (not necessarily relative to academia) or intellectual pursuit. An Air sign child: Libra, Aquarius, Gemini, or the time of one of those zodiac signs.

An interesting concept, as yet undeveloped. A technological pursuit.

Figure 144 – Person of Swords 1

PERSON OF SWORDS 1

An *Air Sign* person: Libra, Aquarius, Gemini, or a person with the qualities. I have been asked if the person cards can represent someone with the qualities of those signs of the zodiac. Of course. But the traveler would then, as a matter of course, understand—innately or through study—what that would entail.

Our Person of Swords can be a fair-haired or grey/silver-haired, light-skinned person. A person of intelligence unless they fall in a story of detriment, whereby they become a person with a cutting tongue or wit.

Figure 145 – Person of Swords 2

PERSON OF SWORDS 2

See our other Person of Swords. This image is originally for a bloke. Can't spae it myself. People are people.

(Approximate dates will vary yearly)

Fledgling of Swords and Lovers –
	the time of Gemini: 21st May to 21st June
Fledgling of Swords and Star –
	the time of Aquarius: 21st January to 21st February
Fledgling of Swords and Justice –
	the time of Libra: 21st September to 21st October
Fledgling of Cups and Chariot –
	the time of Cancer: 21st June to 21st July
Fledgling of Cups and Death –
	the time of Scorpio: 21st October to 21st November
Fledgling of Cups and Moon –
	the time of Pisces: 21st February to 21st March
Fledgling of Coins and Devil –
	the time of Capricorn: 21st December to 21st January
Fledgling of Coins and Hermit –
	the time of Virgo: 21st August to 21st September

Fledgling of Coins and Hierophant –
> the time of Taurus: 21ˢᵗ April to 21ˢᵗ May

Fledgling of Staves and Temperance –
> the time of Sagittarius: 21ˢᵗ November to 21ˢᵗ December

Fledgling of Staves and Strength –
> the time of Leo: 21ˢᵗ July to 21ˢᵗ August

Fledgling of Staves and Emperor –
> the time of Aries: 21ˢᵗ March to 21ˢᵗ April

These dates can be decided exactly using an ephemeris.

PART 7

FÁIDH GIFTED

Figure 146 – Fáidh Training NZ

SPAE THAT DEEP SHIT, CRITTER!

FÁIDH TRAINING

Not surprisingly, all non-literate cultures train their memories. Their very survival depended on them doing so.

Dr. Lynne Kelly,
Grounded, Indigenous Knowing in a Concrete Reality

Studying the preceding information, you are ready to set sail. Buy a pack of tarot cards and archive any extraneous ones. While you're at it, compost the booklet that comes with the box.

ORALITY

Find a quiet place and lay out a cloth, placing the pack on it, face down. Beginning with the one on top turn over each card and recall as much as you can from your notes by the visuals only, saying as many of the key meanings *out loud*. This is especially important as it establishes the habit of verbal interaction with tarot. Do this for the entire pack and repeat this until each image is intimately associated with its meanings.

OPENING PATTERN AND 3 CARD RESEARCH

1. Keep a record of your experiments
2. In your quiet place, at a self-designated time 'open' your cards by placing them, one at a time, in the following

diagram (as mentioned earlier in this book). *Never shuffle them yourself.* Shuffling them at any stage is likely to contaminate the cards with your own future experiences

Figure 147 – Opening

This process is ordered randomness and if none of the cards have stuck together the last card you lay out will fall on 3.

3. Pick up the packs in any order and place them together
4. Take the bottom three cards from each pack and turn them face up, side by side, and
5. recognize what they are saying as a group (exactly like a sentence). When you have an understanding, say aloud what will happen with the mental intention of recognizing what you spae the following day in however small or large their capacity
6. If you don't already, start checking news for local and world events because these maps of 3 cards will show their outcomes here, most often in the not-so-in-your-face-news
7. Throughout, keep refreshing your knowledge of the story-meaning of each card

NEEDING WILLING ACCOMPLICES

1. Ask friends if you can experiment on them. Use one or more of the maps in the following examples, always opening the cards as described earlier, or in whatever pattern you want
2. Suggest that they also keep a record of what you have foretold and to let you know when the event/s occur
3. Keep to basics. Don't elaborate, or generalize, as these are an enemy that can become a habitual bully. Only tell what the cards say

Do all this as often as you can for several months, slowly introducing more than one map, until you have a clear understanding of the story, while constantly refreshing your knowledge of meanings, and your proficiency at reading the maps.

When friends of friends contact you, letting you know that so-and-so recommended you, that is when you need to establish a means of payment. You can begin with a barter: they bring you fresh fruit or vegetables, or other things you might require. When there are way too many patrons wanting you, charge them.

...

MAP 1 — DEAD RECKONING
PRESENT, FUTURE, PAST

The traveler shuffles the cards and cuts them into three packs. They often ask whether the packs they divide need to be of equal size, or whether they should use a certain hand to cut them. It doesn't matter.

The group taken from the top of the pack is always: THE FUTURE

The group in the center of the pack is always: THE PRESENT

The grouping on the bottom of the pack is always: THE PAST

Watch carefully how the deck is cut because people have many ways of doing so. Once they have divided the deck, you will lay the three packs to one side of the Dead Reckoning map, and you ask the traveler's zodiac sign.

If, for example, that person is a Leo then they were born under the element of fire, and the Person of Staves will usually represent them.

From now until question time, caution your visitor to say nothing and to respond as little as possible to what you *spae*, so you remain impartial. Sometimes this becomes impossible because when you touch a nerve for them, they can become quite emotional.

Sometimes these three maps are so clear and precise that I wish I didn't have to go further, and I will tell my visitor so, but they always want to know more and so, you will usually lose the beauty of the moment in the details of the events that ensue.

The cards are then laid out in the following map:

DEAD RECKONING

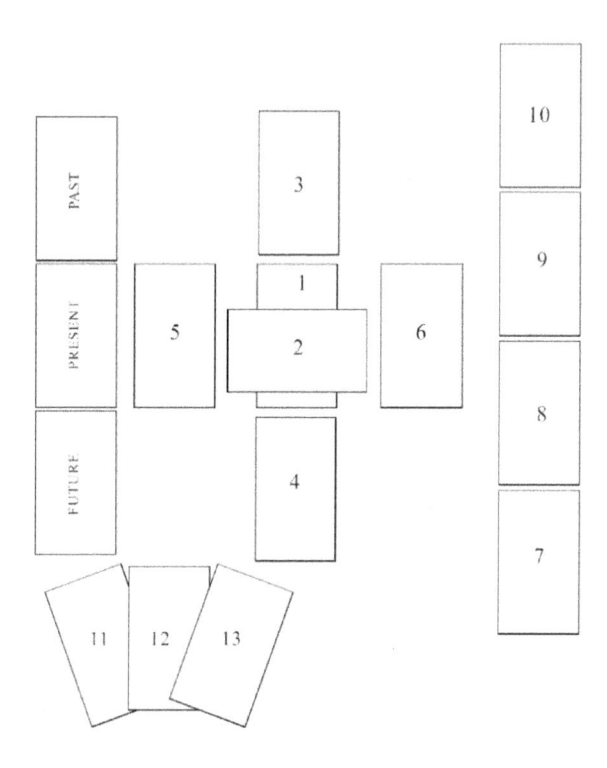

Figure 148 – Map: Dead Reckoning

Once you have laid out the map you place the remainder of that pack to one side, with the card on the bottom of the pack placed on the top, image facing you.

This card is the *stabilizer* and is significant to the overall story. Start with the pack that represents the PRESENT because you want to spae what is of immediate influence. Then do the same with the FUTURE group and, last, the PAST.

A NOTE ON THE PAST

I have a dream that my four little children will one day live in a nation where they will not be judged by the color of their skin but by the content of their character.

Martin Luther King Jnr.

Why I spae in this way is because the past that they show you is what remains – for the traveler – unresolved, or that represents ongoing events and/or influences, or, in some cases, other people. This latter is for many reasons: the other person is someone, yet unmet, who will be important and readily recognized when they talk about themselves to your visitor. This person might already be known but will have an ongoing impact in the future and, sometimes, this other person is body-dead and has left things undone. They could well be a wayshower, like Martin Luther King. Maybe his body is dead but, as the above quote teaches, he is alive, important in so many ways that I am sometimes unable to breathe.

How to navigate *Dead Reckoning*—
1. The first card laid out is in the center of your table and this card can (although not always) represent the situation, or person, at the center of the story
2. The second card is laid across the first, adding information—grace or detriment—to the first card
3. The third card, laid above, is what is in the person's mind or

what is happening, at a distance, that is influencing the current experience

4. The fourth card is the foundation of events, or is the environment of the traveler
5. The fifth card is a past or current situation
6. The sixth card is what is to come, where fate is leading or, if a person card, someone who will influence the story
7. The seventh is your visitor, who or what represents them or, in the case of a person pictogram, other than who is in front of you, an ally
8. The eighth is the environment – home, work or otherwise – in which the traveler will be
9. The ninth represents hopes and fears – it has no tangible reality in terms of the manifest destiny
10. The tenth is the outcome, or where events on the map will lead
11. The eleventh, twelfth and thirteenth cards are to be spaed as a whole pattern and will always show extenuating circumstances or other events that are occurring simultaneous to the above. They will be key information for the traveler's understanding

MAP 2 – THE GROVE

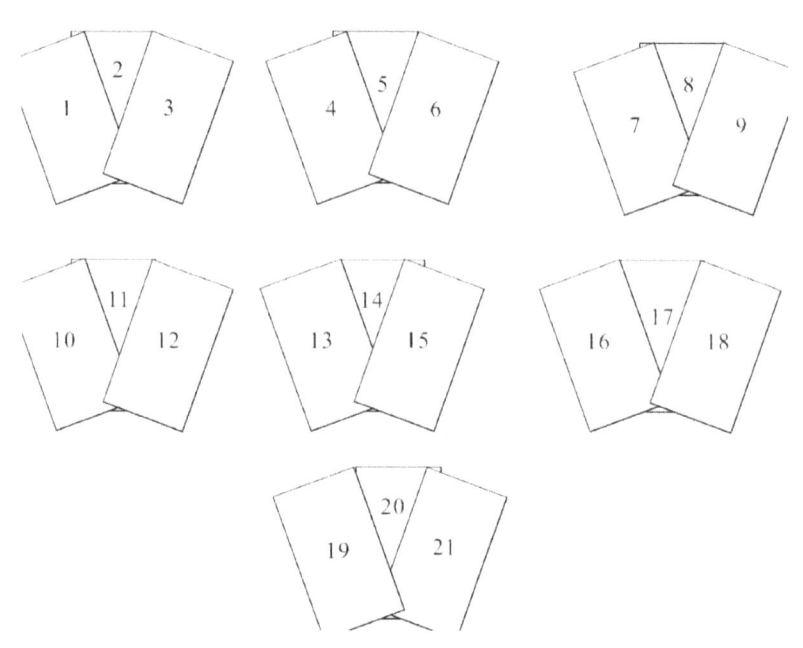

Figure 149 – Map: The Grove

These sets of triplets are all like gatherings of plunder or people in a grove. Each has a personality, and each group has something to offer the whole gathering.

You can spae them as individual outcomes, or they can interrelate depending on the entirety of the map. Often you will encounter correlations with the other maps.

The triplets are interpreted in no particular order, but the three cards off the bottom of each pack will always be the strongest influence.

MAP 3 – FAMILIAR FACES

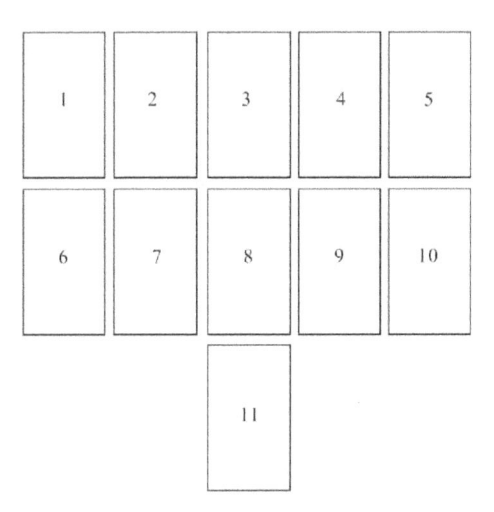

Figure 150 – Map: Familiar Faces

For this map (and those similar) discard the first six cards of the pack and lay out the seventh, face up. Repeat until you have two rows of five cards. Continue the process until the second-last card is placed at the base of the pattern and is considered the *stabilizer*.

As the third map this is often about people or events that are second-hand to the traveler but that will have an impact, however fleeting or seemingly inconsequential (research Butterfly Effect) through their reflection on the event through the pattern the traveler will realize specific obstructions or inspirations. Your interpretation will depend on all other cards on the map, and no card will mean anything on its own.

The layout is the same for the maps of the Horse Latitude and the Question/s.

Card 11 is the *stabilizer. They* are like a referee at a Muay Thai spar. The two lines can be one event, person or situation, or each line can be a separate story. On many occasions you'll understand that the top line is a straightforward situation and the cards from 6 to 10 are underlying influences
.

MAP 4 – STARGATE

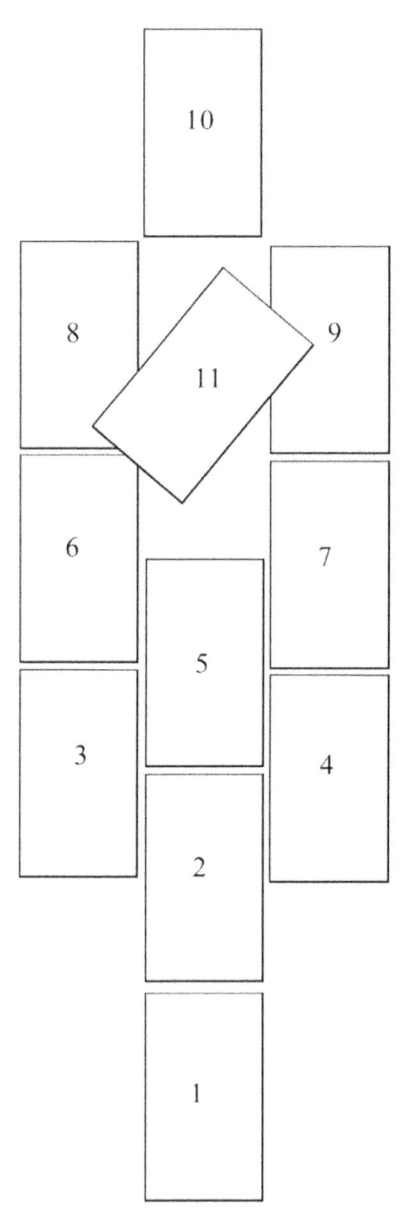

Figure 151– Map: Stargate

PORTAL 1 is HOME. The traveler's knowledge of what that is, a known environment or landscape, and a theoretical *everywhere else*. Port 1 represents the entire Mother Forest, pristine wilderness or slum falling into the monsoon sea. Or their bedsit, or their mum's house. 1 on the Stargate map is the heart of the voyage and landscape of the journey and is the foundation of your visitor's life: where they live, the places they will be, the state of these environments, ecological conditions, the bottom of the building or the base of the mine, the graveyard or the ancestral burial ground. Where they will travel, where they know, the plants that feed them, the food they consume, the state of the road or the conditions of the weather – all in the future. Health-related problems will include the feet and legs, also undermining by circumstances.

PORTAL 2 represents home's orbiting, astronomical and astrological moon. Is TIDE, and spaes events that are occurring at a distance, or deep thoughts within the traveler's consciousness. It can also be things behind: behind the traveler's back, in the alley behind their house, what they have lost, what's in the background. In health matters this region is the genitals, reproductive and urinary system, colon, anus, lower back, pelvis, hips, bum, thighs and knees.

PORTAL 3 is the astrological mercury. NAVIGATION and will foretell of travel, journeys and movement of any kind, transportation, communication and/or the spoken and written word. If using this map as a health indicator it relates to the effect of words, language and/or communication on either your visitor or those with whom they have connections, and in particular circumstances, the state of a person or other animal's teeth and anything dental. Also, the effect of verbal brutality on the flight or fight response on a body.

PORTAL 4, ART, represents the astrological venus. It represents any of the arts: festivals, parties, celebrations. It is motherhood, or a mother or grandmother (the traveler's or otherwise); it is sex, intimacy, fecundity, eroticism, femininity, gardening or gardens. If using this map for health-related matters this directional image will relate to any dysfunctions of the sexuality of the individual, including all sexually transmitted diseases, sexual abuse or abuses, deviant sexual aberrance. It can be the work of the traveler, or the sex-slave trade. Or any variation between.

PORTAL 5 is the astrological sun and is called the CORE, so represents the traveler, or those people or situations that clearly influence. The other cards in this and the other maps for this person will inform you as to whether someone, other than your visitor, falling in this place is an ally or of detriment. In all health matters card 5 is the solar plexus and major organs of the body such as the heart, liver, lungs, stomach, small and large intestines.

PORTAL 6 is the astrological mars and this aligns it with everything from family and community to war, unrest, uprising, protest (peaceful or otherwise), energy, vitality and stamina. The military, scouts, survival training and the martial arts. In health-related matters this place represents gall bladder, spleen, adrenals, musculature, tendons, sinew and ligaments, and other cards in other areas can aid in identification. Port 6, out of balance is violent or—the opposite—weakness and the inability to defend. Portal 6 is PROTECTION.

PORTAL 7 is EXPANSION and is the astrological jupiter and is the traveler's work and their workplace, their financial situation and their position and reputation in a society, culture, clan or tribe. In health matters it relates to metabolism, on the one hand, therefore also displaying their state of body-mass (or lack of it) in the future, and on the other, any viral, fungal, bacterial infections or cancers (anything with the ability to expand) as well as the training required of an individual who is bodybuilding, bricklaying, dancing or asthmatic.

PORTAL 8 is saturn's home. STONE. Cards falling here have a relevance to age or duration, to history and all things old or ancient. To institutions. Antiques or deep-time phenomenon. Concepts of such. Stone and metal. Health-related issues: the skeletal system, the joints. Long-term illness or dysfunction, inherited traits, disease. Cultural ideas of what represents health or illness, dysmorphia, debility that is chronic, and/or the right shoulder, arm and hand, latissimus dorsi and ribs. Can be prisons or genealogy, indigenous lore or the memorizing of a Shakespearian play.

PORTAL 9 is uranus and represents astrology to technology, from extreme disorder or chaos to electricity, electrical systems, nuclear technology. We call them LIGHTNING. In health matters it refers to the central nervous system and the left shoulder, arm and hand, latissimus dorsi and ribs.

PORTAL 10 is CHALLENGER DEEP, the astrological neptune and in this position refers to an outcome, or the next phase of life unfolding, completions and, in some situations, fame or notoriety. It is all things aquatic and if a person's work or excitation is scuba diving, deep sea exploration, marine studies or fishing it will show itself here. In health matters it refers to someone's head, one's intelligence and wit, the ears, eyes, nose and mouth (not including the teeth), back of a neck and/or brain. They are

PORTAL 11 is called the SEED and is represented by the astrological pluto. It gives the traveler knowledge not gleaned through orthodox means. A person of significance who is already known to them, and who will be of assistance at any crucial time. A way of thinking that will be invaluable. In health matters it represents both thought and obscure dysfunctions that defy diagnosis. Physically or mentally it holds one earthbound and can, therefore, represent any culturally stigmatized physical distinction. Throat, larynx, voice, thyroid, cervical spine and atlas.

Oh, and wonder. And mysticism. Better not leave them out.

...

Map 5 — Horse Latitude

The layout is the same as for Map 3. As the name suggests this is a WARNING that is, or will be, easily recognized by the traveler so that it can be avoided, averted, or prepared for in advance.

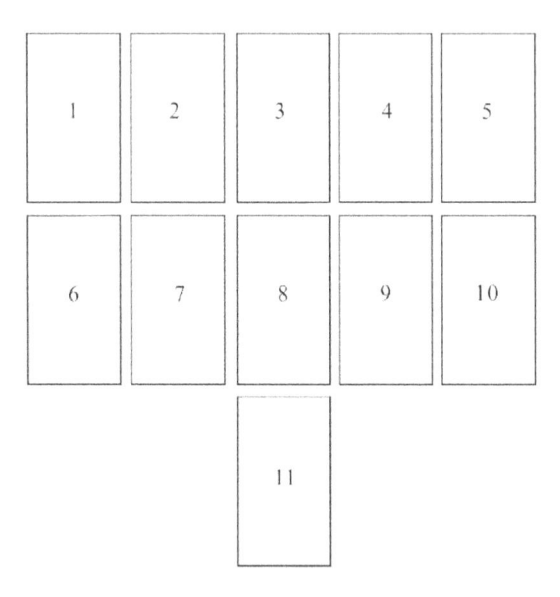

Figure 152 – Map: Horse Latitude

MAP 6 — THE CONTINUUM

Your visitor shuffles the cards and cuts them into 3 stacks. They are to choose one stack. You put the other two groupings aside and only spae the story the traveler has chosen.

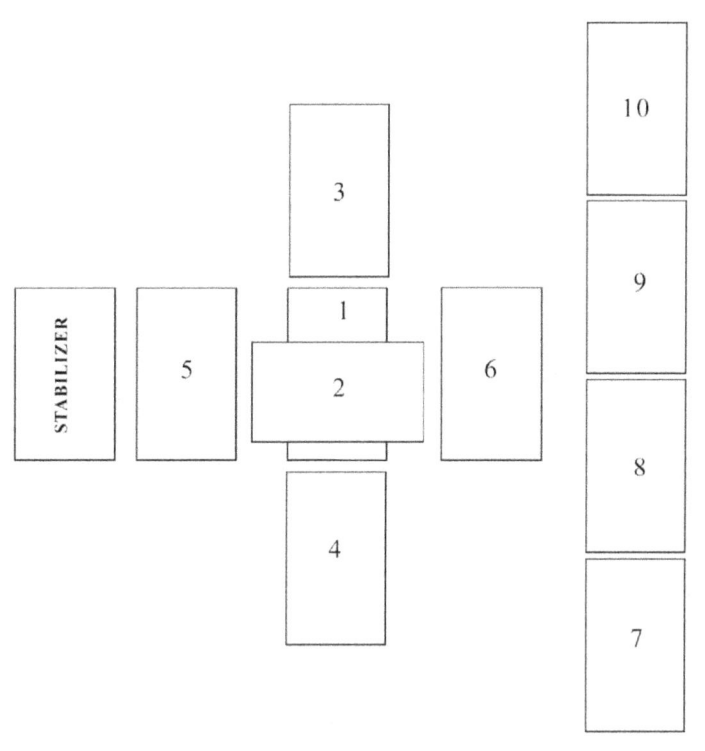

Figure 153 – Map: Continuum

The image that is at the bottom of the pile they chose is the *stabilizer* and is placed in sight so that its significance is reflected on during the interpretation.

Map 7 – Question

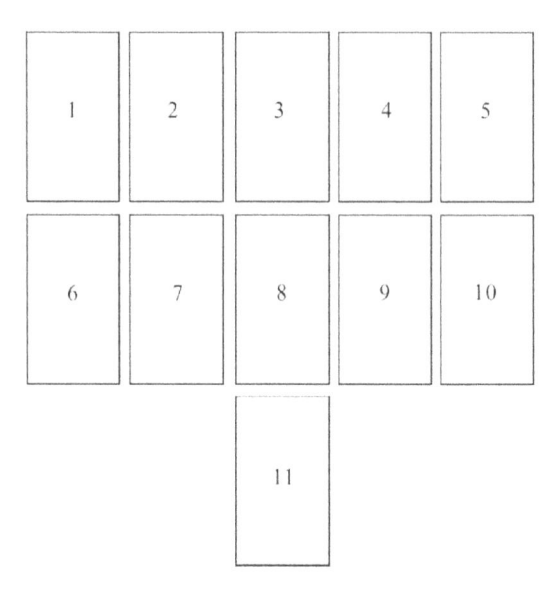

Figure 154 – Map: Question

This map is also the same layout as for maps 3 and 5 but the traveler speaks their question aloud as they shuffle so that their intention is embedded.

From now until the completion of the consultation, several things are going to happen. First the mysteries, plus the entity that is tarot itself, will often join in to discuss the answers. This can be disconcerting if you are unused to it because the story can, when not straightforward and specific, vary from hilarious to hostile depending on the context.

This is where the traveler talks with you: verbally communicating their concerns, thoughts – anything at all that is important to them *other* than pertaining to what has already been said– *while* they shuffle. And here's where glitches can often happen because if their questions are:

1. not in alignment with what you've already spaed
2. if the question has no future
3. if the visitor asks a generic question such as "Tell me about love," or "Tell me about money," or simply says the word "Relationships." You need to discuss what they might mean as an exact answer requires explicit questions. A body can have a relationship with just about anything. You can't assume what they mean (tarot won't) so ask them for clarity as they shuffle
4. if the answer to their question has already been given then tarot will interject with an altogether different story and:
5. in the case of naïve questions such as "when will I find my soul mate?" tarot can be downright rude and obnoxious in response
6. if your visitor seeks to have tarot remove free will from the equation by asking "should I…" or "if I do this or that…" example: "I'm pregnant. Should I have the baby?" or "should I get my dick cut off?" Not your job, dear fáidh-skilled, to take that decision away from them. Talk about it, sure, but future actions regarding the "should" must be their decision

These kinds of questions *will* be asked. They're a crossroads and you are a seer not a fiddler.

I advise visitors, at the outset, that these variables could occur and if, and when, they do I always allude that tarot can be obnoxious. They have a choice, then, in what they ask.

You'll know, believe me, when this is happening because you'll understand enough to realize that, as with the soul-mate question, the answer is as likely to be about a cat or dog as it is to be the Devil or the 7 of Cups.

What do you do if the traveler asks when they will marry, and will they have children and tarot answers "Never"? What do you say if they ask if they will be happy for the rest of their lives and there is the Tower, the 10 of Swords, the Devil, the 4 of Swords, the 7 of Cups on the top line; the 8 of Cups, the 5 of Swords, the 9 of Swords, the 2 of Swords and Judgement on the bottom line with Death (meaning No) as the *stabilizer*? Because it is a stupid question, is why.

PART EIGHT

BETWEEN THE DEVIL

They take us all for idiots
But that's their problem
When we behave like idiots
It becomes our problem

Kate Tempest, *Hold Your Own*

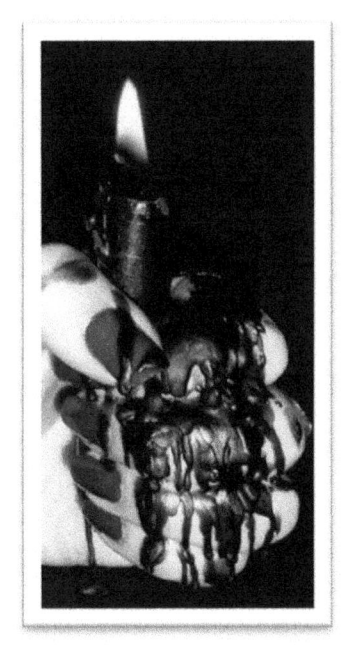

Figure 155 – Between the Devil

AND THE DEEP BLUE SEA

WATERTIGHT

Between the devil and the deep blue sea – faced with two dangerous alternatives. The *devil* is the seam between the deck planking and the top plank of the ship's side. It would have to be watertight and would need filling or caulking regularly, which would require a sailor to stand on the very edge of the deck or even be suspended over the side. A dangerous place to be.

Even though you are going to tell the traveler events, sometimes down to the minutiae, it is important that, if you get the chance, your experience suggests possibilities to lessen the impact of what could be, potentially, a dunking in shark-infested waters. This is the work of the fáidh-gifted and it is achieved by your spaeing of journey cards: with what has traditionally called *the minor arcanum*. I am wary of the ideology of *major* and *minor* as these terms imply that one thing is greater than the other. That is akin to saying a noun is more significant than a verb.

Each sitting with a traveler is a short, but impactful story. Nothing should be of greater precedence than your visitor's safety… unless it is your own and that of those you love.

Please note:
- the *Messenger cards* are rarely (if ever) people
- the four sets of elemental pictograms are words in a sentence
- nothing is interpreted alone
- persons/persons can be, but also are not, gender specific

INTERPRETING SENTENCES AND MIXES

FOOL

With a person card, or the Hermit – someone who will randomly and inadvertently teach the traveler an importance, or will trigger something of importance, but when the Fool is also in this position the traveler does not know the person yet.

With Hanged and Moon – anything from a diving expedition to a person falling from a cliff.

With 8 of Coins, Messenger of Coins – a professional comedian

With 8 of Coins, Ace of Cups – an amateur comedian

With ace of Staves, 8 of Coins – a satirist

With 8 of Coins, Fledgling of Cups, this can represent a cartoonist (usually a satirist)

MAGICIAN

With the traveler, or a card representing a person – someone self-focused, independent and/or displaying a great deal of personal charisma, individually and/or professionally, this means the person, or even the seeker sitting with you, is self-centered (this is as it should be) and self-motivated.

The Magician with the Seer – the person or situation alluded to is unique. I am reminded of profound thinkers, people whose work in the world I have already mentioned. I call them the Great Reflectors.

Lighthouses along the deadly shore of broken ships. From Nan Shepherd to Robert MacFarlane, Lynne Kelly, Martin Shaw, Wendell Berry, Jon Young, Robin Wall-Kimmerer, Ta-Nehisi Coates, Aldous Huxley. People who have broken an anachronous and obsolete dialogue that, to a degree, most of us have fallen prey. Until we wake up.

Words, with this pairing, are beyond most of us. We have had millennia of explanations. Answers when there are none. in the current era. My love, Da Vinci, in others. People who have pulled the mythic rug out from the illusion of separation—the people-trap—from a vast family. Of landscape, sea and impossibly great galaxies. There is an *otherness* to the being of this pair. I have rarely seen them together. I am struck speechless each time.

With Devil – selfishness

With Ace of Swords – a controlling and overtly fussy individual. If it falls with a person, it describes their attitude/energy, they will certainly influence the traveler (for good or ill)

With Chariot – a person who has passed final exams and is now accredited in their field

With events – exploration

SEER

With 2 of Cups – hidden, occulted sexuality, or covert sexual encounter

With 2 of Cups and a person – a mystic, practitioner of revelatory, ceremonial and/or ecstatic rites, psychic and/or philosophically open-minded individual

With Emperor – academic or accredited training in mystery practices: philosophy, anthropology, indigenous lore, medicine, music, science and story-lore

With the Fledgling of Coins – private study in the above

With Hierophant – a public figure, considered acceptably qualified to teach some mystery-practice (in difference to a fraud)

With Sun, 8 of Staves – can represent lands like Egypt, Morocco, Mesopotamia, indigenous desert regions everywhere

With Hermit – older, mystery regions or significant god-sites, usually mountainous or wintery

With Empress – same as the above but more equatorial and tropical

EMPRESS

With Moon and a person, or even illness imagery – hormonal dysfunction

With Ace of Staves – pregnancy

With Hermit and a person – someone older, matriarchal (grandmotherly, or wise woman)

With Seer – a mature, sexuality-assured ciswoman, or person identifying as woman

With Hermit, and in relation to place – majestic geological high places, or deep cave-like environments

With 8 of Staves – agriculturally fecund

With Moon – wetlands, or lush, damp, moist or humid places

EMPEROR

With Justice – Federal or international law or legalities
With 5 of Coins – welfare
With 8 of Staves – local council
With a person card – an individual who works for an institution, or a (usually) bigoted, patriarchal person, the ones who always want to be the boss
With 9 of Swords – treatment in a hospital or other orthodox therapy
With Star /World – cathedrals, old architecture such as the Louvre in Paris, tribal longhouses, machine-made satellites, the Internet

HIEROPHANT

With the Devil – more fundamentalist-type religion, potentially dangerous. A religious institution that tarot dislikes
With Justice – legal marriage of any modality
With the Seer it can represent more than one thing, and attending imagery (and intuition) are necessary to interpret this story: it can represent Judaism (matrilineal), religions or spiritualities that revere a *femininized* concept of deity, or it can also show women-of-the-veil, anyone from a Muslim woman to catholic nuns
With Chariot – it very often represents Islam
With Star – places that are known for their exquisite and grand architecture: Switzerland, Austria, France, Italy, Czech Republic, Jerusalem, Palestine, Sheikh Lotfollah Mosque in Iran, Carcassonne, Petra, Cappadocia, Kata Tjuta, Chichen Itza, Ankor Wat (to name a

few)

LOVERS

With 7 of Cups – choices are illusions, there is only one way to proceed
With a person card – someone of the sign of Gemini
With the Fledgling of Swords – the time of Gemini
With 2 of Cups – a choice between two lovers, group sex or polyamory
With Sun – can be twins
With World – a choice of where to go
This can, occasionally, just represent people who are sexually involved

CHARIOT

With 10 of Coins – caravan, bus, house on wheels, temporary dwelling
With Emperor – passing exams. If it also falls with a 3 of Coins, then it represents acceptance after an interview
With Temperance – passing physical examinations
With Devil, and any pictograms of illness or distress, it is the end of the period. Can also be hazardous travel and dangerous driving
With Strength – can indicate places such as the Middle East, Arabia, parts of North Africa

STRENGTH

With Emperor (also, but in context) – hospitals or the study of physical things. When falling with a person, they can be a stone mason to a grave digger to an architect

With 9 of Swords – physical illness

With 10 of Swords – physical pain

With 10 of Staves – a literally heavy load

With 8 of Coins – bodywork

With 2 of Coins – can be a weight loss program

With 5 of Staves – martial arts

With 4 of Staves – performance such as dance

Falling on the STARGATE, the portal known as ART, is sculpture, metallurgy, or other tactile arts

With Ace of Coins – rock solid or non-specific matter

With Ace of Staves – I have seen it as *new matter* for a traveler who was in the last stages of terminal cancer and wanted to know, from a reading, what would happen after death

With the Devil – undomesticated (wild, although I do not agree to the binary distinction of wild/tame) animals, large animal/s, dangerous animals, like humans, or species trying to defend their territories, family groups, tainted ground

With 10 of Coins it can represent a gymnasium or other fitness studio

With the Moon and the Fledgling of Cups this card has represented sea creatures such as whales

With the Tower it can be either earthquake or blasting as with mining

With the Empress – equatorial lands

With the Chariot – the Middle East, Arabia, Mesopotamia

The Emperor – England, Portugal, Spain, America, Germany, France – any country that has sanctioned the invasion and corporate takeover of another people's lands, usually for profit

With the Sun – desert

With the Star – America, the Arctic or lands around the Arctic Circle, Antarctica

With Sun and Moon – oasis-type environments: desert regions with waterways or desert regions around the Mediterranean such as Morocco

With 8 of Staves – an arid region

HERMIT

NB: in the early Marseille packs this image was known as "THE SPY". As in SPAE, and as such also represents a seer

With any of the Fledglings: a wise, or spae-gifted child, or an older child when relevant to several children in a family

With Star and World – a long way overseas/international

With 7 of Coins – archaeology, geology, history, genealogy or similar

With 8 of Coins – any form of work dealing with that which is old or antique

With 8 of Staves – inland terrain that gets very cold in winter

With 6 of Swords – somewhere prone to cold like Tasmania or New Zealand (a place over water but not far off the mainland) whereas in Europe it can be anywhere from Ireland to the islands of Skye, Man,

Scilly and Lewis. In the USA it could be Manhattan or any other island off an east coast

With 2 of Staves – Melbourne, Adelaide, New York, Chicago, London, Ontario, Moscow, Zurich, Wellington, Tokyo. A large, sprawling city in a place that gets very cold in winter

With Star – alpine places, mountains, stars on snow, a crystal ball or scrying bowl

WHEEL

With Messenger of Staves, Messenger of Coins or Messenger of Swords – wheels on vehicles

With Devil – addiction to gambling, seasonal gluttony or overindulgence, like for christmas

With 5 of Coins – caught in a cycle of poverty

With Chariot/Ace of Coins – a win at gambling, a gain on the stock market or affluence through cryptocurrency

With Empress – a yearly or planting cycle, almanac, indigenous knowledge through the generations

With Moon – a lunar cycle of 28 days, or a lunar calendar

JUSTICE

With Emperor – federal and local government, international legal matters

With 5 of Coins – bankruptcy, forced seizure of property and/or goods, the closure of financial institutions due to recession, eviction supported by police presence, valid or otherwise

With Devil – enforced control, illegal graft, corruption

With 8 of Swords – imprisonment or entrapment

With 10 of Coins – the contract relating to a rented or leased dwelling

With 10 of Cups – the contract or deed of ownership on the sale or buying of a home

HANGED

If *Death* is present it can be self-destruction for a cause or ideal/assassination

With 3 of Swords – separation: no point fighting. Rejection or dismissal

With Moon – diving or fishing

With Death /10 of Swords – can represent the victim of a murder or a suicide by hanging or strangulation, or being pushed off a high place

With Fool and the 4 of Staves – extreme sports such as bungee-jumping, abseiling, free-solo rock climbing, skiing, base jumping

Similarly, with the Star and any pleasure story – parachuting, hang-gliding, any aerial sport or high circus stunts. Stunt work for film or other media

DEATH

Star/Tower/Death – Any shock-and-awe disaster

Devil/Tower/Death – appeared just prior to the London bombing in

2005

5 of Swords/Tower/Death – The use of air-to-ground weapons, incendiary weapons, Molotov cocktails, pipe bombs and any high-powered assault rifles, intercontinental missiles

With Chariot – passing tests or exams

With 5 of Swords, Ace of Swords – war, or violent civilian/military/police clashes. Rubber bullets, live ammo, indiscriminate killings, machete or even bludgeoning. Whatever kills or maims brutally

With Moon – seeming *failure*. Rejection

With 8 of Swords – a stalemate

With Ace of Swords – a natural physical death

With 10 of Swords – violent death. Can indicate self-inflicted by self-injection and overdose as in the case of addiction. Messier types of death, violent accident. Don't be fooled, I have had same with the *8 of Coins* (the woman was an ambulance driver in inner-city Sydney)

Ace of Swords, 9 of Swords, Death – the contemplation of death/suicide

With the 5 of Cups – mourning

TEMPERANCE

With Magician – represents a person involved in alchemy, scientific and medical/practice, or a research chemist

With Emperor – medication or medicine

With Emperor and the 10 of Coins – a medical practice (physical or psychological), a pharmacy or drugstore

With persons and persons – will represent a doctor, pharmacist, chemist, someone involved in medical research

With Devil and a person – will represent a recovering addict or alcoholic

Still with the Devil, where there is no indication of a person or addictive situation, and often *with the 9 of Swords* – a sick person on some form of traditional medication

With the Ace of Staves – verbal exchanges; the dialogue process

With an 8 of Staves – plains, large tracts of farmland, acreage, savannah

DEVIL

With 6 of Coins – corruption/bribery/graft

With Messenger of Coins – problems with car or finances, the black market and the Dark Web

With 7 of Coins – it can represent either a marijuana crop or a form of physical cancer, warts or fungal infestations, infestations of any bacteria or virus

With 4 of Coins – a thing is stuck, unable to move

With Messenger of Staves it is dysfunctional communication or travel delays

With Ace of Swords – fear of violence or the ability to commit violence

With 8 of Staves – the person will need to be careful in relation to property or property dealings. Can represent land and environments poisoned through chemical use or otherwise. Chernobyl, the Marshall Islands, Maralinga, Tahiti, any of many

With a Person of Coins – often a Capricorn person

With Strength – in an environmental sense it can be caves or treacherous, deep places. Also, dangerous, defensive other-than-human-animals, large (with the *Moon* it can be alligators, box jellyfish, sharks and rips) and if showing in a health map it can represent a deep infection or chronic disease of the bone or joints

With Strength and Emperor – dictatorships

With Strength, Tower – mining explosions, strip-mining, can be nuclear meltdown

With Moon – clinically-diagnosed psychiatric disorder

With Moon and the 8 of Staves it can be someone who works with the psychologically disturbed

With Moon and the Emperor – asylums or psychological institutions

With 7 of Cups – delusional behaviors/attitudes

With 10 of Swords – deep pain, extreme violence or violation

With 5 of Swords – violence, a dirty fight, terrorism, bigotry/relationship-related savagery

With 2 of Cups – sexual abuse and/or assault, fear around sex, sexually transmitted disease

With 9 of Swords – insomnia, long-term illness

With 6 of Cups – heavy drug use, pharmaceutical or illicit

With Hierophant – extremist religious ideology or deeply dysfunctional marriage

TOWER

With Ace of Staves – literally: an inferno, a hearth fire, the word fire

With Star – satellite or plane crashes to earth. Missiles, bombs, missile defense systems employed in a war scenario

With Strength – rock explosion as in open-cut mining. A bomb, A mobile telecommunication tower

With 5 of Swords – individually: vicious argument. Large groups: street protest that turn violent, military clashes

With Moon – meltdown, inner explosion. Can be a person or a nuclear reactor. Jaw-dropping storms

Tower/Moon/Star – severe weather patterns

In the place of LIGHTNING, on the STARGATE map – electricity danger of some kind

With the Fledgling of Staves and Tower (anecdotally) – sore throat, laryngitis, tonsillitis

Empress/Strength/Tower – New Zealand or places of high cragged mountains, usually volcanic or on fault lines

STAR

With Coins – technology or technological, scientific or research projects

With 7 of Swords – a commitment of over seventeen years

With 10 of Swords – broken glass

With World/Star – long-distance flights

With an 8 of Coins – can represent an astrologer

With Sun – can represent astrology itself

With Strength – can represent gemstones, geology and seismology

With Ace of Coins – long-term investment; can also represent scientific knowledge or breakthroughs, especially if attended by the Emperor

With 3 of Staves – a coastal place, usually in a clear, warm area

With 2 of Staves – any west-coast city

With 10 of Coins, Emperor – an airport, rail, ship or bus terminal

MOON

With Empress – biological-women's bodies

With the Fledgling of Cups – critters of the sea (not mammals)

With 4 of Staves – full-moon parties, raves and doofs

With 9 of Swords – worry or depression. Insomnia or other sleep-related dysfunctions

With 8 of Coins – often represent night shift work

With 4 of Swords – boredom. The frustration of waiting. Dreaming and sleep-related phenomenon

With Ace of Staves – communication difficulties or misunderstandings, or, conversely, deep levels of communication. The difference will depend on the surrounding images

With 2 of Cups – sexual disappointments or naivety

With 6 of Swords – a boat, surfboard, kayak, or other watercraft

With 10 of Coins – it often represents a spa, sauna or an indoor swimming pool or plumbing

With 2 of Swords – ocean frontage

With 8 of Staves – lakes or large inland bodies of water

With Devil, 2 of Swords – dangerous waters or dangerous, unseen things below the surface

SUN

With Star – astrology, astronomy, navigation, with a sextant or other such devices or knowledge

With Ace of Staves – a biological birth

With Ace of Coins – wealth: rarely monetary or fiscal unless stipulated by cards close by

With imagery of activities (doing and being) this always represents successful outcomes

With Strength – hot, dry, stony places

With Empress – hot, moist places

JUDGEMENT

With the Fledgling of Staves – dental work

With Empress – can represent the seasons of a year

With any activity (being and doing) pictograms (such as the Wheel) – changes, delays, misdirection, or re-directions

With Death – the changes are complete (for now)

With Moon – changes of mood, changes of mind

WORLD

With 6 of Swords – long overseas journey

With Star – the internet, information technology, international flight

With Emperor – international affairs and organizations like the U.N.

With Ace of Coins, Emperor – large financial institutions such as the I.M.F.

With 5 of Swords and/or Strength it can represent a world war

With 10 of Coins – a communal gathering place like a community, evacuation or detention center

With 10 of Coins, Emperor – the dwelling-places of government or organizational bodies

…

STAVES

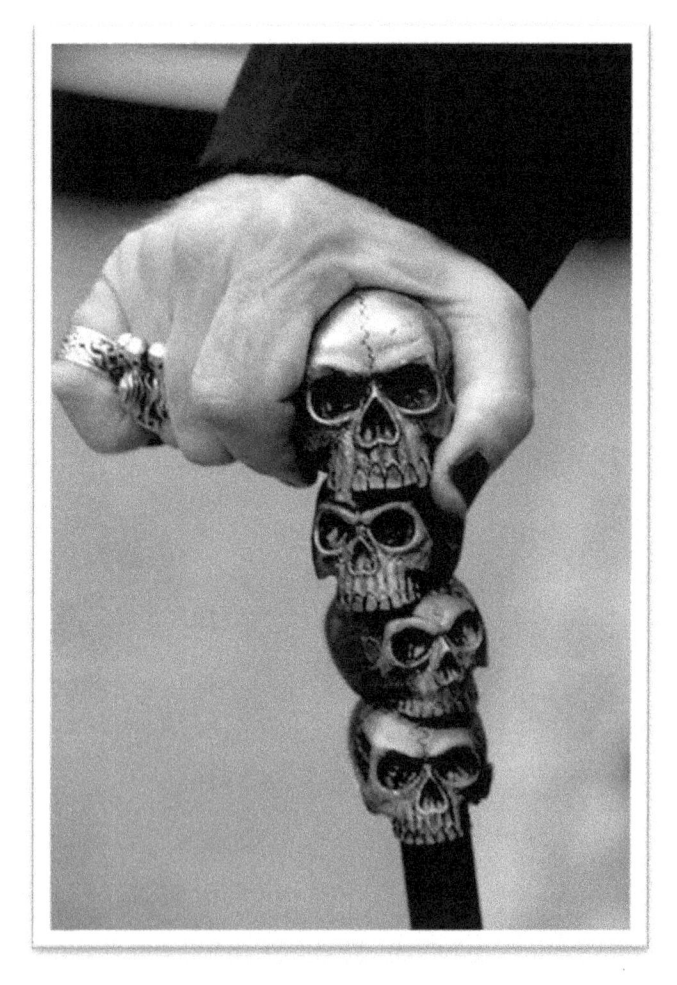

Figure 156 – Staves

Ace of Staves

With Star – internet, media, celebrity, social media influencer

With 10 of Staves – written research or compilation
With Empress – pregnancy
With Sun – birth
With Tower – fire, explosion, catastrophic burning event
With 5 of Staves – a musical band or a dance troupe
With the Fledgling of Staves – a letter, any paper &/or mailed document. Manuscript, screenplay, poetry, oratory
With Ace of Staves, 10 of Coins – a publishing house, newsstand or a library

2 of Staves

With 10 of Cups – the/a person's home is, or will be, in a city
With an individual represented – a person at the pinnacle of their field
With 8 of Staves – inland cities
With World and other significant place information – large cities somewhere else in the world. A journey indicator – like the Messenger of Staves: light-hearted travel, or the Messenger of Coins: a journey for practical or business purposes – would most likely fall close by, often with the Star, indicating flight
With Strength – London, Glasgow or Edinborough, New York, Montreal, Prague, Krakow, Kiev, Moscow and similar
With Strength, Seer – Middle Eastern or North African cities such as Istanbul, Cairo, Jerusalem, Addis Ababa and Petra
With Ace of Coins, Star, Seer – Kuwait, Dubai, Kuala Lumpur, Bali, Tahiti, Hawaii
With Ace of Coins, Star – any extremely brightly-lit capital city:

Perth, Las Vegas

With Star, Hermit – cities such as New York, Zurich, all heavily populate centers of human habitation in mountainous and alpine countries

3 of Staves

With 2 of Staves and the Hermit – a coastal city or town that's cold in winter

With 8 of Staves and the Hermit – an inland city or village that's cold in winter in the same country as the traveler

With 6 of Swords and the Hermit – an island off the mainland of the country of the traveler, never far, also that gets seasonally cold, somewhere like Tasmania off Australia, New Zealand, Victoria Island off Canada, Long Island off New York, USA, Inish Mór off Galway

With 2 of Staves and Empress – a more-or-less tropical destination, in the same country as the traveler

With 8 of Staves and Star – the west coast of a country: Perth, San Francisco, Galway, Lagos, Winnipeg

4 of Staves

With 2 of Swords – a surprise party, or a party next door

With 10 of Coins – opening a shop, restaurant, gallery

With Ace of Staves and the 8 of Staves – an outdoor party or celebration

With 5 of Staves – bands, music, live performance

With Moon – modelling for the fashion or image industry, faces and appearance

With 8 of Coins – a person who works in the hospitalities industry

5 of Staves

With Emperor – red tape, bureaucracy

With 5 of Swords – industrial disputes, strikes, protesting

With a Person or the Fledgling of Swords – can indicate a Gemini

With 9 or 10 of Staves – mess to be picked up

With Strength – physical discipline like martial arts

With 10 of Coins – building materials for an unfinished house or house being renovated

With 7 of Cups – false communication, Mulengro (see Endnotes)

With 8 of Staves – multiple occupancy or community/company title land

6 of Staves

With Emperor – always schoolteacher

With Star and the 5 of Staves – internet chat, email or communication

With Messenger of Staves and the 7 of Staves – a person speaking many languages

With Ace of Staves – a public speaker or public announcement

With places – where a phone call is to or from

With 10 of Cups and images indicates the buying or selling of real estate – an auction

7 of Staves

There are no consistent correlations, *7 of Staves* is a verb. A *doing* or *being* word.

8 of Staves

With 5 of Staves – multiple occupancy, community or company titled property

With Ace of Swords – subdivisions, boundaries or fences in relation to rural land

With 5 of Swords and the Ace of Swords – struggle over borders or boundaries (can be local or international, as this sequence has shown up in relation to the dispute over territory between Palestine and Israel)

With 8 of Swords there will be difficulty with access (road or driveway)

With Emperor – local councils or government lands departments

With 2 of Staves – a small coastal town

With Empress – rural but tropical environments

With Strength – arid landscapes

With Hermit – cold, dry climates

With Empress, Strength – desert, but lush like Kakadu, the Arctic Tundra

9 of Staves

With Ace of Staves, 8 of Coins – can represent a writer of some description who either has *writer's block*, or is having their words censored in some way

With any relationship cards there is communication imbalance

With Justice and any other pictograms representing legal situations – the person to whom the pattern refers is not speaking or refusing to communicate

With illness information (such as the 9 or 10 of Swords) – often represent laryngitis, tonsillitis or some uncomfortable throat or larynx, vocal aberration

10 of Staves

With Emperor – any form of research

With the 10 of Coins – often represents a building being built of wood, or else moving to a new rented or leased dwelling

With Empress – From the responsibilities of motherhood, to those of a busy chef or permaculturist

With Strength and a person – a physically strong individual

Messenger of Staves

With 7 of Staves – a letter, phone call, public speaking, teaching

With Star – airmail, email, online communications mediums

With Ace of Staves – language

With Emperor – learning a language or the study of literature or like subjects

With the Fledgling of Staves (not a child) – communication, a small to medium-sized package or a letter on the way

With a Fledgling card (a child in this instance) – a child who is talkative and able to communicate easily

With Moon – an internal dialogue, psychic or intuitive

communication

With 10 of Staves and World – backpacking

With 10 of Swords – can represent a car accident where damage is incurred

With the 9 of Staves – can represent an inability, or lack of desire, to communicate

Fledgling of Staves

With Strength – time or sign of Leo

With Sun – time or sign of Aries

With Temperance – time or sign of Sagittarius

With Ace of Staves – books or publications

With 8 of Coins – speaking with words

With 4 of Staves – a production has begun. A creative venture has begun

With Moon – descriptive art of any kind

With Tower – sudden, acute illness affecting the throat

With Messenger of Staves or Messenger of Coins – a communication device such as phone, pamphlet or letter (not Internet or email, text or other social media – that would require *Star* to be somewhere close on the map)

Person of Staves 1 and 2

With Temperance – likely to be a Sagittarian

With Strength – likely to be a Leo

With Emperor (or, without any logical reason, *Chariot* or *Magician*) – likely an Aries

CUPS

Figure 157 – Cups

Ace of Cups

With 8 of Coins – for the love of work, work that one loves or amateur work (vocation)

With the Fledgling of Cups and Hierophant – can mean the catholic religion (it's a eucharist/body/blood thing: a brief description of a past even similar to this was seeing *8 of Coins*, *Ace of Cups* and *Hierophant*. I was at a momentary loss and I mumbled aloud *This doesn't make sense unless you're a priest*.

He advised that that he was, indeed, a Melbourne bishop who also had an interest in all things mystical, even tarot, and was involved, unbeknownst to his peers, in a magical order. In all other instances it defines love.

2 of Cups

With the 8 of Coins – can represent the sex industry: the first time I ever realized this was when the 8 of Coins fell on the branch denoting sexuality on the map of the Stargate. The traveler was a *Madam* who managed two pleasure houses. The person in this story could as easily sell sensual, sexy underwear

I have had this card *with Emperor and Ace of Staves* for an academic who writes books about sex and sexuality

With Devil – depraved, forced sexual extremes. Rape

With Devil and the 9 of Swords – can represent sexually transmitted disease

With Judgement and any of the Messengers – easily the transformation into puberty

3 of Cups

With Empress and 4 of Staves – a women's festival or party

With 8 of Coins –represents friends or family in business together

With 10 of Coins – can represent people sharing a rented house or apartment

With Messenger of Staves and distance imagery – represents either people traveling together or people meeting as planned

4 of Cups

With 3 of Cups – reunion, but with unforeseen and additional events in the story

With 3 of Coins – an interview that will result in perks not initially seen. Same applies when with *8 of Coins*

When in conjunction *with 10 of Cups or Coins and Justice* – indicates offers relative to contractual arrangements and alternative opportunities

5 of Cups

With Moon, 4 of Staves or 5 of Staves – can represent the Blues (as a form of musical expression)

With Death – a wake, funeral, or mourning ceremony

With Hierophant or 2 of Cups – indicates past failed relationships or repeat let-downs in a single relationship

With Moon, 9 of Swords – depression or remorse

With Justice – can indicate the loss of a prolonged legal case (the

3 of Cups mean that there would have been more than one instance of appearance, an appeal or an application)

6 of Cups

With 3 of Cups – a reunion

With Moon – things of the past can have a psychological effect on the traveler or person represented, or can be the cause of disillusionment

With Emperor – can represent archives or antiquated people

With 8 of Coins – indicates work within an arcane field such as history, archaeology, genealogy, DNA analysis
With 8 of Cups, Wheel – a return to past work
With Hierophant – a past marriage
With 2 of Cups – a past relationship
With 4 of Staves – a reunion or reunion celebration
With Ace of Staves, the Fledgling of Staves or Messenger of Staves – information or documentation of events to do with the past or history

7 of Cups

With Devil – addiction or delusion and psychosis
With Moon – psychological illness
With Moon and 8 of Coins – a person who works with the people diagnosed with psychic illness
With *Moon and Emperor* – the institution or places of learning associated with psychic illness
With Ace of Staves or the Fledgling of Staves – an imaginative process (or the idea) such as writing a fictional book or story
With Ace of Staves and the Fledgling of Cups – an impressionist work of art or a work of art not based on traditional portrait or landscape
With Ace of Staves and Strength – the idea for any form of 3D art such as sculpture, decoration, 3D printing

8 of Cups

There are no consistent correlations with the *8 of Cups*. You will know the circumstances by whatever falls in this story. *8 of Cups* is a verb, a *doing/happening* word

9 of Cups

If falling with a person – the individual concerned can be either happy, a buffoon or a pompous git
With 10 of Swords, Devil – a situation where cruelty gives pleasure
With Devil, 2 of Cups – a situation where deviate sexual extremes give pleasure
With Devil, 4 of Staves – can represent gluttony or an illicit drug/alcohol event
With Devil, Strength – obesity due to gluttony
With Devil and many other words – a range of self-serving self-indulgences

10 of Cups

With Justice – can be contracts of sale
With Justice, 8 of Swords – delays or constraints concerning contractual property deals
With 10 of Coins, Death (or the 9 of Cups) – the completion of construction of a house
With 3 of Cups – a group reunion
With Moon, 9 of Swords – plumbing or water problems
With Emperor and Tower – disaster will occur involving the

insurance of home and contents issues

With 7 of Swords and either Moon or 2 of Swords – there are thieves in the area of the person's home

With 8 of Swords and any inauspicious information – this person is (for whatever reasons) house-bound

Messenger of Cups

It is of detriment when it shows up *with Moon and 7 of Cups* – opiate-based drug abuse

With 4 of Staves – an invitation

With 7 of Cups – the offer is untrustworthy or comes to nothing

With Hanged and 9 of Swords – someone who gives too much and is easily hurt

Fledgling of Cups

With Death – time or sign of Scorpio

With Moon – time or sign of Pisces

With Chariot – time or sign of Cancer

Also, with Moon – visual arts

With Moon, Emperor – the study of art but, with *7 of Staves*, it is still study (or teaching) but not necessarily through a traditional institution

With Hierophant, Sun – christian catholicism (see *Ace of Cups*), in difference to Judaism or Islam, as the latter do not express their religions through golden artefacts

Person of Cups 1 and 2

With Moon – the sign of Pisces

With Chariot – the sign of Cancer

With the Death – the sign of Scorpio

(The above will depend very much on other attending information)

With 6 of Swords, 10 of Coins – often a person of the sea: a boat, yacht, barge or ship

With 6 of Swords and 4 of Staves – a surfer or someone who gains pleasure from the water

With 8 of Coins and Ace of Cups – from a swimmer to a swimming coach to a plumber, but a professional

With 8 of Coins, Empress – a midwife, perhaps an OBGYN or a gynecologist. Can sometimes represent a medical doctor if around *Temperance* or the *Emperor*

COINS

Figure 158 – Coins

Ace of Coins

With Ace of Staves and an accompanying Messenger of – new matter

With Strength – rock solid, solid rock, stone, foundations (as in a building), geology

With Sun – material wealth

With Justice – money gained through legal means (the sale of property for example)

With Emperor – also represents an official grant or a scholarship

2 of Coins

With Ace of Coins – a large sum of money (in the traveler's considered opinion), or settlement, divided between two or more parties

With 10 of Coins – shared accommodation

With 10 of Coins and Moon – sharing shop fronts or displays

With 8 of Coins – part-time or casual work; unstable employment or financial situation: things can go either way

With 2 of Cups – friends or lovers who share financial things in common

With Moon, 7 of Cups – can represent bipolar symptoms, or some form of delusional behavior

3 of Coins

With 8 of Coins – a job (or some kind of) interview

With Emperor and Temperance – a medical consultation

With home, or dwellings, such as *10 of Coins or Cups*, accompanied by such images as *10 of Staves, Moon, 5 of Staves* – either the building of a place or work/renovations being carried out on a place. The *3 of Coins*, in this instance, is the traveler discussing the plans with the tradespeople

With Justice – legal discussions

4 of Coins

With Ace of Coins – a deposit or part thereof

With Strength – extraneous body-fat, or obesity

With Moon – fluid retention

When representing a person – a miser, or someone holding onto what they have very tightly

With Seer – hidden possessions; same with *2 of Swords*

5 of Coins

With Strength – can represent such dysfunctions as anorexia or bulimia. Starvation or malnutrition

With 7 of Swords and Moon – a theft

With 8 of Swords – indebtedness that one cannot escape, or a heavy fine

With Devil – poverty or financial loss due to obsessive or unwise spending

With Moon – poverty of mind; poverty of emotion; entrenched poverty

With Emperor and Ace of Swords – departmental or governmental cuts to funding

With Tower and 10 of Coins – crashes on a stock exchange (large or small)

With Justice – extreme legal expenses

With Temperance, Emperor – it can represent the state of having no health insurance due to lack of money

6 of Coins

With 8 of Coins – can represent either the wages paid or a person who pays wages

With Magician and a Person card – can represent a human being who patronizes or belittles others (of any species)

With 5 of Coins and a Person card – they value themselves poorly or feels/is impoverished by others or circumstances pertaining to other people or critter-people

7 of Coins

With Devil and 4 Swords – a controlled or dormant cancer

With Devil and other relevant information on the map – any plant crop considered officially illegal: anything from marijuana (which is commonly seen) to the opium poppy and coca plantation

With 3 of Swords and Devil – the removal of a possibly dangerous or carcinogenic growth (mole or tumor) but can as easily be warts. Information surrounding it on the map will advise of the severity of the condition

With Devil and Empress – rampant growth such as occurs in tropical locations; or unwanted growth such as happens with an unwanted pregnancy, mold, fungal infections, infestations, or inundations of any kind except flood

With 8 of Coins – work in a growth industry

With Fledglings as children – growth spurts or a rapidly growing child

With Strength – a person may put on large amounts of weight

With Wheel of Fortune – annual or seasonal growth

With World – population growth of critter-person

8 of Coins

There are no specific correlations – it simply means *work*, or employment, and its interpretation will depend on the circumstances

9 of Coins

With 8 of Coins, Ace of Swords – an editor/editing/censoring

With 10 of Cups or 10 of Coins – a dwelling that is small but adequate

With a person card – an individual who has nothing to prove

With Ace of Staves (and perhaps the Fledgling of Staves) – a publication with no extraneous or unnecessary embellishment to make it appealing

With the Ace of Staves – clear, concise communication

The same as the above applies to any form of art or business

With Star – advertising (or PR) that does not insult the public

With any of the Messengers – quality transportation or a journey that is short but satisfying

10 of Coins

A house of information if attended by *Emperor* or a story of study and learning

With Seer – a place of the study of the ceremony, lore, knowledge based on ancestral teaching

With Temperance – indicates a place where the healing arts are taught

With the Fledgling of Cups and Temperance – a place where visual arts are taught

It is not *10 of Cups* but can become so – an incomplete dwelling

With Emperor – houses where money moves: banks, credit companies. Also, government departments, and such places as school or hospital buildings

With Messenger of Coins – caravan, bus, mobile home

With 5 of Staves and 10 of Staves – a dwelling being built

With 2 of Coins – a shared rental/house; a shared business venture

With Strength – building societies, gymnasiums or other sporting establishments

With Strength, Temperance – places where physical disciplines or therapies of an alternative nature are conducted

With Strength, Emperor – military buildings, physical training institutions

With Justice – a courtroom; the signing of leases or property contracts

With the Fledgling of Cups – Blue Chips. So-called strong investments on a stock market

With 6 of Swords – houseboat, yacht, launch or ship

Messenger of Coins

With 10 of Staves – carrying heavy loads

With 2 of Coins – part-time financial venture

As a form of transportation – a larger vehicle, such as a 4-Wheel drive, a bus or a train

With 8 of Coins – the process of one's work or someone who works with money or within a financial institution

With Justice – the paperwork

With an Ace of Staves (sometimes *Messenger of Staves* or the *Fledgling of Staves*) – a large parcel or package

Fledgling of Coins
> *With the Empress* – the time or sign of Taurus (not Hierophant)
> *With the Devil* – the time of or sign of Capricorn
> *With the Hermit* – the time or sign of Virgo
> *With the Messenger of Staves and the Wheel* – craft markets, fetes, food markets, fairs
> *With Strength* – a big kid, or an adult behaving irresponsibly

Person of Coins 1 and 2
> *With the Empress* – quite likely a person of the sign of Taurus (not Hierophant)
> *With the Devil* – quite likely a person of the sign of Capricorn
> *With the Hermit* – quite likely a person of the sign of Virgo
> *With Strength* – very physically fit
> *With Ace of Coins* – wealthy. Bearing in mind that *wealth* is sometimes conceptual rather than literal, it will always be determined by the traveler's concept of such
> *With 5 of Coins, 9 of Swords* (or *10 of Swords* if severe) – a person with a physical disability, like arthritis or osteoporosis
> *With 7 of Coins* – a gardener, or person who likes to garden
> *With 8 of Coins and 10 of Cups/Coins* – a person in real estate or one who works from home

SWORDS

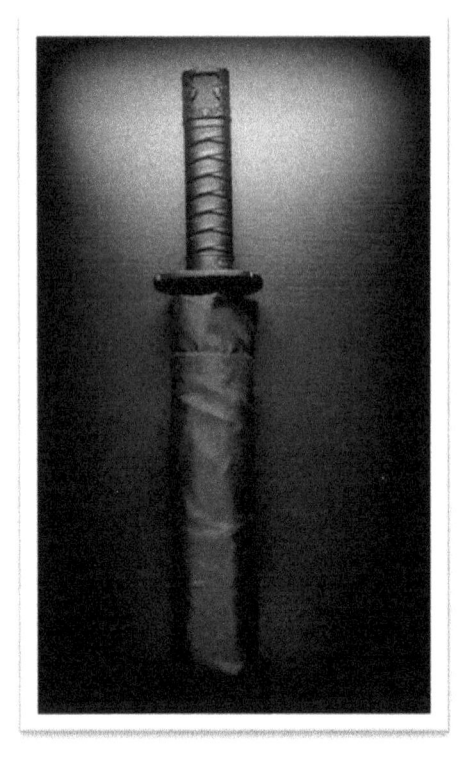

Figure 159 – Swords

Ace of Swords

With 7 of Swords – bound to a commitment and can't escape

With 8 of Staves – boundaries around land or property

With 8 of Staves and the Lovers – sub-division of property

It can literally represent a sword as occurs within traditional martial arts

With the Emperor and 5 of Swords – it can represent a soldier, their training, their weapons, or war itself

With a person card, the individual depicted is quite likely to be an *authority* but that would depend on other information on the map because add a 10 of Swords to this and we have either back pain or cruelty

With 8 of Coins the situation changes again. An example would be *Person of Swords, Ace of Swords, 10 of Swords, 8 of Coins, Temperance* – this person is in the business of healing, utilizing such skills as acupuncture, osteopathy, and chiropractic adjustment

With Death – death

2 of Swords

With Star and any slight medical or health issues – can indicate eye-sight problems or things to do with limited vision

With Moon – it can represent living, or being by or near, the ocean or a large body of water

However, *with Moon, 7 of Swords* – looks to me like a thief is casing a joint under cover of night

With 10 of Cups or 10 of Coins – a dwelling out of sight to the general public

With Seer – no matter what else is around it this indicates unusually mystical situations or people, like poltergeist stuff, or other forms of haunting

3 of Swords

With Tower or ill-health – heart attack or related illness

With Tower, 10 of Coins – the demolition of a building

With a map indicating surgery – the *3 of Swords* is the process of whatever is removed from the body

With Hierophant – marital separation

With 2 of Cups – separation between lovers

With Empress, 9 of Cups – a baby born

4 of Swords

4 of Swords is a verb card. *Doing/being.* This represents waiting and stillness. There are no multiple correlations necessary here.

5 of Swords

With 5 of Staves/Emperor – industrial dispute or strike

With Devil – drunken, or drug related violence; domestic violence

With Tower, Death or any of the Dark-Night-of-the-Soul pictographs – violence, war and/or battle, from local to international

With Ace of Staves, 3 of Cups – debating, choir, musical production, but small

6 of Swords

With the person indicated on the map – surfers, divers or people who fish (with *Hanged*)

With Messenger of Staves or Coins – boats, boat travel, or medium to large watercraft

With Messenger of Swords – fast moving things on or in the water

With Moon and 8 of Coins – a professional fisher, the fishing industry on a personal scale

When Death is assured – it is not going to happen for a long time

With World – long international journeys

With 10 of Coins – houseboat, a water vessel on which one can live or stay awhile

7 of Swords

With Moon – someone disseminating rumors

With 5 of Coins – loss through theft

With the Emperor – can indicate anything from a governmental body planning in secret to graft or corruption

With Devil and 9 of Swords – can indicate a virus or bacteria (can't be seen) that will make someone ill

With people added to the map the variations are endless—

Person, Justice – undercover police, or agency of some description

Person, Justice – the opposite applies: a criminal avoiding justice, or, as in many anti-hero stories, an individual who takes justice into their own hands because of a lack of it, or bias within a system, that does not, otherwise, aid the so-called perpetrator. Examples of this are legion: two come to mind, Claudette Colvin who, in the era of segregation, refused to give up her seat on a bus to a person of pale complexion, and here, in Australia, Eddie Mabo. Wade vs Wade. **Wajeha al-Huwaider**

In most every country or under so many law-abiding states of officialdom, thus termed *breaking the law* is covered by *Justice*

Person, Emperor – a spy or intelligence agent. Probably attended by other information, such as *7 of Swords*, even *Devil With 8 of Coins* – either a person who is a snitch in a work situation, a lazy person (*Devil*) at work who is avoiding their job through subterfuge, a person who is working on the sly, a human being working a black-market job

8 of Swords

With Justice – can indicate anything from legally-binding contract, to imprisonment, to losing a driving license for some illegal reason

With 8 of Staves – stuck somewhere without transport

With Star – a commitment lasting for upwards of seventeen years—like parenthood. Delays, or cancellations, around airports. Computer or network failure

With Moon, 9 of Swords – sleeplessness, or insomnia that is chronic

9 of Swords

With Emperor, Temperance – the health industry

With 8 of Coins – night shift

With 8 of Coins, Temperance or Emperor – a nurse, medic, paramedic, or carer of ill or disabled people: human or critter-cousins

With the Moon – insomnia, disturbing dreams, PTSD and/or nightmares

With 5 of Staves, the Fledgling of Cups, Moon – singing the blues, a R & B or hip-hop, usually including more than one person

With Ace of Staves (and other *Staves* and/or *Messenger of Coins*) – working on a speech

With a Person or people, it is either of detriment or advantage depending on the nature of the map. Some people work things out by so-called worrying at them

With Strength, 10 of Swords – physical pain

With Death, 5 of Cups – mourning, bereavement, unassailable grief

With 7 of Cups – worry over what will not even eventuate

10 of Swords

With 8 of Coins/Ace Swords – a person working in any field such as: tattooing, piercing, acupuncture, chiropractic adjustments

With Star – stabbing pain in the eyes (vision); injury from broken glass

With Judgement, the Fledgling of Coins – toothache

With 3 of Swords – heart attack; radical severance

With Death – violent death

With Death, Hanged – violent, extreme suicide such as would be for suicide bombers

With 5 of Swords – war-inflicted (of whatever kind) injury/pain

With Emperor, Devil – officially sanctioned torture

With a person/people, Devil – either someone being violently abused, or the abuser

Messenger of Swords

With 10 of Coins – a mobile phone or tablet

A vehicle with two wheels – bicycle, motorbike, scooter or skateboard

With a card representing a Person – either an aggressive, quick tempered and/or impatient individual, or one who moves swiftly in whatever circumstance shows itself

With Star – quick or short flights

With Messenger of Staves, and/or Chariot – fast cars

With Strength and the Fledgling of Swords – fast horse or horses. Racehorses

With Magician – brisk, no-nonsense people

With Devil – amphetamine-type drugs or cocaine

Also, *with Devil* and financial gains (*Ace of Coins, 7 of Coins*) or losses (*5 of Coins*) this story relates to horse-racing as a gambling addiction

With 7 of Swords, Justice – lost driver's license because of speeding

With many of the Staves – haiku, short stories, articles, people with quick tongues: often thoughtless

With any Fledgling (a child in this instance) – a hyperactive or one unable to do things at a steady pace

With Justice and other auspicious alignments – a quick resolution to a legal case

Fledgling of Swords

With Person of Swords – a young person, usually pale-skinned and/or blonde (bottled or born)

With Lovers – the time or sign of Gemini

With Star – the time or sign of Aquarius; ideas, a thought process

With Ace of Swords – intelligence, also ideas

With Justice – the time or sign of Libra

With Strength – critter-person, pale-colored, from a lion to a greyhound, to a ginger tomcat

With the Ace of Staves – inspiration, thoughts

With Messenger of Coins – intellectual pursuits

Person of Swords 1 and 2

With Justice – quite likely to be a Libran

With Star – quite likely to be an Aquarius

With Lovers – quite likely to be a Gemini

…

PART NINE

TO WILL, TO KNOW, TO DARE, TO KEEP SILENT

Figure 160 – Know Will Dare Silence

MAPS IN REAL TIME

EXAMPLES OF INTERPRETATIONS

Sweet dreams are made of this
Who am I to disagree?
I travel the world
And the seven seas,
Everybody's looking for something.

Annie Lennox/David Allan Stewart,
Sweet Dreams

What we call HOME—*Earth*—is in the transitional epoch between Expansion and Stone, and it is sometimes difficult to keep abreast of events. In of 2020 we are in a vast forest of world-altering social, economic, ideological upheaval as old guard regimes seek to control and contain an untenable colonialist attitude to wealth, status, food, religion, the imposition on the rights of other species and the unavoidable consequences of environmental apathy.

As fáidh-born and elder lore-holders, what kind of a teachers are we if we remain mired in tired terminology? If we disregard rights to gender equality, queerness, individual quirkiness, and individual expression and if we shut our mouths relative to what tarot is? There is always backlash to issues of significance, and now is as important as any other historic moment to get this work right. To update our understanding of what is acceptable.

You who are learning to become fáidh-skilled, are also wayshowers. You have a responsibility to change your language. To not sit idly in the mold of *Matryoshka* dolls, rather to really spae, to question everything you might have been told will make you popular or financially secure (if such a thing exists). We are on the historical brink of earth shifts, and the environmental refugees will shatter preconceived ideas of border and ethnicity. There is a time for truth-telling. For recognizing that we are animals even though, like Srinivasa Ramanujan, we seem capable of wonders. Even though I can cite the *Danyang-Kunshan Grand Bridge* as a feat of the extraordinary, the same could be said of the amount of weight carried by one ant.

Gender has not, to my knowledge, been discussed in traditional tarot circles, and the mapping and charting of events has not changed, is not questioned. I must do this. I am constantly amazed at inequality and its attending violence and assumptions of rights. It is nonsense. Bigotry is nonsense. So many of the *do-not-pass-go* dynamics, not *tapu*, are currently acceptable. The use of cybercrime, the gathering of personal data through social media, the use of robotics to calculate debt or statistics (*robodebt,* in Australia), homelessness because we are forbidden to hunt, fake news, algorithms, the addition to food of carcinogens, the trade in cosmetic surgery and medicine for the gratification of the few. Work it out, those who seek to apply this witchcraft to your lives. This is new to us. Such as this must, by the very nature of tarot, change from moment to moment.

The idea that other species are less important to us is deplorable. And ignorant. During the bushfires here, in Australia, with those out of control in New South Wales covering a larger mapped area than the entire country called Wales, media only mentions loss of human life and habitat. That these fires, the European floods, ice storms and arctic vortices are now common, should be a wake-up call to all of us, to be courageous enough to say what we know is to come.

To dare to warn.

To adjust our personal stories accordingly.

REALTIME (AS WE UNDERSTAND IT)

Three explicit, *realtime*, maps. I recommend that you record the meaning of each map, and that you lay down the individual pieces of these puzzles respectively because your first question is likely to be *How does this person spae this?*

By contemplating the map, holistically, you'll understand. You'll recognize, then, how one piece of information melds with others. It is like a medical diagnosis where a healer takes several variations of the same, or interconnected, observations into account, to give an accurate, appropriate cure. Like a jigsaw puzzle cut-out's completed picture.

These are consultations utilizing whatever maps available to you, and of course, invent patterns that please you, because it's easy to do that and still correctly prophesy.

Reminder – *no card is interpreted in isolation*

Any map will, in most cases, tell you *one* thing, *one* event. One immediate fate.

First thing—Observe all the pictures on the map, contemplate your sensations and feelings and understand, in essence (because you have learned all the many various meanings of the pictograms), how they fall together to tell either an exact series of events, or one specific event, then, until the questions you, as a fáidh-trained seer, need to remain unbiased. Although aware of thoughts and sensations, the traveler is silent. Quite often what you spae and say will trigger an emotional reaction, and you could need time out for weeping and tissues.

EXAMPLE SESSION FOR DOM

MAP 1 – DEAD RECKONING

Figure 161 – Dead Reckoning for Dom

1: 5 of Swords
2: 5 of Coins
3: 10 of Coins
4: Ace of Staves
5: Chariot
6: 4 of Coins
7: Emperor
8: Lovers

9: Person of Saves 2
10: Devil
11: Person of Swords
12: 6 of Staves
Past: 3 of Swords
Present: Person of Staves 1
Future: 7 of Coins

At a Glance

Dom is a Leo. That's a Fire Sign. They have achieved success already. Money, however, is an issue and, with the Emperor and the 4 of Coins their choice is hindered by financial lack. An Air Sign (perhaps Gemini) person is a quizzical addition to the map, their involvement not yet established.

Breaking Things Down

What has influenced the interpretation? What are you looking for on the surface of things in relation to the images before you?

The central theme of the map, and the three pictograms covering the packs of past, present and future, indicate a seeming progress.

Note the position of the *Chariot*, telling of hard-won achievements that are influencing current events. Let your eye wander from this to the *4 of Coins*.

Do you recognize what's happening? Can you spae the problem?

I have not mentioned the loss or separation (*3 of Swords* in the past) because, as yet there is no indication of its significance.

I'd say *Your position in life, right now, Dom, is hindered. That can be by a lack of money, acceptance, evaluation and there is much fear or bigotry. Your words – either spoken or written – will have consequences.* This is due to understanding the collusion of *Lovers*, *Devil* and *Ace of Staves*, the latter also giving cause for optimism as does the pictogram covering the pack of the future.

The *10 of Coins*, however, indicates that we're not talking about an owned home, here but rather a rented dwelling or temporary accommodation.

The other *Staves Person* (2) lies in the place of hope and fear and this is interesting, but of unknown impact.

Would the traveler have the same difficulties if they were a bloke? It's worth your consideration because, yes, this is what gender discrimination can look like.

This is a typical map of an individual who has recently been accepted into an educational/institutional program (*3 of Swords, Emperor*) based on whatever the criteria of the institution, but has to find the money to complete a degree as they have relocated from an unknown place—can often apply to a person who has been granted asylum—and has to prove themselves both financially, and in reference to qualifications gained in another country. They are torn between living here and being in their homeland. They will experience bigotry and obstacles. I want to know more about the Gemini, because with all those *Staves* there is a connection with communications. They have completed a phase of training, or preparation, and has more to come (as occurs when an individual is at university), but they have a paper or thesis (*Ace of Staves*) to write, or a proposal of significance.

Does the map indicate someone working in a poverty-stricken area as the central theme of *5 of Swords/5 of Coins* indicates? The *Ace of Staves* shows they are writing/communicating about such. There is threat. More will show itself in subsequent maps.

What is obvious, by the *3 of Swords*, *Lovers* and *10 of Coins*, is that they are not living in their family home and, with the *Devil*, both their environment and general situation is threatening or claustrophobic.

With the *3 of Swords*: reserve your opinion until you have read the map of the PAST. It will indicate whether circumstances are environmental or personal.

What is also obvious is that this is not a map indicating ill-health, as could happen when *Devil* and *Emperor* appear together, and there is also no indication that the institution is law.

FINAL COMMENT

Dom will, retrospectively, have the realization that any hardships, most certainly challenging, have—for now—passed. This is in direct reference to the *7 of Coins*—the focal card of the pack representing the FUTURE, as each of the stabilizer cards is a part of each map.

When you have deciphered all there is to unpack from each of the three maps you pick up the cards and hand them to Dom to shuffle again.

...

MAP 2 – THE GROVE FOR DOM

Figure 162 – Grove for Dom

1. Ace of Cups
2. 3 of Staves
3. 9 of Cups
4. Strength
5. Person of Coins
6. 4 of Coins
7. Messenger of Cups
8. 9 of Coins
9. Judgement
10. Person of Swords
11. Tower
12. World
13. 6 of Coins
14. 9 of Swords
15. 5 of Swords
16. Death
17. Messenger of Swords
18. Moon
19. Hierophant
20. 5 of Staves
21. Person of Wands 1

At a Glance

This second map, for Dom, shows a marriage, or marriage-like situation, is in discord. The whole middle row shows environmental disaster, looking suspiciously like a hurricane and given a female name (as so often happens). The map does not indicate in what capacity the traveler acts, although both the earlier map and the central theme of the layout indicate that there is a crisis of funding, or aid, and that would not show itself here unless the traveler has an involvement in this but, in difference to such organizations as Médecins Sans Frontières, more in the capacity of aid distribution. That they do this in a smooth, quality, fashion, is based on honor and compassion, is obvious.

The top line changes the map. The layout indicates that Dom will live a great deal of their lifetime away from home, but that home is secure. There is a big, strong, solid, dependable Earth sign person in Dom's life, who does not appear *to participate in Dom's involvement in anything other in this map. The top line however, whichever way I look at it, is about love.*

Breaking Things Down

Look back at Dead Reckoning and note how things have suddenly opened out.

Note the foundation: *Hierophant, 5 of Staves, Person of Staves* (Dom). The *Hierophant* indicates a marriage, or marriage-like situation that is not in detriment but that is quite complicated. The *5 of Staves* verifies that. I am no longer just looking at this map in isolation. I put two and two together based on the first map.

The central line of pictograms, in three groups: In this instance the *Person of Swords* no longer looks like a human person. This is a disaster of massive proportions that has a feminized name, as do many hurricanes, cyclones, and violent storms. The fact that in the first map they were messy by nature is an understatement, only from a human perspective. Storms do what storms do.

The *6 of Coins*, *9 of Swords* and *5 of Swords* indicate aid provided to those battling despair, *Death*, *Messenger of Swords*, *Moon* indicate how quickly this event happens, and how deadly.

From a personal perspective it has all the appearance of either Hurricane Katrina, Cyclone Debbie, Hurricane Loreno, a Polar Vortex, the wildfires that decimated much of Australia in 2019, and corona virus of 2020. Although we are learning from the past, this story is in the future, so it may be like these but it's yet to come.

How do I know it is devastation by water or ice, and not some other natural disaster? The *Tower* is *not* with *Strength* (which can represent seismic activity such as earthquake or volcanic activity), therefore the devastation may have begun with a quake, but it is the *Moon* (water) that does the damage (it is not a mudslide disaster either because *Moon* and *Strength* don't fall together).

Now look at the top line. Spae how calm it seems compared to the center? This reflects, in this instance, the love and backup in Dom's life.

The *Messenger of Cups*, *9 of Coins* and *Judgement* indicate that they bring poise and honesty/quality to the situation, whereas the *Ace of Cups*, *3 of Staves* and *9 of Cups* indicates either a distant achievement and/or love at a distance, and both can be mentioned here as being relevant.

Strength, Person of Coins, 4 of Coins? Well, look for yourselves... this person exudes fortitude and dependability. No matter what their relationship to your visitor, they do *not* show as a problem.

...

MAP 3–FAMILIAR FACES FOR DOM

Figure 163 – Familiar Faces for Dom

1. Person of Cups
2. 4 of Cups
3. Young Staves
4. 10 of Staves
5. 2 of Staves
6. 10 of Swords
7. 6 of Swords
7. 2 of Swords
8. Messenger of Coins
9. Moon
10. Hierophant

At a Glance

This one had me perplexed for a moment but, on further contemplation, things become clear. The sea is unpredictable. No one should ever turn their back on the sea. Ocean is going to cause some major damage in the future. The Water Sign person (Pisces, Cancer or Scorpio) or the person associated with water will, therefore, take this into account regarding oceanic phenomenon. I'm rather excited by now. Dom is cool, and is involved with diverse and interesting people.

Breaking Things Down

Are we still in the reading for Dom? Yes, we are.

So, who is this *Person of Cups*? And why are they significant? Considering the previous maps, it's easy.

We have a natural disaster by water – hurricane or flood. Many critters are injured, in need, or dead.

This information explicitly discusses a Water Sign person, or one associated with the sea.

The top line shows their research and written reports. It indicates a coastal environment, or a city tapestried with water, like Venice or Amsterdam, Port au Prince or Fukushima.

The bottom line indicates coastal adaptation from flooding or storm. Erosion from when the big sea arrives. The *6 of Swords* beside the *2 of Swords* and the *Messenger of Coins* can tell of a boat or other seafaring craft.

Hierophant is again present, indicating some form of marriage or religion. I'll remind you here that this can be a legal collaboration and/or a humanitarian quest or undertaking.

And Another Perspective

On a different note, but worth bringing up because you'll get maps that are this interesting. Two things: one is an indication that the *Person of Swords* has done the research necessary to present (*Hierophant* can be a conference or parlay amongst several people holding some superiority complexed religious high ground) to an environmental group, specifically about oceanic life. This person could easily be advancing a cause against deep-water sonar use and its effect on our ocean-going kin, or the opposite: I have recently watched a documentary on the Inuit and their demands for fishing and hunting rights, in alignment with the traditional people of those lands. Interestingly, *Hierophant* can represent the seeming good will of groups protesting this practice.

Japan presenting documentation regarding their right to hunt whales for *scientific purposes*. Norway doing the same, for ancestral reasons, as are the Inuit and other indigenous hunter-gatherers.

You may be confused because this is on paper, but you won't be when this traveler sits at your table.

...

MAP 4 – STARGATE FOR DOM

Empress
Magician
Star
Devil
Person of Staves 1
3 of Staves
7 of Swords
2 of Staves
Death
Messenger of Coins

Figure 164 – Stargate for Dom

At a Glance

Has Dom gone through gender reassignment? Looks that way. Has the process been difficult? With the Devil card in this position, yes. Will this sort itself out? Dom is temporarily discombobulated but that doesn't last. They are very sure of their research and, with a little weirdness from the public over and done with they continue on with their lives. The only thing that is an oops-factor is LIGHTNING. What is Death doing? Will there be some sort of technological crash? This is BIG but it doesn't seem personal, like a system crash. Someone of Dom's intelligence (and I do spae them as such) would have their data backed up, and in this currently-defined twenty-first century many people have more than one device anyway.

Now...

I'm writing this bit on my birthday, and a friend comes and drops me off a gift. They are going through gender reassignment themselves and I show them this. That LIGHTNING portal? Death? Do people of unspecified gender get death threats? All the time. ALL THE TIME. Just take it into consideration, because about now, with this, I'll be talking to the traveler, suggesting they be aware.

Breaking Things Down

Initially I ceded that it is Dom in the middle of the map. They showed up previously, but in the position of *hopes* and *fears* in the Dead Reckoning map. The very issue of so much information on them here (the story oozes the information that it's all about them), suggests the person is either Dom or a highly relevant other.

Look at HOME (living places, environment, or the landscape/dwelling/situation as a foundation). The *Empress* means many things but, in this position, it shows a place of lushness, fecundity, sensuality and/or luxury. Or it's the world of womankind, and all that is represented by the concept of *her*. TIDE shows a completeness that does not require breaking down. Is this physical? Of course. Is it also a state of consciousness? Of course.

Now let your eyes take in ART (love, sexuality and sex, beauty, eroticism, art, femininity, fecundity, fertility, motherhood and birth, feminization). *Devil* is prejudice. *Devil* is fear, *Devil* is bigotry and *Devil* is religious misappropriation based on doctrinal interpretation. I'm reminded of the disgust directed to women undergoing abortion, the trade in designer vaginas and FGM, and I'm also aware of malevolence directed to people of gender diversity where ambiguity still hinders acceptability. Will Dom have a hard time here? Yes. Could it even be with their own mother? Yes.

NAVIGATION, PROTECTION and STONE are all indicators of place and vision. None of the images presented are in detriment. Whether the Star pictogram is flight or film, PR or place, it is graced. The *3 of Staves* simply indicates both distance or timing, while the *2 of Staves* is a city of age and establishment, like New York, Geneva, Paris, London, Prague, Amsterdam. It's not very Australian, in STONE, because cities here are under two hundred years of settlement. That's too young to be considered… by me anyway.
Dom may very well be living in Sydney.

As I wander the inter-orbiting network of the Stargate, to EXPANSION, the *7 of Swords* is either snooping, or the necessity to resolve arguments.

Considering the *Fledgling of Coins* in the place of the Seed, and the *Messenger of Coins*, in CHALLENGER DEEP, I'm not worried, and neither will the traveler be. They will just get on with it.

...

MAP 5 – HORSE LATITUDE FOR DOM

Figure 165 – Horse Latitude for Dom

1. 5 of Swords
2. Strength
3. Person of Coins
4. Ace of Coins
5. Justice
6. Chariot
7. 10 Cups
8. Person of Staves 2
9. 6 of Staves
10. Ace of Staves
11. Temperance

At a Glance

In a previous map/s there was mention of the Person of Coins and this time the information relevant to them comes to light.

Who are they? A fighter? A warrior? A military person? I love them! The entirety of the HORSE LATITUDE indicates that Dom has a champion. That it's okay to have them do certain amounts of work, legal, monetary, in the form of a settlement. It is always interesting when the warning is of an event (or sequence) is productive. The traveler is being asked to, in some way, allow. For the earth person to stand for them, to draw them into their home venture, to partner with them, in earned trust, sufficiently that they agree to the other representing them in a sale or purchase of place. As a follow-on to the Stargate I can also spae that a legal suit may very well have been represented by the Devil in ART—slander—and that this is resolved.

This is what I call a reverse warning insofar as the traveler knows, or will know, this earth person and they would be wise to allow them to mediate or negotiate on Dom's behalf. They will come out of any legal process unscathed, happy and with a victory.

Breaking Things Down

The top line: *5 of Swords* with *Strength* is a *rammy*—a fisticuffs—heavily populated with people-critters or gang warfare. Put these together with a person and you have a warrior. Add that to the *Ace of Coins* (can mean money or capital but can as equally represent knowledge) and *Justice* and you have a very proficient individual.

The second line shows your visitor's response. They are happy with the outcome of a difficult time (*Chariot*, *10 of Cups*). No doubt at all that they are a writer, journalist, or communicator (*Person of Staves*, *6 of Staves*, *Ace of Staves*).

The foundation, *Temperance*, shows the balancing and harmonizing effect as a result of the *Person of Coin's* involvement.

Again, Dom shuffles, and cuts into three packs. I ask them to choose one of the packs. Once they've picked, I lay the unchosen piles to one side. The pack Dom chose is spaed, in the described format, until the entire sequence is complete, providing anything else required to complete the story.

I'll tell you now, that the pictorial maps I'm showing here are not random. I'm reading for a flesh-and-blood Leo person, and this is exactly what happens. I couldn't invent this stuff.

...

MAP 6 – CONTINUUM FOR DOM

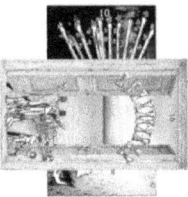

Figure 166 – Continuum for Dom

1. 10 of Staves
2. 10 of Cups
3. 5 of Staves
4. Person of Staves 1
5. World
6. Ace of Coins
7. Ace of Swords
8. Person of Coins
9. 3 of Cups
10. Hermit
11. Messenger of Coins

At a Glance

This has all the appearances of a long-term view of destiny and it is very satisfactory. There is a sense of achievement in worldly matters that will over-ride anything else that may come from following maps.

Breaking Things Down

Dom needs only continue what they are already doing (*Messenger of Coins*). The *Person of Coins*, ally in the previous map, is shown here as being in the same house or place-situation– due to the central theme of *World*, *10 of Cups*, *10 of Staves* and *Ace of Staves* this person shares the traveler's life. Now this life could be an actual dwelling (as indicated by the *10 of Cups*) or the home/world that they occupy together. That they do/will know each other for an awfully long time is indicated by both the *World* (literal or longevity) and *Hermit* (can represent a long time, old age, an elder). *Hermit* also applies to an individual with nothing to prove. The *Ace of Swords* indicates both Dom's authority and their awareness of boundaries. This can harmonize, also, with the *Hermit*, indicating that both people can respond individually to events.

The *10 of Cups* coupled with the *10 of Staves* can also be interpreted in an altogether different fashion, particularly being followed by the *Ace of Coins*, insofar as it can indicate the building or renovating of a house for sale or profit. It can indicate that the property is a place of solidity and security, away from the *5 of Staves*. And, with the *3 of Cups* in the position of hopes and fears, a place of reunion, and/or a gathering place of likeminded others.

MAP 7 – QUESTION FOR DOM

Until now Dom hasn't said anything, but now they ask: "You never mentioned children. Will I have children?"

Figure 167 – Question for Dom

ANSWER: No. You'll get a rescue dog—or maybe rescue a horse from going to a knackery—whatever, they'll be with you for life and it will break your heart when it's their time to die. Leave it alone until you decide to get another one.

Breaking Things Down

The *6 of Coins* indicates what the traveler pays for the species-cousin-critter. The heartbreak with animal cousins is that they don't live as long as us. The *3 of Swords* is the separation issue in a nutshell. The *8 of Cups* explains that it'll be quite a while before the traveler gets over the loss. *Ace of Staves* is that they will, but the entire story indicates they will never quite get over the loss.

Tarot does not put one species above another. If there was going to be a child that would have been mentioned in part one of the reading. Quite often, however, Dom won't have heard that.

...

EXAMPLE SESSION WITH JESSE

MAP 1 – DEAD RECKONING FOR JESSE

Figure 168 – Dead Reckoning for Jesse

At a Glance

Jesse's an Aries and is involved in a legal case. Victory is assured but for the present the challenge is fraught with discord. At first glance I spae the 5 of Cups and understand that this legal matter is associated with the past, but I don't know what yet. It is difficult to place a gender on either Jesse or their partner, the Water Sign person, as both are people-critters. Jesse has sadness or disappointment behind them, either a loss or grief over a death or ending, and their future is, as yet, hidden, or obscure.

Breaking Things Down

Jesse, here, is represented by the stabilizer card. There's no need to muck around in the mess of how difficult the legal matter is. *Chariot/Tower*, in relevance to the triplet of *2 of Coins, Justice, Death*, is extremely significant, and this triplet also indicates a partnership or the dividing up of money/material goods involving either the justice system or police.

The *Star*, at this stage, means many things, from the end of a long process, to flight away to an altogether different destination than the rural one (*8 of Staves*) in which the present scenario is unfolding, a plane crash that requires an enquiry, even a hint at astrology (reference *Seer*, later) but I'll reserve my judgement until I learn more. The *Messenger of Cups*, in the place of self, indicates a time of trust and *Strength*, as the outcome (which of course, still is malleable) seems to indicate a solid conclusion to current issues.

In the destination of place is a *Person of Cups*, but present, also, is another *Person of Cups*, and this human being shares Jesse's environment, although the relationship is not, as yet, obvious.

…

MAP 2 – GROVE FOR JESSE

Figure 169 – Grove for Jesse

At a Glance

Jesse will rent a house or studio from which they conduct private business. It looks busy. Both a writing project, and a connection with pain that is satisfying, such as tattooing, piercing, will cause pleasure and satisfaction.

Four other events: a reunion, or gathering of seeming collaborators, will end in disappointment, the Water Sign friend *going through changes that will have unforeseen consequences, rather happily so, an Air Sign person who, without knowing why, moves away, and an emotional separation (bet you that's the legal drama in the map of the present) costing heaps which means that Jesse's superannuation (money for their retirement) is hit hard.*

Breaking Things Down

The triplet of *10 of Coins*, the *Fledgling of Coins* and Jesse, represent Jesse's main place of living and/or working. The *3 of Swords*, *5 of Coins* and *Hermit* represent poverty into old age. The *Person of Swords*, *Fool* and *3 of Staves* indicates an unknown person at a distance, and the *Messenger of Staves*, *3 of Cups* and *8 of Cups* is that disappointment with the reunion or group of people, all seemingly on the same page.

The foundation triplet—pleasure in pain—is blatantly obvious. It is not acupuncture or chiropractic, osteo, or physio work as there is no *Temperance*, which would, of course, indicate a healing technique.

...

MAP 3 – HORSE LATITUDE FOR JESSE

Figure 170 – Horse Latitude for Jesse

At a Glance

Legal recognition, a clear road ahead.

Breaking Things Down

Top line— *3 of Coins* is a professional discussion – *Moon*, souped together with *Justice*, *Chariot* and the *9 of Cups* indicates an excellent legal outcome. The second line: sees the back-and-forth – or return journey – to the city (*Wheel*, *2 of Staves*) as effortless, and Jesse is in their element (*6 of Staves*) and comfortable with this. After a time of relaxation (*4 of Swords*) Jesse adapts to this next phase of life in full independence, and with self-determination and a well-earned self-respect. The *Star*, again, features prominently and reflects a clear future.

...

MAP 4 – STARGATE FOR JESSE

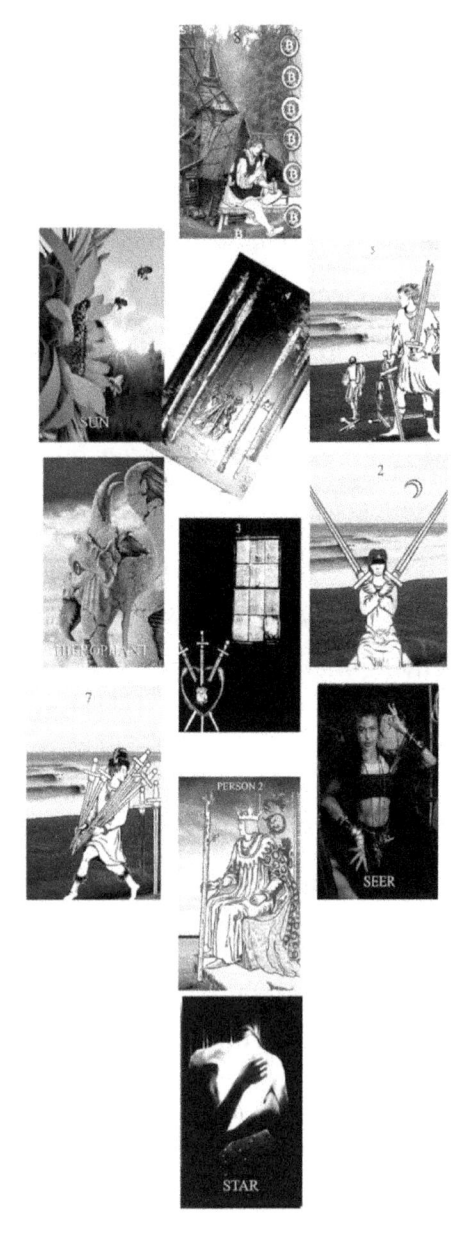

Figure 171 – Stargate for Jesse

At a Glance

Other than the quizzical nature of the 3 of Swords in the CORE, this map is fabulous. There is sense of finally being oneself and understanding riches of a philosophic and, not including money, in the nature of being. I'm interested, however, in the maps that the traveler also displays. That Star is moving you with the wisdom of a sextant. They will be a parent, whether of a biological child or a project, is irrelevant. I get a strong hit from this that they'll land at their next home, and in which life will be right up there with the best of them.

Is it pointless to suggest they look after both their physical heart and their emotional grief at having left the place they may have called home, for this better life? I'll do both, anyway. There's likely to be a child or children from a past relationship to consider. We never get over leaving them, and we never stop loving them, despite these changes.

Breaking Things Down

The *Star* features here as their way of life/living environment. It can also represent fame and or celebrity status. They are obviously involved (*Seer*) in covert femme-type matters and (*7 of Swords*) are careful with whom they discuss this, and the way they do so. This is likely to be one of two things: a. a pregnancy/birth, that is unusual, but becoming normalized as we move through society's pathologically religious roadblocks or b. work (cosmetic or plastic surgery, fillers, injectables) being undergone privately.

The *Hierophant* indicates a future marriage dynamic—either involving the past or resulting from personal dislike of the institution, or family involvement with the religious elements of the traveler's loving partnerships. The *Sun* represents two things: a) long-term ongoing relationships with a child or children, human animal or other and b) success within an established industry.

The *5 of Swords* is not a bother, it simply indicates that transactions and communication of a confrontational nature take place online, rather than in person, whereby the *8 of Coins*, is both their intellectual work, and the successful outcome to ART.

Getting out of a past partnership (or contract) has liberated them and, working as they are, in a freelance style, is perfect for both career and self-worth.

...

PART TEN
DOCKING IN A SAFE HARBOR

Figure 172a – When to Trust

WHEN TO TRUST

A GARDEN OF CAVES

My first book on tarot, *Tarot Theory and Practice*, 2007, was just like this, insofar as I thought I shouldn't, or couldn't, write it. That stabbing the words onto paper would be akin to capturing a wild thing, and a mystical system of orality, into some trap, a gentle wild thing—wolf, crocodile, orca, golden eagle—in a zoo, just so I can say *See? I know about these things.* Or so you can read it and say, *There, I am fáidh-gifted.* You very-well could be, and I might know nothing. But today I'm just about to close the laptop for a while because I have a traveler is due to arrive. They didn't understand, when I read their future a few months ago, that their romantic, intimate partnership would turn violent. How could that be real? They are in love. They are a lawyer, their lover isn't. But the drug *ice* can get anyone. It has. And so, we will, today, spae if there is anything to learn from this personal shock of unexpected violence. And what comes next.

Often it is the small things: the warning not to drive too fast and the traveler coming by tram because they didn't heed it. Didn't realize that they saw their own future catastrophe, seeming small except they also drive an ambulance for a living and they now don't have a license. I wonder, then, if anything is little. If you can have a small rape, or a bit of persecution, just a few years in detention for daring to escape certain death in a country that once housed your laughter, and your great grandparents. If a hill, now bombed to rubble, that your ancestors rendered homage as a garden of caves, was ever insignificant.

Twice now I have thought it impossible that I both could or would write about tarot. Just goes to show how constantly one can fool oneself into perceived limitations.

But hear me out: should you be fáidh-skilled, and tarot kicks in for you, you take care not to burn.

Even now, after all these years, I take a deep breath when people—strangers—are due to arrive, and sometimes I catch myself toying with the idea of retiring, but from what? Me?

People everywhere, are under all the usual stresses, likely to hot up in the next few decades, and you have the right to say no, to be sick, tired, over it, frustrated at people's anxiety, demands, stupidity, ignorance, neediness; to ask that if they have a cold they not come. To be unavailable or otherwise inclined to make a few talismans, hang out by a hearth with other fáidh-born, speculating on ancestry.

CERTAIN GODS WILL TEACH YOU

The pictograms, in their groupings and positions on specific maps, expose destiny. Fate. Other senses are always at play – clairvoyance (clear and psychic sight), clairaudience (clear and psychic hearing), clairsentience (clear and psychic sensory perception) and always when you look at a map a multitude of other faculties are at work. For me it's clairolfaction. The so-called dead will rattle you with their incessant desire to let the person seeking your spae-gift know they are around. The earth-self will speak pleasure or pain. Unknown people, from the future, will tell you their names. Unborn children will explain, to the grieving woman who recently miscarried, why they chose not to want a body right now. Certain gods will teach you. Alternate selves of the traveler will tell all about themselves, and who they are, and where they live and what they do, and the secrets that only the alternative traveler can know.

I have stared, dumbstruck, when an unsuspecting first-time seeker says "So, do you just read tarot?" as though the skill of looking beyond the world-as-it-seems, and life of individuals and nations, and knowing what will happen, and then *having* it happen, is the same as cooking spaghetti.

THE PLATEAU

Each of you, who pass the *PLATEAU*, mentioned way back at the start, have my most profound respect. Those of you who can heal – often without knowing – a distress and a dilemma that is yet to occur because you spae it coming, and the person you read for knows, then, that the thing is destiny. I bend the knee to those of you who have the courage to take the risk of feeling foolish, because what we do is both an art and a science and it has been disrespected, feared, even persecuted for millennia.

Tarot is like a crop circle – the universe's palette: grasses. The unraveling of *What ifs* and *maybes* into a paradox of the unanswerable. Its presence leaves us feeling touched by an awesome wildness.

The focus of this book is the changing patterns of both liberation and gender. While many are still caught in the *christmasness*, and *white-lightedness,* and *It's a boy!* story, at the birth of a person, a fáidh-born, fáidh-gifted and fáidh-trained person is not.

The reality of us as a species must be considered with every stranger that sits opposite us at our table. They are not us. Many are nothing like us. Many think they are and will impress themselves with anything from their *kundalini yoga* story, to their *christ-consciousness* story. Most of the time you'll let it go. Sometimes that's not going to be the story you, and tarot, throw back at them. When you learn a thing, and you know—in your rivers, meat, marrow and dust—that what you have is real, the hypocrisy of agreeing to the delusion will take its toll. Do I leave you with that as a warning?

Yes.

...

THE DARK NIGHT OF THE SOUL

It's the heart afraid of breaking, that never learns to dance
Its the dream afraid of waking, that never takes the chance
It's the one who won't be taking, who cannot seem to give
And the soul afraid of dying, that never learns to live

Writer, Amanda McBroom
Sung by Bette Midler,
The Rose, 1979, based on the life of Janis Joplin

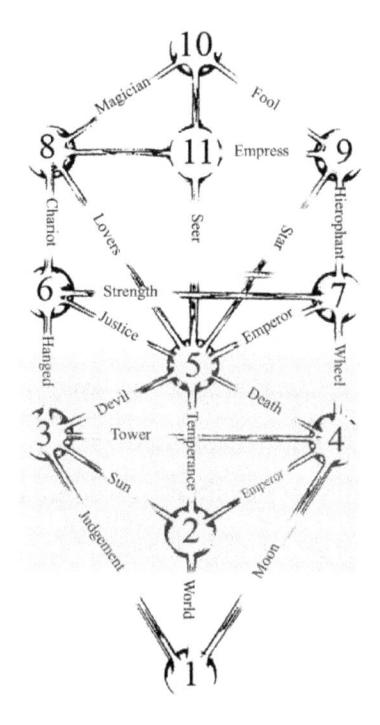

Figure 201 – Dark Night of the Soul

DARK NIGHT OF THE SOUL
DEVIL, DEATH, TOWER... AND TEMPERANCE

The experience of the *Dark Night of the Soul* was mentioned somewhere, earlier in this work. Now, as we head for the final gate, is where this experience has to be discussed in all its seeming hopelessness and sincerity, because if I don't warn you, then you, or those you love, or someone—anyone—won't know how to find their way out of the vast, fearful place that they were not taught to interpret—were not given a map through—when they are lost. When everything becomes too hard and the ocean seems too deep; when you are too far from shore to consider hope an option, when you feel too weak. That's when people die. Of grief. Of despair. By their own hand. Because they don't cope. Don't know how to be what they're not. Don't even know how to be who they truly are. Because there is no one to say *this* is what they are experiencing. In all its immensity.

No way can I or anyone else, even though we may care about you deeply, know about your private terror or despair. This slipping off sure footing. Your life gone crazy. You, sitting at the kitchen table, hardly able to breath and repeating over and over, what just happened? Whatjusthappened? Whatjusthappened? Whatjusthappened, like some litany of confusion because what are words, all said and done, if they leave us in a tangle of tapeworm-type congestion where even our eyes ache? We can only ever compare. We can only ever hold you as safely as we can.

This is the DARK NIGHT OF THE SOUL. And the truth—the secret—is that you all experience it. Some of us—oh, yes, me also—hide it from anybody else because what happens to the weak? The ashamed? The beaten and infantilized?

You're with a booze-crazed partner caught (and trapping you) in a delusion-fueled rage—a bitter parent—and you don't know what to do when they hurt you. You are raped but you know, or think you know, how bad things can get if you report it. When you're fourteen, at a family get-together, and you say you have an announcement. And you come out. And no one wraps you in their arms, and whispers softly in your ear, *It's okay, I gotcha*. That *thing* in your gut that twists your ability to think right, so it's senseless, and then drives you to the edge of the cliff and whispers *Go on, GO ON!*

You have a choice. They had a choice. Some never knew that, though.

Without a level of insight, they jumped. They never knew of the *Temperance* card. There was no wise elder. No inner voice that said *you're grand, valuable, beautiful*. They took that extra jack, they put the gun to their own head and hoped like almighty fuck they could do it right. They went to bed and never got up. That's been me, that's… is it you? Do you recall that moment? You *know* you will never recover from those words of cruelty. That absurd degradation. If only there was someone—anyone—who could explain what just happened. Or, when you finally cotton-on to the fact that you are *not* the problem; that you've been sucking on the straw of that bullshit from your mother or your brother, or your father, or the government,or a doctor who thought antidepressants were a great idea when all you really needed was for somebody to say I'm sorry. For someone to hold you and really mean it. For recognition and mutual respect.

WHAT?

Am I explaining this okay? I know it's a piss in the ocean of the muck you've been drowning in, but I'll say it anyway. I'm sorry. For the whole filthy, uncaring, inconsiderate, off-the-cuff throw away insult. I'm sorry. For the injustice in your family, for the snide jokes at the expense of your outraged, dangerous, sullen, ratbag, anarchistic self who maybe has to hide behind a fucking perm, or an old lady face, or a suit, or boardies and a pair of snow-white Adidas, when all you want to do is put on that red dress, Roxanne, and go out, and make out with someone whose name you'll never know, but who is liberated enough to agree to a condom, or maybe to just have a home that feels like one, and not some upright coffin.

Devil, Death, Tower, making a triangular trap between your instinct for self-preservation and the safety of those you love, and the desperately beautiful acknowledgement of who YOU are, in all of this. *Devil Death* and *Tower*, like a double-spring steel bear trap. You know the one. With the chain and the spikes on its jaws that point inward? With the *Come this way, little kiddie, I'll look after you*, sign just above where it's buried, in a shallow pit, covered with flowers and a box of chocolates like some callous and deceitful 1950s Rock Hudson movie.

RING PASS NOT

If you have no level of insight you will return to the soil. A not-person. Identity-less. You will have accepted the humdrum demon of deceit, and the invisibility that seems someone agreed was love. If you followed the rules. Behaved like you weren't who you are.

So don't. *Temperance* is your way through. Go to the deep places. Yes. But hold the rope your ancient grandmother tied around the log that spans the chasm, the abyss, with the little note in the bottle, hanging from the end that's just above the river far, far below that reads, *I gotcha, I won't let you drown, child of my future.*

SKYWOMAN

> *It is good to remember that the original woman was herself an immigrant. She fell a long way from her home in the Skyworld, leaving behind all who knew her and who held her dear. She could never go back.*
>
> Robin Wall Kimmerer,
> *Braiding Sweetgrass*

Temperance is medicine. Not the kind you get from a physician, but the medicine that is forest, island or fjord wisdom. The little inlet by the river, surrounded by ancient old pines. It is the medicine of plants and silence and, as Robin Wall Kimmerer suggests, it is having someone braid your hair with those real hands. *Temperance* is that log across the seething waters and the boulders at the bottom of the ravine. Temperance says, *Jiggle the stick, don't look down, feel, feel your feet on the raggedy bark, I have made it like this for you. You can be safe if you take your time and remind yourself of what you have learned.*

DON'T LOOK DOWN

See, that's exactly what we do when we are in grief, when we despair, when we doubt. Right down at our feet, when it's the sky calling, sighing, whispering, *Straight ahead to the other side, kid of mine. I gotcha. Eyes on the horizon, darlin'.*

When even one of these three cards turn up on the table, I ask that you recollect this final section. That for a fleeting second you recall that you've been here and know this ache. Then, and only then, can you spae. You think that being lied to, being accused, being ignored is poison? Someone fed it to you once, like a metaphorical *deathcap* toadstool instead of a *goldtop* psilocybin one. And yet, here you are. So, hold their hand when you see these.

Be kind. Rough is okay, just like the bark on that log. But don't lie to the traveler and have them think you never knew this cruelty. There is a time for looking another human being in the eye, to say, *I gotcha.*

...

CONCLUSION

THE FRAGILITY OF THE FÁIDH SKILLED

Figure 172 – Circe Invidiosa

A man's mother died, and when she was well-buried, he went about disposing of her things. Emptying her house. Making it ready for a sale. Her? She'd arrived after the Second World War, from Europe, a refugee, a voiceless woman. She married somebody. She gave birth to this boy/man who is currently erasing her. She hummed while cleaning, or washing, or shopping, or she put on the telly and sat silently staring at its endless consumerist conning. She baked palačinky or deruny (she learned to knead the dough for the pastry before what happened, happened), she went to fat, grew whiskers, got old, wore slippers to the corner shop, ignored the cat, was forgotten, and seemed never to know, not once, how to speak.

Almost everything was cleaned up or taken. Or thrown away. There was only what he hadn't known. He lifted the manhole cover to the space between the ceiling and the slant of the roof. The panelling was covered in flat, schoolbook-type diaries.

His mother, nameless woman, had been the mistress of Eduard Roschmann, an SS *Obersturmführer*, titled the *Butcher of Riga*, and she recorded everything he did to her, and *everything* she witnessed. The terror. The humiliation. The almost elegant lies and *Wagneresque* style of him.

No one, once she eventually escaped, and finally landed — a refugee from a futile Europe — in Australia paid her heed. Not one person, living, in her lifetime, knew what she knew. Her son did not realize who his mother really was. He'd never thought of her as young. Or beautiful. Violated, molested, tortured, horrified. She'd baked, shut up, disappeared, died. But…

I know how it's been, or is, for most of you. Wildlings in boxes called houses. Upright, windowed coffins for us privileged, while some, on the streets, ask where their next fix is coming from, or where'd ya score the tent, mate? People being weird... I mean, fearful or lovely, when for most of your life they've been strangers who've ignored you. The confusing maelstrom of media exploitation. But I guess, just for a moment, all that exhaust, and all those big-mouthed bullies telling you what to eat and how to look better than your beautiful born bodies already are, shuddering in their rhinestones, their Botox needles looking somehow redundant, have gone as quiet as the dead woman.

Furry bits finally, or momentarily, obtaining their liberation and reprieve from the wax or the razor.

Yes, we've known this was coming. Covid 19. Death. Irrelevance. Me, and tarot, that scammy bastard that throws up the *Devil* card like a random fungal thing between summer toes, where sand and sunshine should be. And yes, I've got my car trunk packed and a chainsaw beside my bed for the next fucker who decides to try breaking in.

But... Stay the course, lovelies. Keep that wildness keen. Hone it. Train. Be as real as you've always told me you are. Cook and plant, stitch and draw, write by hand in some forlorn and abandoned TO-DO diary. Because TO-DO is today. Be covert cabals of witchery and wisdom.

I want to tell you what I know is happening but to do so is a really long rant. I'll save it for a future gathering of us, but... again... this was all predicted. This glitch. This is destiny. I haven't got to Ethiopia yet, but I probably will, if that helps hearten the confused among you.

I'm exhausted. Getting all the images together for this book (excerpts and explanations to come). It will be published here in Australia, through LOTHBROKSIGURD, and I'm running with color and considered-rebellion, all the more to make it uncluttered, honest and viable for you. Because it's YOU, fáidh-trained, or else travelers who've sat with my cards in your hands: the weird, the pierced, the inked, the porcelain, the polyamorous, the artistes of flesh and song, the travelers of abused and forgotten places, the lawyers defending the rights of greyhounds and thoroughbreds, the trans, the thief, the mother and the battered, the cop who arrested the dealer's boss, who have inspired me with every, every story you have shared, or that we have exposed. You are all so courageous and so fucking gritty.

We've been groomed, Wildlings, into submission. How about that? Look in more directions than left or right, because they are not changing. Only in and out and down are open now. Your bravery is what is required of you now. And me. And the person, whose name I never knew and was never destined to know anyway.

What are we to make of all this, hmm? Something rare, my darlings.

Something of a treasure of tales, and a raven-chair of storytellings. I know you have, hidden, that which you dare not say aloud. So here is a moment… Write. It. Down. Who you are. What you dared tell no one. Then hide it. Let tomorrow's child find it and wonder who the fuck you really were.

I could, if I was a wanker, suggest you buy one of my books for the time you spend in solitude, but nah. Go get Ta-Nehisi Coates, *Water Dancer*. Go watch Lynne Kelly **or** Jon Young on YouTube.

I'll be back…

…

ABOUT

Figure 173 – Ly de Angeles, 2020

LY DE ANGELES

Website www.lydeangeles.com

In print since 1987 Dorset, England, Ly is a scholar, deep ecologist, mythographer, feminist, and master storyteller. She also has the *sight*, is an exponent of several martial art and healing techniques. She casts a jolly-good curse. She has three living children and five grandchildren. De Angeles is still a seer of tarot after forty years, as of the year known as 2020 on the Gregorian calendar.

"My preferred writing style is magical realism. Because realism is over-rated and usually by someone claiming an authority biased by Medieval monks, and an opinion that just makes me sigh. Again."

BIBLIOGRAPHY AND WORKS REFERENCED

Ashcroft-Nowicki, D. *The Shining Paths*, Thoth Publications, 1997

Berry, W, *World Ending Fire – The Essential Wendell Berry* Penguin, 2018

Black, C. (Director) *Schooling the World: The White Man's Last Burden* (film), 2010

Bly, R. *Iron John, A Book About Men,* Addison-Wesley, 1990

Brand, R. *My Booky Wook*, Harper-Collins, 2007

Davis, W. *The Wayfinders, Why Ancient Wisdom Matters in the Modern World*, Anansi Press, 2009

Davis, W. *The Serpent and the Rainbow* Simon and Schuster, 1988

Doidge, N. *The Brain that Changes Itself,* Viking Press, 2007

Eide-Næss, A. E. *Ecology, Community and Lifestyle*, Cambridge University Press, 1989

Eisler, R. *The Chalice and the Blade*, HarperCollins, 1998

Gibran, Kahlil. *The Prophet*, Alfred A Knopf, Inc, 1923 (136th printing, 2001)

Kelley, L, *The Memory Code*, Allan & Unwin, 2016

Kelly, L. *Grounded, Indigenous Knowing in a Concrete Reality*, Essay, Rounded Globe

Person, Martin Luther, *Letters from a Birmingham Jail*[2], Liberation Magazine, 1963

Knight, C. and Lomas, R. *The Hiram Key*, Century Books, 1996

MacFarlane, R. *Landmarks*, Penguin Books, 2016

---

[2] http://www.africa.upenn.edu/Articles_Gen/Letter_Birmingham.html

MacFarlane, R. *The Old Ways*, Penguin Books, 2012

MacFarlane, R. *Underland,* Penguin Books, 2019

Monbiot, G. *Feral*, Penguin Books, 2014

Monmouth, G. *The History of the Persons of Britain*, 1136

Palahniuk, C. *Invisible Monsters*, W.W. Norton & Company, 1999

Roy, A. *The God of Small Things*, IndiaInk, 1997

Reanney, D. *Music of the Mind*, Hill of Content, Australia, 1994

Shaw, M. *A Branch from the Lightning Tree*, White Cloud Press, 2011

Shepherd, N. *The Living Mountain*, Canongate, 2012

Storm, H. *Seven Arrows,* Ballantine Books, 1972

Wall-Kimmerer, R, *The Grammar of Animacy*, Daily Good e-zine, 2016

Young, J, *What the Robin Knows: How Birds Reveal the Secrets of the Natural World*, HMH Books, 2012

IMAGES

(Sources cited when known)

1. Mask
2. Magician and seer
3. Denial
4. Murder
5. Snowy River
6. Persistent Illusion
7. Seer
8. 7 of Swords – Source: Darkness Light Tarot
9. 2008 GFC
10. 3 of Staves
11. Destination rebirth – Dark Mansion Tarot
12. AIDS
13. Natural Death
14. Exalted End of Life
15. Hand of Staves
16. Y-Node Ancestry
17. Cage of Self Imposing
18. Walking Through
19. Opening Pattern
20. Pied Piper
21. Wealth
22. Lascaux Hunting Magic Art
23. Deep Listening
24. Androgynous

25. Mobius Strip
26. Way of the Navigator – Catacombs Paris
27. Judgement – volcanic eruption
28. Devil – Josef Mengele
29. Hierophant – Gargoyle, Notre Dame
30. Ace Cups, Source: *Darkana*
31. Roman Catholic Something
32. Betrayal
33. Legal Corruption
34. The Language of Loss
35. Pacific Northwest Loon
36. Dead Reckoning
37. Acupuncture
38. Stargate Numbered
39. Earth – Labyrinth
40. Tide – First Crescent
41. Navigation – Fibonacci spiral
42. Schooling the world
43. Art – Ensō
44. Core – Sun – Navajo cave art
45. Extinction Rebellion
46. Protection – Spider Web
47. Silverback
48. Expansion: Jera – A Year
49. Aboriginals in Chains Source: nationalunitygovernment.org
50. Stone – Ankor Wat
51. Motherboard Mathematics

52. Bitcoin
53. Challenger Deep – Horizon at sea
54. Sumerian Cylinder Seal
55. Clach an Truseil, Isle of Lewis
56. Seed – Liberty
57. Pluto – Message in a Bottle
58. Lighthouse
59. Horse Latitude
60. Grove
61. The Continuum
62. Egalitarianism. Source Pinterest
63. De Angeles with a Traveler
64. Ghost Ship
65. Wayshowers
66. Fool
67. Magician
68. Seer
69. Empress
70. Emperor
71. Hierophant
72. Lovers
73. Chariot
74. Strength
75. Hermit
76. Crystal Ball
77. Wheel
78. Justice

79. Hanged

80. Death – Source: Andreas Sundqvist

81. Temperance

82. Devil

83. Tower

84. Star

85. Moon

86. Sun

87. Judgement

88. World

89. The Journey Cards

90. Ace of Staves

91. 2 of Staves

92. 3 of Staves

93. 4 of Staves

94. 5 of Staves

95. 6 of Staves

96. 7 of Staves

97. 8 of Staves

98. 9 of Staves

99. 10 of Staves

100. Messenger of Staves

101. Fledgling of Staves

102. Person of Staves 1

103. Person of Staves 2

104. Ace of Cups

105. 2 of Cups

106. 3 of Cups
107. 4 of Cups
108. 5 of Cups
109. 6 of Cups
110. 7 of Cups
111. 8 of Cups
112. 9 of Cups
113. 10 of Cups
114. Messenger of Cups
115. Fledgling of Cups
116. Person of Cups 1
117. Person of Cups 2
118. Ace of Coins
119. 2 of Coins
120. 3 of Coins
121. 4 of Coins
122. 5 of Coins
123. 6 of Coins
124. 7 of Coins
125. 8 of Coins
126. 9 of Coins
127. 10 of Coins
128. Messenger of Coins
129. Fledgling of Coins
130. Person of Coins 1
131. Person of Coins 2
132. Ace of Swords

133. 2 of Swords
134. 3 of Swords
135. 4 of Swords
136. 5 of Swords
137. 6 of Swords
138. 7 of Swords
139. 8 of Swords
140. 9 of Swords
141. 10 of Swords
142. Messenger of Swords
143. Fledgling of Swords
144. Person of Swords 1
145. Person of Swords 2
146. Fáidh Training NZ
147. Opening
148. Map: Dead Reckoning
149. Map: The Grove
150. Map: Familiar Faces
151. Map: Stargate
152. Map: Horse Latitude
153. Map: Continuum
154. Map: Question
155. Between the Devil
156. Staves
157. Cups
158. Coins
159. Swords

160. Know Will Dare Silence
161. Dead Reckoning for Dom
162. Grove for Dom
163. Familiar faces for Dom
164. Stargate for Dom
165. Horse Latitude for Dom
166. Continuum for Dom
167. Question for Dom
168. Dead Reckoning for Jesse
169. Grove for Jesse
170. Horse Latitude for Jesse
171. Stargate for Jesse
172. Circe Invidiosa, John Waterhouse, 172 a. When to Trust
173. Ly de Angeles, 2020
174. Spell Jar
175. Heartbreak
176. Insomnia
177. IVF
178. Sexual Abuse
179. Religion
180. Insanity
181. Poison
182. Pregnancy
183. Legal Agreement
184. Legal Severance
185. Prison
186. Will

187. Corruption
188. Quiet
189. Illness
190. Stony Ground
191. Fertile Wilderness
192. Middle East
193. Desert
194. Eruption
195. Birth
196. Medicated Illness
197. Acute Illness
198. Fire
199. Tyranny
200. Flood
201. Dark Night of the Soul
202. The Drama Triangle

APPENDIX ONE
PAIRS

Figure 174 – Spell Jar

PICTORIAL EXAMPLES

Here are several pairs that should provide you with an idea of what to look for. These are examples of the center of the DEAD RECKONING map, but they don't take all the other stories into account. That will vary the eventual meanings exponentially. As, also, will be how they appear in the arrangements of other maps. These are snippets of predictions that have proved true.

2 of Cups/3 of Swords

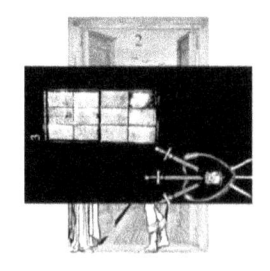

Figure 175 – Heartbreak

The 2 of Cups and the 3 of Swords are variations of partnership blues

Heartbreak

A partnership breakup

A long-distance sexual partnership that is difficult to maintain

Occasionally can be a heart condition, but not life-threatening unless with cards indicating

9 Swords/2 Swords

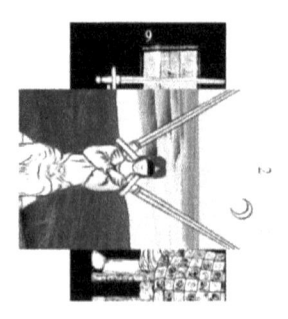

Figure 176 – Insomnia

The 9 of Swords and the 2 of Swords are instability and silent worry
Insomnia or grief
The inability to decide
Anxiety without a cause

Ace Swords/Empress

Figure 177 – IVF

Ace of Swords and Empress are usually a medical procedure
IVF – In vitro fertilization: same sex couples and later life pregnancy, fulfilling the desire for parentness, without a partner
Gender reassignment surgery
Occasionally an outspoken, disciplined, and willful femme

Devil/2 of Cups

Figure 178 – Sexual Abuse

The Devil and the 2 of Cups are gender bias. Can be rape
Sexual depravity
Rape, and sexual predation. Victim grooming and 'priestly' privilege
Sexually transmitted illness or virulence (herpes, gonorrhea, psychosis)

Devil/Hierophant

Figure 179 – Religion

Devil and Hierophant. Tarot perceives all religions as delusional cults.

Religions

Any of the Abrahamic ideologies, evangelicalisms, interferences, morality judgments and indoctrinations

Devil/Moon

Figure 180 – Insanity

Devil and Moon together are likely to represent a person's rights removed from them. They are declared incompetent to themselves and, even, a danger to self and others.

Mental confusion and disorientation, by means of physiological trauma, poison or brainwashing, or an uncontrolled pathology

Devil/Temperance

Figure 181 – Poison

Devil and Temperance are poison.

Alcoholism

Medicine that is either prescribed or dangerous: statins and henbane would both fall into this category

Sugar, white flour, processed once-foods, artificial color, flavor, other

Anything ingestible that abuses an animal body

Empress/Ace Wands

Figure 182 – Pregnancy

Empress with the Ace of Wands

Always a pregnancy

Not necessarily with a biological child, can be creative project

Does not imply a birth

Justice/2 of Cups

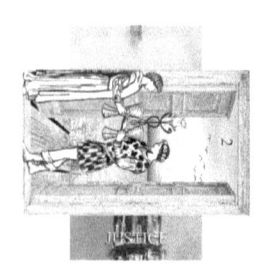

Figure 183 – Legal Agreement

Justice with the 2 of Cups

This is a form of marriage. A legally binding agreement between two *consenting* people

Justice/3 of Swords

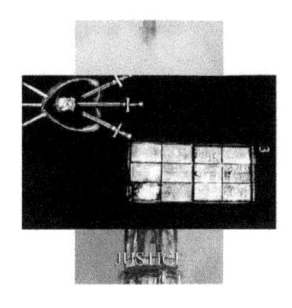

Figure 184 – Legal Severance

Justice with the 3 of Swords

This is the legally agreed-to severance. May be of a couple, a company, or a police intervention, into a family dispute-turned-violent, where one or more people are removed

Justice/8 of Swords

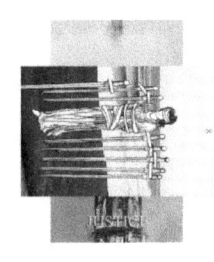

Figure 185 – Prison Sentence

The Justice card with the 8 of Swords

Jail time, a good behavior bond, detention, an AVO or equivalent

Legally binding anything, from a mortgage to a debt repayment, not necessarily monetary

Justice/Ace of Swords

Figure 186 – Will

The Justice card with the Ace of Swords
A court ruling
A last will and testament
Police control or enforcement
The court, or council, justification of property division into more than one title
Forced acquisition of property or goods in response to poverty

Justice/Devil

Figure 187 – Corruption

Justice Card with the Devil

Legally sanctioned corruption: apartheid, slavery, sentencing based on religious-bias, forced detention for refugees

A police state or martial law

A corrupt coup

Strength/2 Swords

Figure 188 – Quiet

Strength with the 2 of Swords

Profound silence

Inner calm

Is always unforced. These pairs can turn up on a map depicting silent protest or lack of action, but that lack of action is never lazy, thoughtless, or ineffectual

The sound of kata Tjuta with no other people-critters around

Strength/9 Swords

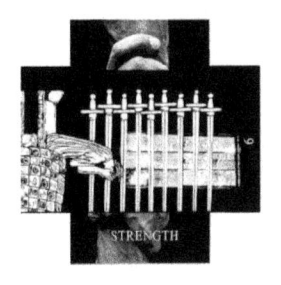

Figure 189 – Illness

Strength with the 9 of Swords

An action has caused pain: after beginning a physical discipline

Pain or illness keeping a person awake

One of the most difficult decision in a person's life is inherent within this pair

Strength/Death

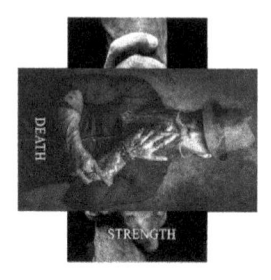

Figure 190 – Stony Ground

Strength with the Death card

A graveyard

A burial ground

Barren ground

Stony ground

A vast expanse, seemingly void of life (no such place)

If personal, it is hard to deal with, but more often than not this pair is an environment

The beautiful creature that Death presents at body-death

Strength/Empress

Figure 191 – Fertile Wilderness

The Strength card with the Empress

Kakadu Wilderness

The Amazon

The Congo

Oases of any kind. This pair is lush, environmentally vast, and fecund

Strength/Hierophant

Figure 192 – Middle East

The Strength card with the Hierophant

Sometimes this pair represents the Middle East, Arabia and/or Spain
Can be any desert-like environment with an overtly religious human-

people presence

Strength/Sun

Figure 193 – Desert

The Strength card with the Sun
Desert

Strength/Tower

Figure 194 – Eruption

The Strength card with the Tower

Seismic activity

Earthquake

Volcanic eruption

Catastrophic mine disasters

Catastrophic environmental damage, but not by water or wind

(The above 'catastrophic' descriptions are based on a human evaluation)

Sun/Ace Wands

Figure 195 – Birth

The Sun card with the Ace of Staves
Birth

Temperance/9 Swords

Figure 196 – Medicated Illness

Temperance with 9 of Swords
Really sick
Too many examples to add more
The person is definitely medicated in some fashion, whether this is working to heal them or not will depend on destinations on the maps

Tower/9 Swords

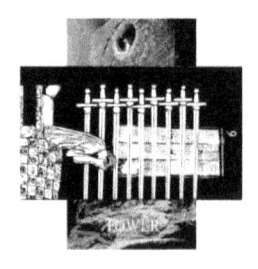

Figure 197 – Acute Illness

The Tower with the 9 of Swords
An acute illness, one with a generally high temperature as for a virus or infection
Extreme pain
Acute injury
Impending catastrophic situation
Unquantifiable grief

Tower/Ace of Staves

Figure 198 – Fire

The Tower with the Ace of Staves
A bloody-big fire

Tower/Emperor

Figure 199 – Tyranny

The Tower with the Emperor

Tyranny. Whether that tyranny is on a huge scale, condemning human people-animals or cattle-people in life-sentence stalls, zoos, live animal circuses and ocean-people entertainment venues, wet markets or forest-people-sanctioned environmental destruction... when you or the traveler is trapped by a tyrannical partner or jailer. It's all tyranny.

Tower/Moon

Figure 200 – Flood

The Tower card with the Moon card

Flood, hurricane, tidal wave, cyclone, overwhelming mass of 'destructive' water

APPENDIX TWO

CROWHEARTED

ON BEING RAGGEDY, AND WISE WITH STUFF

IT SEEMS like an illness. This weird pitter-patter music where a heart should beat. Rain overflowing the gutter in a steady, Zen-garden-bamboo-night rain tonkle. I think I was maybe three, when crow first tore into me and took away my capacity to grow into other kids. Set up this nest. A thing that felt like awe. A scarring that I'm proud of.

Later on, he paired up. In love for life. Year after year, breeding storytellings into the dreams of others a bit like I was becoming. Having me live 'em first though. And that was hard. Fledgling, working out her wings along the airwaves of the world. I must say predators took a lot out of me. Traps and poison culled… is culled the right word for murder? Culled hundreds of things I had to say: who I was, who we thought we were. Yeah, you too, you know yourself to be like this, eh? Talkin to you about you… What? You thought I'd leave you out of the story? Not ever gonna happen, my friend.

I have a crow inside me instead of a heart. A blackness that is some kind of beauty. Some of you got the same thing. Some of you know what I'm saying. When this wildness savages the UGLIES that people try to plant in you, and who call 'em truth, a bit of us can die.

The rest has to learn how to fight. To be a warrior for the wake. We peck 'em to death and refuse to eat the carcass, cause of the wrongness in it. The wrongness they tried to tell us that we are. I can circle all that in a mess of midnight-blue pinions, and scavenge my way behind them, into their secrets, where the good stuff hides and not what they have discarded.

Crows are corvids. Like ravens and jays and jackdaws. Like magpies and rooks. Making the world new every day. Shot. Maligned. Why?

We've heard it said our chatter is a fucken racket. But it's really a language that people don't know—don't recognize as something—because they only hear the voices of the red blood hearts, so easily broken, so casually betrayed. We're having a meaningful conversation when we sit on the barbed wire or the electricity lines, or on top of streetlights, calling to the families two miles away that here's the black plastic bag, rattlin in the wind, all chokkas with food, calling sunset and no predators in this part of the city.

It's a funny thing... Is it funny? That people think we caw cacophonously? When what's going on is really veryvery important. Like *where's the food? Who's dead? Who's in charge? What's a true name? Where's the bloke with the rifle? How the fuck did you open the bag with the Velcro?*

Crow instead of a heart. Hackle feather sloughing off, and making for ground zero every season. Black thing as wild as the days people hide from. Too hot, too cold. Why can't we control this? Why am I not lucky? Why am I so poor? How can I get more likes? Why did my kids abandon me?

Some big, ol', birch and cedar and spruce forest. That's where crow is from. The maker of the world. The waddler across the asphalt. The wickedness on the beach at Bettystown, County Meath, when shouldn't they be seagulls scavenging the tourist chips, and not us big ol' blackbirds?

The one thing I'm pretty sure about is this, if you're crowhearted as well, nothing is going to seem ordinary. Bits are interesting. Stuff people chuck away make good nest material. Things look different. Talk is not the same.

When crow ate that chunk of me, and set up home, I didn't know anything was wrong. It was like this for everybody. Then I thought I was a mad kid. I didn't know what ribbons of flight felt like, then. Not for years. Thought I'd died. I could have. I just never put it down to an experience I ever recognized from anybody else. When I was big enough, I wrote poetry. Things of the dead. Of god. Of fearing and wanting to know what it really means to not be. Why people kill each other. Even if they don't think they do. Cruelty like that. Crows feed on stuff like that.

Crow instead of a heart. Had to figure out how to sing with that voice. Something like laryngitis. Like there were thorns in what I said when all of it was love. Talking crow comes out strange to lots of people, most of the time. And funny. Funnyfunny and dangerous together. Like chilli-chocolate is, like desire for trinkets and bright, shiny-seeming friendships that turn bitter as easy as pissing.

Some kind of mystery tore a hole in normal that night, when I was just a chicken. While I was sleeping. When I was a kid, in that dream, and… was shown a deep valley, to soar through once I worked out what wings were for. Pond water to drink from. Gutter water. Left-over water from storm water type water. Breeding ground am I, for generations yet to be born. And there. That's the bottomlessness of being corvidhearted, isn't it?

Poetry from some wizened, scary, dark un-chainsaw'd forest elder lore. Does it take a long time to get a head around all this? If I'm still working at that, I bet you are too. But. What I know? What I realize? I'm awfullyawfully glad. About crow, that is. I have no idea what NORMAL must beat like. A bloody-great big, raggedy black-feathered crow of a bird, where a heart once was… isn't such a bad way to grow up after all.

…

ENDNOTES

WHAT IS A GOD?
FROM WITCH | FOR THOSE WHO ARE

Just so we're clear, in case the word pops up anywhere in the following stories, *god* is not a person.

A *god* does not have a true name, and *god* is not a *god*, as we have been indoctrinated to think of a *god*. They have no gender and they are never an it. They're an *us*… and we are not just people.

Just so you know, if I use the word *god*, I don't mean a deity. Because I have no religion. I do not worship. We are belonging. In the way of present-continuous. A *god* is the whole, being the sum of its parts, but not greater than them. *God* is the land you are, and have been since before you were recognizably human, and that of your ancestors of every species, of every flora, of every river, each wave upon the sand of an atoll. Each susurration that laps the shingles of a Cornish beach. The macaw within the Brazilian canopy. The blue fungus that teaches the dreamer sight. What you know of it. That it knows you. The names of plants and the plants that are unknown and unnamed. That you are it, long after your body has ceased to be the you people think you are now. Or even that you think you are.

God is love and wildfires and volcanic eruptions. A *god* can be a certain rock, along the Birdsville Track, in Australia, when there was no Birdsville Track. That rock is a wayshower. Its name is sung and danced and painted by indigenous people who know that to pass it by, and head north at a certain time of year, will lead them (and with the guidance of many other such *gods*) to the trading bay with the people who travel the sea routes (also *gods*) from elsewhere for that trade.

So now we have established what I intend, should I use the god word anywhere in this (or any other book). When a tall, dark-skinned man named Hunter, introduces himself as a forest *god*, he doesn't necessarily say which forest. And he only appears to be a *he*. Hunter is everything in the forest and, as such, could be any forest. At any time. Could also be the forest long since devastated for logging. Forgotten except as myth.

As you work your way through this lore, this gathering of teachings, this story-telling of ravens, please spare a thought for the effect any of us have on a god, or the gods, if we grade a road and remove that stone on the Birdsville Track, bulldoze a forest (a *god*) and cover the earth (a *god*) with concrete, build a dam where a free river (a *god*) once ran, construct a city, desecrate the bones of ancestral dead, of any species, terrorize the penned herds (*gods*) that are descended from what once were seasonally migrating aurochs. Spare a thought pertaining to our ignorance at treading roughshod over what has lived for a million years.

...

MULENGRO

Mulengro is like a disease passed from one person to another using seven dysfunctional manipulations:

ENVY

GREED

GUILT

DECEIT

DENIAL

EXPECTATION

ASSUMPTION

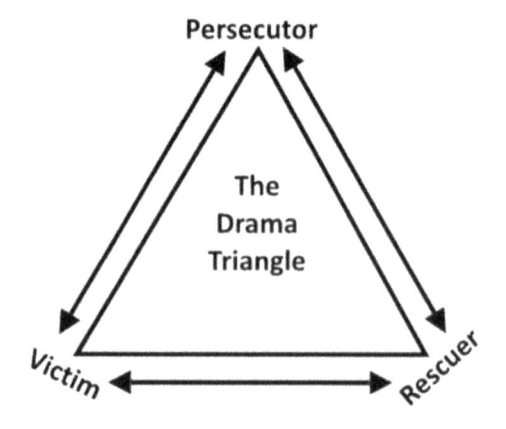

Figure 201 – The Drama Triangle

When someone attempts to entice, control, coerce or otherwise warp seeming-facts to suit an agenda they will use one or more of these techniques. The only way to prevent despair from overwhelming our well-being is to cease Mulengro in our lives. I've done it; several students have done it; most of my friends have stopped it. The outcome to being infected by Mulengro is *always* resentment, rejection, blame and despair.

And Mulengro *is* infectious. Mulengro is like the *Karpman Drama Triangle*:

I read an article about a couple living together. I'll call them Gabe and Kelly to ensure gender neutrality because this happens in every partnership at least once.

Kelly is at home and Gabe phones from the office, explaining there is an after-work function they were required to attend, and it could go until late.

Kelly asks, *So Gabe, will you be home for dinner?*

I doubt it, says Gabe, *so don't bother cooking for me unless you want to. I can always microwave it later.*

Okay, says Kelly.

OH-Oh.

The problem begins when Kelly thinks to make dinner for two anyway, just in case Gabe comes home unexpectedly and is hungry. Partners do that for each other, right? They love each other. But

Gabe does not come home and does not call.

Kelly, alone, does not get on with the evening and read a book. The thought is there, but thoughts also stray to the time, and how late Gabe is. And has there been an accident? Or is Gabe having an affair. Or…

Finally, exhausted, Kelly goes to bed, but cannot sleep because Gabe's absence is now a monster.

At 3 in the wee hours of the morning Gabe comes home drunk, closes the door quietly, removes the shoes and creeps upstairs to the bedroom. Kelly switches on the light.

Where were you? Why didn't you call me? I made us dinner anyway but then it just dried out and was ruined so I threw it away. Why are you so late? What have you been doing? I've been so worried. I didn't know whether to call the hospitals or your mother or what! I've been terrified you were mugged or dead.

I've got to pee, Gabe slurs, swaying towards the bathroom.

You're drunk! You've been partying and you're fucking drunk! Kelly bursts into tears.

Gabe returns to the bedroom, undresses, gets into bed and is snoring in seconds.

…

What just happened? A happy couple is now on the slippery slide to an eventual end. Both are party to the drama triangle, also to every aspect of Mulengro. At one stage Kelly enacts all three characters of the triangle whilst both enact assumption, expectation denial and envy. Through Gabe's silence deceit is employed, as is denial and greed as Gabe *gaslighting* and *muting*.

GASLIGHTING

Named for a 1944 film called *Gas Light*. The term refers to a psychological abuse and is used to describe an attempt to destroy another's perception of reality, very often by sociopaths or narcissists, but there are grades of that. Very often an individual will lie to another, thinking to save them from the hurt of knowing, for example, that they had sex outside the relationship and both do not want to admit it out of guilt, or wants to keep the external relationship as well as remain in the current partnership. The problem arises when one person's body (gut) gets the jitters. Adrenalin. Bodies read more than intellects and when one knows a partner as well as an intimate partner, or a parent/child relationship, bodies do the talking. Small things. A phone call not returned. A scent one cannot identify. Over time unknown patterns arise and the person being *gaslit* can become extremely ill. Anxiety. Fear.

Confusion. If they ask the partner if something is going on, they should know about and the partner says no. The relationship is, again, doomed. At the extreme, the victim of gaslighting kills themselves.

MUTING

When you have something important to discuss with a sibling, partner, offspring, parent, boss, misbehaving or inappropriate work colleague and they suggest you stop bitching, moaning, whining, complaining. They say, I don't want to discuss the matter, or you're talking out of turn, or I don't want to hear this again. Or, you want to keep your job? Do you do it?

It's aggression. It's avoidance. The person raising the topic is effectively shut down. It can be threatening. You run the risk of being cast out, unloved, unemployed, disbelieved. How do we function as a society?

The need to tell the truth. To also admit when we're wrong. To not inflict these psychological savageries onto people we love or admire when we would not inflict them on a total stranger. Because all the above are dishonesties. They seek to avoid personal responsibility. Accountability.

AUTHORITY

What connotations. The word *authority* has come to represent a pinnacle – the epitome of a powerful person. The word *authority* is very different, in truth, to a *master* (such as a master carpenter, a master of the sword, a master chef) because a person who has mastered a skill is a practitioner whereas, in many instances, an authority is someone with an opinion who confers with other people with opinions and who, therefore, could be considered educated in opinions. Of *course,* I'm generalizing but it is worth your consideration as quite often those who consider themselves authorities do not condone having that authority questioned and *that* is, and has been, despotism or tyranny or psychopathy. Whether the presumed authority is a parent, the president of a company or country, an educator, a five-star general, or a pope, it is the responsibility of a truthful person or society to consider the individual, or the institution, open to fallibility.

I once sat on the loo of a friend's house in Victoria pondering the poster he had on the back of the door. The image on the poster was of a skeleton in a bathtub in the bathroom of a hotel that is discovered in the far distant future by a team of archaeologists. They document the sarcophagus (the bathtub), the roll of paper used to send messages to the gods via an aqueduct (toilet paper and flush-toilet), mirror used for divination, various *holy* objects (like razor, toothbrush etc.) kept on the altar, the obvious sacredness of water (realized, of course, from the profusion of taps), the quirky plastic crown worn by the king or priest of this temple (the shower-cap). On and on went the description. I understood that no one could truly understand the past from the standpoint of the present and that all such sciences employ educated guesswork.

When I watch a documentary on ancient people depicting them bent-over, ugly, hairy primates I tend to cringe as nothing in life is ungainly in its natural habitat so why depict humanity, alone, as having been so? And *primitive* is merely deemed as derogatory in comparison to us now. To take upon oneself the responsibility of informed questioning ensures that *authority* does not take upon itself the presumption it is better-than another, person, system, lore or knowledge just because it may not understand. It allows for possibilities, it allows for alternatives, it allows for error and it ensures that its own authority remains accountable.

Religion (from L: *religare,* to bind back)

THE JESUS MYTH

Pope Leo X, who reigned 1513-21, said: "It has served us well, this myth of Christ." By this he meant that over the centuries, the vatican managed to acquire enormous wealth and power in the name of a personality it called *Jesus Christ*. In the twentieth century, the man most responsible for making the Vatican a financial powerhouse was its investment manager, Bernardino Nogara. Speaking of him, one cardinal Spellman, of New York, once said, "Next to Jesus Christ, the best thing that ever happened to the catholic church is Bernardino Nogara." Anticipating that Europe was heading for war, Nogara invested heavily in armaments factories, buying several of them outright. This allowed the Vatican to reap huge profits when Mussolini invaded Abyssinia in 1935. Later, in World War II and beyond.

RELIGIOUS FUNDAMENTALISM, DOGMA, BIGOTRY

It's driven into children, in war-torn countries, brainwashing them into hating one another without them knowing exactly why. It is the arrogant racist who believes in an imperialist, white supremacy that presumes anything can be bought. It is in the neo-Nazi and the Ku Klux Klan. Fundamentalism is in the office worker next to you who feels her faith is superior to yours and that you will be damned for your viewpoint and your sexual activity and she, to a place thought of as paradise. Fundamentalism is the reason people mail anthrax to abortion clinics because they don't believe a woman should have a right to choose. Fundamentalism is the man who bullies, beats or represses his wife because he believes women are inferior – the source of all wickedness because of some Middle Eastern myth from life only knows how long ago – and passes on seeds of tyranny to his children. Fundamentalism is the people who mock same-sex love; people who shun unwed mothers, the poor, and those infected with HIV-AIDS calling such a terrible illness "the wrath of God". It is people who smile politely to those of another race in public but, condemn them in private purely because of the color of their skin or *their* religion. Religious fundamentalism; religious laws, rules, arrogance, moral condemnations.

A jolly productive way of controlling people, don't you think? Divide and rule? *Divide et impera*, the practice has been used socially, politically and militarily since documentation began. Philip II of Macedon (circa 365 BCE) is the first person quoted as utilizing the tactic. Divide us to conquer us. Diminish us. Instill doubt, envy, threat, fear. It is happening as I write, in politics. The year of this update is 2017 and politics wages a chess game of brinkmanship in league with big business and media. Do we buy into it? The challenge is to *not* allow it to. The challenge is to be very alert but to *not* become angry. They have us when that happens. Shouldwe declare organic food our weapon, or peddle-power, or cloth bags instead of plastic, recycling over the next iPhone, if we should meet in an age of text-isolation, use pencils to retain the knowledge of how to write, gather in large numbers to protest the cruelty of factory farming and the imprisoning of refugees in offshore detention, if we could stand together so that education returns to being education instead of big business, not eat their garbage. Well, I'm with you on that.

The same applies, I am stunned to be informed that, in the post twentieth century 'west', so-called spiritual practices known as paganism, shamanism, druidry, wicca and some groups that even call themselves witches, charge money to teach. To hold retreats. They sell products that we used to always make ourselves.

The challenge of this essay alone is for us to learn. For us to hold our freedom and not be undermined because we spae what is being done. To learn and keep learning, Then, to unlearn when necessary; to deepen. To thunder into the future as creatures of art.

A future where wonder is revered, and the wildness and the beauty of life is honored, where such terms as *man conquers…*, *in the battle to control…* and *in the war against…* are no longer used to discuss natural phenomenon like mountains, space, death – actually, to not use this terminology for anything.

Who else we are …?

Religions? What *is* valid about them? Whom do they serve? Religions demand worship. They demand divisions and employ dualisms like good and evil, us and them, sacred or profane. Always divisive. Religion and the words *worship, faith, belief* all to go together. Inherent within these words is possibility of doubt. When we can gather for feasting and mutual learning, building a barn, a community, a cleaner environment, without religion to bind us, we'll have achieved a metaphorical *grail quest*.

The spelling *MULENGRO* is a shortening of the form *mulengero*. This shortened form is used quite commonly in some varieties of Romani < mulhengero *mulo* (fog ghost) <*Mulengero Di (All Souls Day)* < *mulo (dead)* [these terminologies are from the Burganland Romani dialect]

...

ALSO BY THE AUTHOR

The Way of the Goddess, England, 1987

The Way of Merlyn, England, 1990

Witchcraft Theory and Practice, A Wiccan 101 Approach, 2000

When I See the Wild God, Urban Celtic Witchcraft 2002

Pagan Visions for a Sustainable Future, Essays, 2004

The Quickening, 1st in the Traveler Series, Magical Realism, 2005

The Shining Isle, 2nd in the Traveler Series, Magical Realism, 2006

Tarot, Theory and Practice, 2007

Magdalene, A Grail Epic, 2012

The Feast of Flesh and Spirit, 2013

Priteni, the Decimation of the Indigenous Britons, 2015

Initiation, A Memoir, 2016

The Skellig, A Shapechanger Epic, 2017

Witch, For Those Who Are, 2018

Under Snow, 3rd in the Traveler Series, Magical Realism, 2019

…

ACKNOWLEDGMENTS

To Serenity de Angeles, photographer, trivia-assassin, and outspoken daughter, you have been here for me with your lens and your honesty for years now. Frankie Valentine, Queer Stripper & Performance Artist, it is through you and your sexy, loud and talented network that I have learned so much, and for agreeing to be what you are: Empress.

Arian Levanael and Nick White, thank you for the cover, Nila Chandra, inspiration for the Temperance card and Jordie Scott for the four in the morning vigils, despite the Arizona heat, and their addition to the imagery of Lightning of the Stargate map. Being in the wild heart of uranus' embrace is not for the coward, that's for sure; and Tannah, and the arroyo with bows and camera. To Zelia, inspiration for the Seer and Andreas Sunqvist for mutual agreement to the Death card.

Thanks to Bonnie for your eagle eye and understanding that I can be sluggish with technicalities. I bend the knee to your generosity.

For the apprentices that have already done the work, and those online who are waiting patiently. The art of foretelling is not for everyone, but here's everything I've got… for spaeing, that is. Muses of Mystery, Melbourne, for backing my launches.

Thank you to Yantra de Vilder and Arian Levanael for agreeing to provide feedback on the early drafts.

To Eldritch Forest, for disagreeing with me on so many things, and for running through the wild woods after words that, to others, seem irrelevant... but are not. To Jade, for yelling at our conversations from a slight and guarded distance.

Most recently of all, to Grace Kelly, for walking me through the tragedy of legal paperwork towards an authentic identity. We are not there yet, but land-ho, me hearty, and deep, deep into yesterday, Lisa Engeman for the organic Stargate design.

And for every one of my apprentices over the many years.

...

CONTENTS

INTRODUCTION

7.	Broken – The Subtle Bigotry of the English Language
9.	Mutiny
15.	Masks
16.	Mascara
17.	Foolishness
18.	The Price of Authenticity
22.	Unpacking in a Safe Harbor

PART 1
AN ACKNOWLEDGEMENT OF WONDER

27.	Of Maps
27.	The Magician and the Priestess
29.	Denial
30.	Say It as You Spae It
32.	Tarot and Amnesia
35.	Bite the Weird and Real
36.	Time, the Great Initiation
36.	The Persistent Illusion
37.	Tarot as Healer
38.	Gender Bias
39.	Witchcraft
39.	Fáidh-Skilled
40.	A Questionable Propaganda
44.	Whispers

45.	Landwisdom
47.	Responsibility
48.	Taking Care of You
49.	Saying It Anyway
51.	Leaving a Safe Harbor – The Voyage Begins – Initiation
53.	Death, and Days of Condescending Folly
55.	You Died and Didn't Know
55.	What is Initiation?
56.	Metamorphosis – the Larval Stage
58.	Prophesy – Moths to a Flame
59.	Death – Destination Rebirth
62.	HIV AIDS
64.	The Observation of the Living
67.	Recycled in a Songline
68.	Jumping Mouse – Couple of Billion Years
70.	Exercise – Pebbles and Pools
71.	The Theory of Everything – The Arrow of Time
73.	Practice – Digging for the Roots of Your Ancestral Tree
75.	Mind, Thought and Light – A Cage of Self-Imposing
78.	Close Encounters – Walking Through What Happens
80.	Opening Spell of Tarot
81.	Hope – Truthsayer
83.	The Random Factor and the Fool
84.	Being Psychic and Other Weather Auguring
84.	What is Tarot?
86.	A Fáidh Trained Navigator in a Jaded World

88.	Deep Listening – Tracker Language
90.	Orality
91.	Black and White on a Rainbow Spectrum
92.	Sei Chu Tu – Frog-Skilled

PART 2

94.	Revolution – Beyond Stereotype and Gender
94.	Being Present
95.	The Muck of Language
96.	Weird
97.	Earthtalk
101.	Training – Traveling to Nowhere
105.	Training in Godlessness

PART 3

107.	The Way of the Navigator – *Tapu*, and *Rāhui* – Wrong Turn
108.	Judgment – True Seeing
113.	Devil – Tapu
116.	Language and Being, the Abundance of Loss
118.	Hierophant – False Promises
120.	Agreements Written in Dust
121.	Houses of Stone and Bone
122.	Soulmates
123.	Poison – Tapu and Rāhui – *Tapu*
125.	*Rāhui*
129.	Semantics – Hiding the Suture Line

130. The Language of Loss – *3 of Swords*

PART 4

133. Maps and Spaeing – the Art of Prediction
134. Trapped in a Cliché
135. 1st Map – Dead Reckoning
137. Present, Future, Past
141. 2nd Map – The Stargate
142. *Inntrenger* – Invader Mentality
143. Underworld
145. The Stargate – The Eleven portals
146. HOME
150. TIDE
154. NAVIGATION
157. Gendering
158. Heretic – The Right to Choose
159. Fungal Neurons
161. ART
162. Your Mother's Death
163. Sensuality
164. CORE
164. Queen After Queen After Queen
166. Love is Love, and Rebel is Rebel
169. Heart Attack
170. Blowin' in the Wind – Grain and Species
172. Self-Awareness

174.	PROTECTION
176.	Boss Cocky or Silverback?
177.	AR15 Assault Rifle
178.	EXPANSION
179.	Education vs Schooling
182.	Epic Flatulence
183.	Tipping Point
184.	STONE
185.	Bad Rap
187.	Major Tom's a Junkie
188.	One Plus Zero Equals One
190.	LIGHTNING – Motherboard & Crazy Genius Zapzones
192.	A Vast Intergalactic Bridge
184.	CHALLENGER DEEP – Unfathomable
196.	Heaven and Hell
196.	Balderdash
198.	Seal and Whale and Spawning Cod
199.	Ancient Messengers
201.	We Are Gods
203.	SEED
204.	Gateway of the Abyss
205.	No Matter
207.	3rd Map – Horse Latitude – Great Voyages or Brutal Truth
208.	Bring Out Yer Dead
211.	Warning
212.	4th Map – The Grove

213. Rosslyn Chapel
214. 5th Map – The Continuum
215. Other Maps – A Fáidh-Trained Witch's Journey Log

PART FIVE

217. Going Pro – What's a Person? What Actually *is* a Person?
218. Lore
220. Cassandra's Fate
221. Dualisms and Puzzles
222. And… Go!
224. Thuggery
226. Still Burning Babies
226. Transference
227. Codes of Silence and Selective Memory
228. First Do No Harm
231. Self-Protection and Psychic Clag
232. That Gunky Stuff
232. Best Friend Syndrome and Personal Privacy
233. Tip of an Iceberg – You Won't Spae What Won't Happen
234. Safety and Responsibility
235. To Buy or Not to Buy
237. Tax Files and Other Evils
238. Communication vs Babble

PART SIX

241. Wayshowers and Journeys – 78 Omens and Portents

242.	The Cards
243.	Navigation
247.	Wayshowers – Big Words, Big Islands, Deep Currents
248.	From Fool to World
297.	The Journey Cards – Staves, Cups, Coins, Swords and Time Sequences

PART SEVEN

356.	Fáidh Gifted – Spae that Deep Shit, Critter!
357.	Fáidh Training
357.	Orality
357.	Opening Pattern and 3 Card Research
359.	Needing Willing Accomplices
360.	Map 1 – Present, Future, Past
361.	Dead Reckoning
362.	A Note on the Past
364.	Map 2 – The Grove
365.	Map 3 – Familiar Faces
367.	Map 4 – Stargate
372.	Map 5 – Horse Latitude
373.	Map 6 – Continuum
374.	Map 7 – Question

PART EIGHT

377.	Between the Devil and the Deep Blue Sea
378.	Watertight

379.	Interpreting Sentences and Mixes
379.	Fool with –
379.	Magician with –
381.	Seer with –
381.	Empress with –
382.	Emperor with –
382.	Hierophant with –
383.	Lovers with –
383.	Chariot with –
384.	Strength with –
385.	Hermit with –
386.	Wheel with –
387.	Justice with –
387.	Hanged with –
388.	Death with –
389.	Temperance with –
389.	Devil with –
391.	Tower with –
392.	Star with –
392.	Moon with –
393.	Sun with –
394.	Judgment with –
394.	World with –
395.	Navigating the Journey Cards
395.	Staves with –
403.	Cups with –

410.	Coins with –
417.	Swords with –

PART NINE

425.	To Will, To Know, To Dare, To Keep Silence – Maps in Real Time
426.	Examples of Interpretations
428.	Real Time as we Understand It
430.	Example Session for Dom – Map 1 – Dead Reckoning
434.	Map 2 – The Grove for Dom
438.	Map 3 – Familiar Faces for Dom
441.	Map 4 – Stargate for Dom
445.	Map 5 – Horse Latitude for Dom
448.	Map 6 – The Continuum for Dom
450.	Map 7 – Question for Dom
452.	Example Session for Jesse –
452.	Map 1 – Dead Reckoning for Jesse
454.	Map 2 – Grove for Jesse
456.	Map 3 – Horse Latitude for Jesse
458.	Map 4 – Stargate for Jesse

PART TEN

461.	Docking in a Safe Harbor – When to Trust
462.	A Garden of Caves
464.	Certain Gods Will Teach You
464.	The Plateau

466.	The Dark Night of the Soul
469.	What?
470.	Ring Pass Not
470.	Skywoman
471.	Don't Look Down
472.	Conclusion – The Fragility of the Fáidh Skilled
477.	About Ly de Angeles
478.	Bibliography and Works Referenced
480.	Images
488.	Appendix 1 – Pairs – Pictorial Examples
506.	Appendix 2 – Crowhearted,
510.	Endnotes
510.	What is a God
512.	Mulengro
523.	Also by the Author
524.	Acknowledgements
526.	Contents

NOTES

NOTES

Lightning Source UK Ltd.
Milton Keynes UK
UKHW021011231121
394456UK00013B/1224